The
Millionaire
and the
Mummies

The
Millionaire
and the
Mummies

THEODORE DAVIS'S GILDED AGE IN
THE VALLEY OF THE KINGS

John M. Adams

St. Martin's Press

New York

www.stmartins.com

map by Rhys Davies

Library of Congress Cataloging-in-Publication Data

Adams, John M., 1950–
The millionaire and the mummies : Theodore Davis's Gilded Age in the Valley of the Kings / John M. Adams.—First U.S. edition.
    p. cm.
Includes bibliographical references and index.
ISBN 978-1-250-02669-9 (hardcover)
ISBN 978-1-250-02670-5 (e-book)
1. Davis, Theodore M., 1837–1915.   2. Archaeologists—United States—Biography.   3. Egyptologists—United States—Biography.   4. Excavations (Archaeology)—Egypt—Valley of the Kings.   5. Tombs—Egypt—Valley of the Kings.   6. Valley of the Kings (Egypt)—Antiquities.   I. Title.
    DT76.9.D38.A33 2013
    932.0092—dc23
    [B]

                                                          2013009111

St. Martin's Press books may be purchased for educational, business, or promotional use. For information on bulk purchases, please contact Macmillan Corporate and Premium Sales Department at 1-800-221-7945 extension 5442 or write specialmarkets@macmillan.com.

First Edition: July 2013

10   9   8   7   6   5   4   3   2   1

For Nancy

Contents

Acknowledgments   *ix*

A Note on Names   *xiii*

Tombs in the Valley of the Kings Discovered or
    Cleared by Theodore M. Davis   *xiv*

One: Thuyu's Golden Coffin   1

Two: Rekhmire's Bronze Bowl   29

Three: Hatshepsut's Quartzite Sarcophagus   71

Four: Kiya's Alabaster Jar   125

Five: Tawosret's Golden Earrings   195

Six: Yuya's Vanished Shabtis   283

Notes   *323*

Bibliography   *341*

Index   *347*

Acknowledgments

The life of Theodore Davis is the story of two distinct and widely separated histories: that of Gilded Age robber barons and of Egyptology. To piece together the tale, I have been extremely fortunate to draw upon the work, assistance, and friendship of scholars in both fields, without whose help the book would have been impossible to produce.

Gratitude beyond measure is due to Aidan Dodson, who plowed through the early drafts and kept me from making a number of embarrassing errors regarding Egyptian archaeology. Dennis Forbes, editor of *Kmt: A Modern Journal of Ancient Egypt,* was of constant and unflagging assistance in clarifying historical fine points, introducing me to other experts, and producing illustrations. Arwen Bicknell spent endless hours refining my work and transforming a monstrous prose outline into a readable text. My agent, Jessica Papin, was wonderfully patient and gentle in revealing to me the realities of the publishing business. My editor at St. Martin's

Press, Daniela Rapp, has been of inestimable help in transforming the manuscript into a successful narrative. Frances Sayers edited the final version to perfection.

Since no collection of Davis's papers has survived, I am deeply indebted to the libraries, archives, and private collections I have been able to draw upon. Special thanks are due to Susan Allen, Marsha Hill, and Dorothea Arnold at the Metropolitan Museum of Art for access to Emma Andrews's journal; to CEO Christopher Lee of the Columbus Chapel and Boal Mansion Museum in Boalsburg, Pennsylvania, for permission to consult the Boal family archives; to Lady Eileen Baker Strathnaver, Alice Newberry Hall, and Mary Newberry Matthews for offering the letters of Ellen Mary Newberry; and to the Keweenaw Land Association for their unpublished company history.

The staffs at the many institutions I have used have been unfailingly helpful. An incomplete list must include: James P. Quigel Jr., at the Historical Collections and Labor Archives at the Pennsylvania State University; the Ohio Historical Society; the New York State Historical Association; the public libraries in Bridgewater, New York, Worthington, Ohio, Iowa City, Iowa, and Pepperell, Massachusetts; the Special Collections Unit at the University of Rhode Island Library; the Redwood Library in Newport, Rhode Island; the Newport Historical Society; the Burke Library of Union Theological Seminary at Columbia University; the State Historical Society of Iowa; the University of Illinois at Champaign-Urbana; and especially the interlibrary loan department at the Orange County Public Library in California. For illustrations, thanks are due to the New-York Historical Society, the Semitic Museum at Harvard University, the City of Birmingham Library and Archives (UK), the Metropolitan Museum, and the Boal Mansion Museum.

Personal assistance at various vexing moments in the project has been graciously given by Dan Gordon, who blazed the trail; Nancy Pritchard, historian for Westmoreland, New York; Dennis O'Connor, for background on Joseph Lindon Smith; John Larson, archivist at the University of Chicago's Oriental Institute; Rush Clark and Rosemary Clark for information on their family; and Janice Kamrin, Geoffrey Martin, John Romer, Betsy Bryan, Don Ryan, Otto Schaden, and Nicholas Reeves. Any remaining mistakes or inaccuracies are wholly my own.

Personal thanks are due to Darrell Baker and David Moyer for books and encouragement; to Debb and Leon Green for Iowa City hospitality; to Tom and Joyce Coultas for the use of their barn; to Mike Hurrelbrink for IT support; and to Aby, Crombie, Desh, and Kem for company.

Finally and forever, my endless gratitude and love to Nancy Ileen, the light of my life, solver of all problems, and repairer of all things broken. She shared her home with Theodore Davis for more than half a decade, and I fear on occasion he was a somewhat inconvenient guest.

A Note on Names

Since the written ancient Egyptian language did not include vowels, translation of names into English has always been varied and a bit arbitrary. As a result Thuyu, Tuya, Tjuya, Tjuiu, Thuaa, and Touiou are all the same person. I have chosen to use the generally accepted current transliterations, per Baker's *Encyclopedia of the Egyptian Pharaohs,* observing the dominant conventions such as "Thutmose" (the U.S. name for the kings) instead of "Tuthmosis" (the usual British choice). In quoted passages I preserve the original authors' spellings to provide a sense of their times, and believe most are similar enough to avoid confusion.

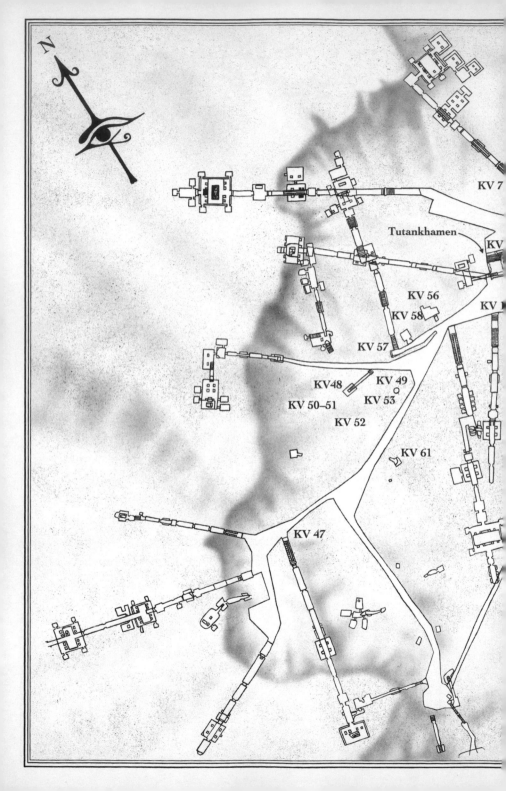

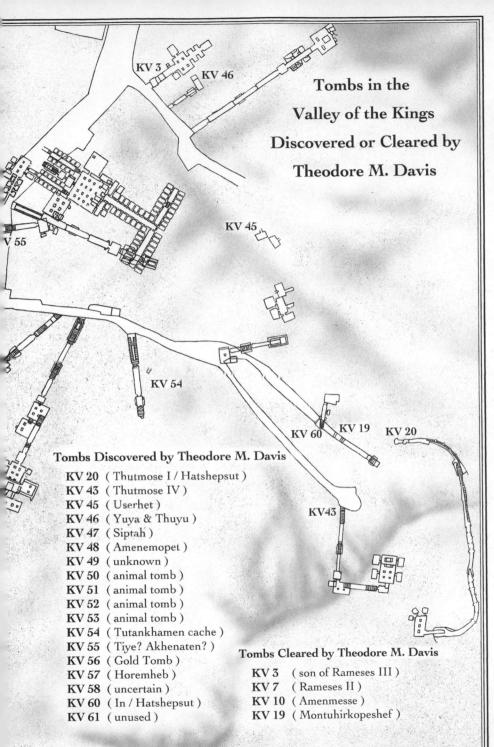

KV 3

KV 46

KV 45

V 55

KV 54

KV 60   KV 19   KV 20

KV43

Tombs in the Valley of the Kings Discovered or Cleared by Theodore M. Davis

Tombs Discovered by Theodore M. Davis

KV 20 (Thutmose I / Hatshepsut)
KV 43 (Thutmose IV)
KV 45 (Userhet)
KV 46 (Yuya & Thuyu)
KV 47 (Siptah)
KV 48 (Amenemopet)
KV 49 (unknown)
KV 50 (animal tomb)
KV 51 (animal tomb)
KV 52 (animal tomb)
KV 53 (animal tomb)
KV 54 (Tutankhamen cache)
KV 55 (Tiye? Akhenaten?)
KV 56 (Gold Tomb)
KV 57 (Horemheb)
KV 58 (uncertain)
KV 60 (In / Hatshepsut)
KV 61 (unused)

Tombs Cleared by Theodore M. Davis

KV 3   (son of Rameses III)
KV 7   (Rameses II)
KV 10 (Amenmesse)
KV 19 (Montuhirkopeshef)

Rhys Davies 2013

The
Millionaire
and the
Mummies

"Outer Coffin of Touiyou," painted by Howard Carter in the Salle Theodore M. Davis of the Egyptian Museum (Summer 1906). From Davis, The Tomb of Iouiya and Touiyou.

One

THUYU'S GOLDEN COFFIN

A blockbuster exhibition of ancient art left Egypt and started touring the world in 2004. It stayed on the road for the next decade and was visited by ten million people on four continents. The largest golden object in the show was a massive mummy case[1] seven feet long, two feet wide, and forty inches high. The refined, elegantly sculpted face was broad, with a wide nose, a dainty chin, and eyes of obsidian and calcite set in blue glass; it gazed serenely into eternity, a slight smile hovering on its lips. It was sheathed from head to toe in gleaming, beaten reddish gold. The overwhelming size and ostentation made the coffin, if not the most subtle or exquisite piece in the show, perhaps the most imposing.

The coffin was made in the royal workshops for a woman named Thuyu who likely bore no resemblance whatever to the face on the cover. Thuyu was perhaps a commoner, perhaps petty nobility. She was a priestess of the god Amen and moved into the palace when her daughter became the Great Royal Wife of the pharaoh known as Amenhotep the Magnificent during Egypt's Eighteenth Dynasty. As a special favor, Thuyu and her husband were given a tomb in the highly exclusive Valley of the Kings. One day around 1370 B.C. Thuyu was placed in the coffin and the coffin was sealed in her tomb. It sat in silence and unremitting darkness for almost 3,300 years.

The two well-dressed men riding donkeys through the afternoon shadows in the Valley of the Kings on February 12, 1905, might have been tourists—an old man and his grandson on a world tour, perhaps, visiting Egypt between stops in Naples and Constantinople. A cold southern wind sent clouds of sand flying around them. The sturdy little animals they rode (the older man using his hand-made English saddle) were available for hire by the day or month, but the two were not sightseers; their donkeys had been rented for the digging season because the men were tomb hunters, returning to work after lunch. Both were excited, although their demeanors remained properly restrained and only the constant cigarette puffing by the older man gave away his anxious anticipation.

For five days their workmen had been breaking apart and clearing concretelike rubble out of a stairway carved more than three thousand years before into the bedrock of the royal cemetery—a stairway found at the bottom of a thirty-foot mound of sand and rock chips that had taken sixty men three weeks to remove. The previous day the crew had reached the top of a doorway and they had spent this morning digging to uncover that. The older man knew the passage might end abruptly in a blank limestone wall, an unfinished mistake abandoned by the ancients. The younger rider dreamed it might lead, as such doors had led his companion twice before, to a pharaoh's tomb.

The older man was Theodore Montgomery Davis,[2] a sixty-six-year-old American millionaire who had been granted the right to excavate in the valley. Davis's agreement with the Egyptian government gave him the authority to lead the exploration and the obligation to pay for it, a familiar role; in America he had dug a canal, built railroads, cut down forests, and opened iron and silver mines. He was an art collector who socialized with presidents and had erected a mansion for himself in Newport, Rhode Island. He had selected the spot where the stairway was found although, as he later wrote, "the site was most unpromising . . . certainly no Egyptologist, exploring with another person's money, would have thought of risking the time and expense."[3]

He was a fit, wiry man, five feet nine inches tall (average for his day) with hazel eyes that were striking for their direct, appraising gaze. His brown hair was turning white and he wore elaborate muttonchop whiskers that had been stylish in his youth but were now considered old-fashioned. He wore a broad-brimmed hat, an expensive woolen jacket, a vest, and a collar and tie; his legs were protected from the donkey's flanks by puttees and knee-high spats.

Davis's companion was twenty-four-year-old British archaeologist Arthur Weigall, the newly hired antiquities inspector for the Egyptian government. Weigall later said Davis tended to regard the valley as his own property, but the young Englishman's job would be to oversee the American's work. Acutely aware of his subordinate position to the older man, Weigall knew that Davis's goodwill would be crucial to his future.

For Davis, the relationship was natural to the point of tedium; almost everyone he came in contact with was a subordinate. Davis's wealth ensured that those who met him were invariably conscious of what his favor could provide, and he was far from stingy. The week before, he and his mistress had inspected the building he had constructed for a girls' school run by Presbyterian missionaries in Luxor (ancient Thebes), across the Nile from the valley. Once Davis decided a man—or a woman, as at the school—was reliable, he was generous and charming. Weigall later said that "thanks to his good nature, the serenity of our work was ruffled by but few breezes."[4]

As their donkeys arrived at the excavation site the two men dismounted and eagerly inspected the hole gashed by the ancients into the bedrock.[5] Davis's diggers had finished exposing the doorway at the bottom of the steep, thirteen-step stairwell; a stone and mud-mortar wall filled the door space. The men immediately noticed that an opening had been made at the top of the blocking wall, proof that something lay beyond the doorway but also a sign the tomb had been entered by ancient grave robbers. It was an unwelcome indication but not a surprise. Every king's tomb in the valley—including the two Davis had already discovered—had been robbed millennia before, leaving behind only broken fragments of the riches they had contained when they were first sealed.

Night would fall before the workmen could clear the wall blocking the doorway, so Davis ordered a halt for the day and sent all his men home except the *reis* (the Egyptian foreman). The day before, Davis had called in police to guard the site overnight, knowing the several hundred natives living in poverty and squalor in villages near the valley were as interested as their ancestors had been in acquiring some of the wealth a tomb might provide. Accumulating his fortune had given Davis a keen appreciation of human frailty; his own wealth was the result of intelligence, hard work, and luck coupled with fraud, perjury, and bribery.

With the workmen gone, Davis and Weigall inspected the
tomb's entry. The doorway at the bottom of the steps was six feet
tall and blocked by the wall except for the top eighteen inches, a
chin-level opening impossible for them to crawl through without a
ladder. Peering through the opening, they saw a steep ramp descending farther into the earth; to one side Davis saw what he
thought was a cane lying on the floor. The young son of the *reis*
was enlisted, and with his turban undone and tied under his arms,
the boy was lifted up to the opening and then lowered into the
chamber. The ramp was clear beyond the door but the space was
almost completely empty. The boy handed back through the opening what Davis had seen—an ancient staff of office—followed by
a neck yolk from a chariot and a stone scarab (a religious amulet
carved as a beetle) covered in gold foil. The frightened child was
hauled back out of the dim chamber after reporting there were no
paintings or carvings on the walls.

Davis wrapped the objects in his overcoat, secured them to the
pommel of his saddle, and headed for home. As he traveled across
the plain from the valley back to the Nile he was surprised when
some villagers told him they knew he carried the staff of a prince,
a large scarab, and a chariot yolk of solid gold. News spread rap-
idly among the locals, and inconspicuous watchers kept an eye on
foreign diggers; Weigall had decided to spend the night at the
tomb since it was assumed Egyptian guards could not be relied
upon and a European's presence was needed to protect the find.
"The mouth of a lonely tomb already said by native rumour to
contain incalculable wealth," he wrote, "is not perhaps the safest
place in the world."[6]

Home for Davis was his *dahabiyeh,* a unique style of sail-
powered houseboat used for travel up and down the Nile. Davis's
twin-masted boat had all the opulence of his Newport mansion: a

grand piano in the salon, a crystal chandelier in the dining room, a library, four bedrooms, and bathrooms with tubs. A large U.S. flag floated across the stern. The crew of twenty Nubian sailors wore matching white turbans and brown cardigans with the name of their ship—the *Beduin*—stitched across the chest in red. The *Beduin* was tied up to the west bank of the Nile, about three miles from the valley.

Seated on deck in one of the brown, hooded wicker chairs decorated with bright yellow and black cushions and arranged around a collection of handmade carpets, waited his companion of the past twenty years, Emma B. Andrews. Emma, a cousin of Davis's absent wife, was a wealthy widow from Columbus, Ohio, and a year older than Davis. Today she would be called his mistress (and that is how Davis's wife referred to her), despite their separate bedrooms in Newport and on the *Beduin*. She was intelligent, cultured, and unconventional. One of her passions was education for young women; now the champion for the school in Luxor, when she had moved into the mansion with Davis and his wife eighteen years before she had been elected vice president of the Newport Industrial School for Girls.

The couple spent every winter in Egypt and preferred to travel with company. On this trip they had brought twenty-three-year-old Jean Hardy from Columbus, a member of Emma's extended family, and Alice Wilson, also in her early twenties and the daughter of Davis's closest friend and business partner. Davis's English valet and Emma's French maid rounded out the party.

Arriving at the *Beduin,* Davis rushed past the cage of live poultry that provided eggs and meat for the five-course dinners served on the boat, past the huge wooden pilings the crew had pounded into the earth to secure the boat to shore, and bounded up the gangplank to share his finds with the ladies. In her journal, Emma wrote that "he had an air of great elation," and described what he revealed: "a yoke of a chariot, finely decorated in gold and color— in perfect condition . . . a wand of office—also finely decorated . . . and a large beautiful green, hard stone scarab, with gilded bands, beautifully inscribed even to the wings."[7]

Davis sent messages to two other *dahabiyeh*s that were tied up nearby. On board the *Miriam* was Gaston (later Sir Gaston) Maspero, director general of the Egyptian Service des Antiquities and the supreme authority for all decisions on archaeological work in Egypt. The French-born son of an Italian political exile, Maspero had been a professor of Egyptology in France since 1869 and from 1881 to 1886 had served as head of the service; he had returned to the job in 1899 (with a substantial salary increase). Maspero, recognized as the world's foremost Egyptologist, was returning north to Cairo after an inspection tour and was the man who had approved Davis to excavate in the valley, referring to him as the American Maecenas (the ancient Roman patron of Virgil and Horace). Davis's note invited Maspero to "come over and see something worth looking at."[8] When he arrived, Maspero said he had already heard in Luxor that afternoon that a tomb had been found in the valley filled with gold.

Davis also invited the Reverend Archibald Sayce, an Oxford professor and ordained minister in the Church of England who never wore anything but the black long-skirted clerical costume and three-cornered hat his religious office called for. Sayce, the world's foremost expert on the ancient Hittites, had largely retired from academic life and spent every winter on the Nile excavating different sites and copying inscriptions. His boat had just arrived in Luxor and moored next to Davis. Like most of the scholarly *dahabiyeh* owners, Sayce had been friends with Davis for years.

It was a dramatic and exciting evening on the *Beduin,* and

laughter and applause echoed over the Nile far into the night. Davis reported that the light had not been sufficient to see what lay beyond the ramp into the rest of the tomb. All agreed that the most likely explanation for the presence of the treasures on the ramp was that the ancient robbers had emerged from looting the burial chamber into better light and discovered the objects were not solid gold but only covered in gold foil. As they examined the finds under the crystal chandelier in the salon, decorated with its Morris green brocades and art fabrics, the group on the *Beduin* could only speculate on what else such picky burglars might have left behind.

Maspero was most excited by the chariot yoke, since no complete ancient Egyptian chariot had ever been recovered. Mostly, the group speculated about whose tomb they had found. "We had not the slightest clue," Davis wrote.[9] None of the objects carried a name, although they clearly came from the ancient royal workshops.

Maspero asked if the tomb could be opened the next day. He had received a telegram from Lord Cromer (the British consul general who actually governed Egypt) saying Queen Victoria's third son would be in Luxor the following afternoon, and the Frenchman was eager to benefit his position with the British by presenting the Duke of Connaught and his party with a noteworthy event. Davis quickly agreed. No one found it easy to sleep that night, as visions of what might lie beyond the tomb's door kept the explorers awake.

Another of Davis's friends joined Weigall at the mouth of the tomb that night when American artist Joseph Lindon Smith and his wife, Corinna (of the publishing Putnam family), arrived to camp out with the inspector and the half dozen Egyptian guards. Joe Smith, a forty-one-year-old native of Pawtucket, Rhode Island, had studied art in Boston and Paris and dedicated his career to painting the architectural glories of the past. Like Davis, he spent

Davis's yacht, the Beduin, *photographed 1902. Reproduced with permission of the Semitic Museum, Harvard University, Lyon Photo No. 142.*

winters working in Egypt; the two had known each other for several years. Davis, whom Smith described as "an eccentric, brusque little man but a good friend to people he liked,"[10] had already promised Smith he would be among the first to see any new discovery. Weigall recalled they slept fitfully until the dawn, although Corinna Smith told Emma the night had been one of the most beautiful she had ever spent, despite the cold; she had risen early to make tea and watch the sunrise from a hilltop.

Davis awoke as usual the next morning when his valet brought him his juice and laid out his clothes for the day; Emma and the girls were awakened by her maid. When the situation called for it, Davis would trade his donkey for a hired carriage, and after a hurried breakfast on Monday, February 13, a stream of carriages left the Nileside moorings of the *dahabiyeh*s. Emma rode with Alice Wilson, who had been ill for several days but could not bear to miss the opening of the tomb, and Davis rode with Sayce. The men chatted nervously as they crossed the country to the valley. Davis told Sayce a story he was particularly fond of, about the time he asked his friend and Newport neighbor Alexander Agassiz, a noted naturalist, why he thought the Almighty had made living things. "To eat each other," had been Agassiz's instant reply.

The group arrived at the tomb around nine o'clock and found Weigall and the Smiths had been joined by the work crew. As soon as Maspero arrived, orders were given to take down the wall at the bottom of the stairs. "It was very slow work, as every stone had to be examined for hieroglyphs and signs, and every basket of sand and debris sifted and examined for objects of interest," Davis wrote.[11]

As the work began, Maspero told Davis there was a location in the adjoining western valley that he thought was promising and asked Davis to accompany him to the site to inspect it. Maspero more likely wanted to talk privately about a problem he was having with an employee named Howard Carter, a young British archaeologist who in 1922 would discover the tomb of Tutankhamen. The first three years of Davis's digging in the valley had been supervised by Carter and they were good friends, but the archaeologist was now embroiled in a controversy that would soon result in his resignation. Davis would hire the unemployed Carter to paint illustrations for his next book.

The winds of the day before had ceased and while Davis and Maspero were gone, Emma and the group waited in the sun, seated on rocks or in carriages (with and without parasols) as the workmen took down the wall to the tomb. Although Davis was entitled to be the first entrant to any tomb he discovered, Emma wrote that when one of the workers came out of the tomb and told Weigall the entrance was free, he and Smith went down the tantalizing stairway. As the two scrambled down the steep ramp beyond the door, Smith noticed a bunch of desiccated ancient onions and a large black wig discarded by the thieves. At the end of the thirty-foot ramp the men found another stairway of seventeen steps. At the bottom was another doorway, again blocked by a wall of stones and mortar. Like the door above, the wall had been breached at the top.

They peered through the hole until, after a short time, they heard the voices of Davis and Maspero outside. Weigall emerged from the tomb pale and breathless. "I thought he had been affected by bad air," Emma wrote, "but it was only excitement—for he ejaculated 'wonderful,' 'extraordinary,' etc." Smith crowed there was "everything down there but a grand piano!" Smith remembered that Maspero, seeing the men's smoking candles, asked if the passageway was clear. Both men agreed it was. Maspero ordered a message be sent to the Duke of Connaught.

Davis, Maspero, and Weigall now descended into the tomb, each carrying a candle. As they passed down the ramp Davis noted a bouquet of dried flowers to the side; a roll of papyrus that proved to be a *Book of the Dead* was also discovered in the passage. At the bottom of the second staircase Davis found a bowl "showing the finger-marks of the man who with his hands gathered the mud and plastered it on the doorway wall" three millennia before. Inspecting the door, Davis wrote, "we found that the opening which the robber had made was too high and too small . . . Though we had nothing but our bare hands, we managed to take down the upper layer of stones, and then Monsieur Maspero and I put our heads and candles into the chamber."[12]

The sight that greeted Davis and Maspero was the most

astounding discovery ever seen in the Valley of the Kings; it would be eclipsed only once, seventeen years later when Howard Carter saw the "wonderful things" in the tomb of Tutankhamen. The candle flames were reflected in what appeared to be a room filled with gold, and as the men's eyes adjusted they began to discern coffins, furniture, statues, boxes, and more, all with golden surfaces glinting through the drifting motes of dust. In front of them was the greatest collection of ancient art and fine craftsmanship ever found in Egypt. With the sole exception of Tutankhamen's, it remains to this day the richest tomb ever discovered in the valley.

They were amazed to see that while the tomb had indeed been robbed, it was not seriously disturbed. A huge wooden sarcophagus—a box eight feet long, six feet high, and trimmed in gold intended to hold mummy cases—was directly opposite the door; its top had been lifted off and set aside by the robbers. Within were three nested coffins, their lids also removed, and in the innermost gilded coffin lay a mummy. Its wrappings had been torn from the face and hands, revealing an elderly man whose features reminded the artist Smith of Abraham Lincoln. To the left was a similarly opened sarcophagus, the inner golden coffin containing a woman's body. At the far end of the chamber was a perfect chariot. The robbers had clearly searched the mummies for jewelry but had left the chamber crammed with ancient funeral goods. The tomb, according to Maspero, "was violated with discretion by persons who almost possessed respect for the dead, and who were in too great a hurry to despoil it thoroughly."[13]

Struck dumb, the men gaped at what the world press would soon trumpet as the greatest find in the history of Egyptian archaeology.

It was a moment of personal triumph for Davis. The archaeologists of the antiquities service—including Maspero—had emphasized how unlikely a discovery on that spot would be. Davis insisted he chose the location simply to finish exploring the section of the valley they had already almost completed. With uncharacteristic pride, Emma wrote that although the experts did not think the site worth working, "Theo in his thorough way said he should go on clearing up both sides of that side valley."

The moment finally passed, and the men set about entering the burial chamber through the opening in the top of the door. Davis was the first to go through and made the entry with little difficulty; at age sixty-six he still rode horseback and played tennis every day in Newport.

Maspero faced a greater challenge than Davis. The director general was an extremely large man who enlisted Weigall's help in getting through the hole. After what must have been a prodigious effort by young Weigall, Davis's moments alone with the treasure ended when Maspero's considerable bulk was heaved through the opening into the chamber. As Maspero himself put it, "There is no slit behind which an archaeologist suspects he may find something new or unknown too small for him to get through. He undergoes much discomfort, but he manages to squeeze through."[14]

Weigall entered the tomb last. As he described the scene later, "We saw a sight which I can safely say no living man has ever seen. The chamber was pretty large—a rough hewn cavern of a place. In the middle of the room were two enormous sarcophagi of wood inlaid with gold." He recalled being most moved by the apparent timelessness the scene conveyed; he likened it to entering a town house that had been closed for only a few months. "We stood, really dumfounded, and stared around at the relics of the life of over three thousand years ago, all of which were as new almost as when they graced the palace."[15] He was impressed by alabaster vases, two beds, and three wooden armchairs decorated with gold. "In all directions stood objects gleaming with gold undimmed by a speck of dust, and one looked from one article to another with the feeling that the entire human conception of Time was wrong." He felt as though he were "mad or dreaming . . . Maspero, Davis and I stood there gaping and almost trembling."[16]

Maspero echoed Weigall's emotions; he felt he had "left behind him all the centuries that have elapsed since the dead man was alive; the mummy has just descended to the vault, the celebrant performs the last rites, the acolytes finish placing the furniture and the offerings . . . Fortune, which often betrays us, has this time deigned to shower its favors on Mr. Davis."[17]

Stepping gingerly among the objects through the still, slightly stale air, they searched for the owner's name, marveling at all they saw. Davis wrote their candles "gave so little light and so dazzled our eyes that we could see nothing but the glitter of gold." It was Maspero who found the tomb owner's name, inscribed in gold on the sarcophagus. The tomb belonged to a man named Yuya, a chief officer in the Egyptian chariotry, and his wife, Thuyu. The men recognized the couple's names from the "marriage scarabs"— palm-sized carved stone beetles with an inscription on the underside announcing the union of King Amenhotep III and his Great Royal Wife, Tiye. "The name of her father is Yuya. The name of her mother is Thuyu," the scarabs read, and Amenhotep had them widely distributed (some fifty survive) to spread the news through Egypt in 1386 B.C. The explorers had not found a king's tomb; they had found an almost undisturbed burial that a king had provided his in-laws as a very special favor. The mummies were the grandparents of Akhenaten, the "heretic pharaoh"; they were the great-grandparents of King Tut.

In the excitement of reading the inscription, Maspero handed his candle to Davis and leaned closer to the giant wooden box, which was painted with a flammable tar called bitumen. Davis moved the candles closer to illuminate the characters until the Frenchman broke the silence by shouting at Davis to get the candles away from the pitch-covered box. "Had my candles touched the bitumen, which I came dangerously near doing," Davis wrote, "the coffin would have been in a blaze. As the entire contents of the tomb were inflammable . . . we should have undoubtedly lost our lives."[18] Having avoided by inches what would have been the most bizarre archaeological disaster ever to occur in Egypt, the three men decided it was time to leave the burial chamber. They set the workmen to taking down the wall and returned to the sunlight; Maspero invited the rest of the group to inspect the tomb—just as soon as electric lights were strung into it.

As Corinna Smith entered the burial chamber Maspero assisted her over the dismantled wall and commented, "Doubtless you are the first woman that has been in this tomb chamber alive—there's a dead one over there,"[19] as he pointed to Thuyu's coffin. Corinna broke down in tears at the sight of the treasure; Emma recalled "a dim glitter of gold everywhere and a confusion of coffins and mummies." Sayce found the tomb "historically interesting and full of treasure . . . Wherever we stepped we trod upon fragments of gold foil."[20]

After they had seen the tomb the group adjourned to a nearby plateau where the *Beduin*'s crew had assembled a full sit-down luncheon. After lunch Davis, Weigall, and Maspero reentered the tomb and the archaeologists began recording the conditions and started to inventory the objects. Davis spent the time gazing at Thuyu's mummy. "I studied her face and indulged in speculations germane to the situation, until her dignity and character so impressed me that I almost found it necessary to apologize for my presence."[21] That he could sit and calmly reflect in the company of a desiccated corpse belies a familiarity with death. In fact, his earliest memories were of a funeral sixty-two years before.

Birds had chirped cheerfully as they careened through blue skies, oblivious to the four-year-old boy below who walked solemnly with his mother and big brother through the mud of the Middle Village Cemetery in Springfield, New York. The ground was still soaked from a freak snowstorm that had hit the week before, on June 11, 1842. Two days after the storm the boys' father, the Reverend Richard Montgomery Davis, had died of consumption.

The smell of wet earth rose from the freshly dug grave as the reverend's thirty-year-old widow, Catherine, stood over it with her two sons, seven-year-old Arthur (named after Arthur Tappan, a wealthy New York City abolitionist leader) and Theodore; she carried baby Gertrude in her arms. The cemetery was a short walk down a quiet country lane from the Presbyterian church where Reverend Davis had served as pastor and where the funeral had been conducted. The funeral was well attended despite the chilly weather; Davis had added fifty-five members to the church and most of them had come.

At the service, the visiting minister had described Richard Davis's conversion to Christ in his early twenties at a Methodist camp meeting during the "Second Great Revival" in 1821, where he found religion and felt a call to the ministry. After graduating from Union College he enrolled at the Auburn Theological Seminary, a hotbed of antislavery sentiment where Davis helped form the Seminary's Temperance Society in 1828. Fellow students recalled him as "quite eccentric" and "an odd fellow, a queer genius," who "preached a good deal at random." He had been ordained in 1831 and ministered in Parma, Marshall, and Bridgewater before coming to Springfield in 1835—where he was, according to the minister, "successful in leading souls to Christ."[22] As the congregation sang the final hymn Catherine may have recalled the funeral of her infant daughter Angellica nine years before, or that of her own father when she had only been ten. As the coffin was carried from the church, the bell tolled from the steeple Reverend Davis had heightened.

Catherine's future looked bleak as she stood with Arthur and Theodore in the quiet graveyard watching her husband's coffin being lowered into the ground; she had no claim to the parsonage she and the children had lived in, and her husband had left no savings. Springfield offered few opportunities; it had been a busy stop on the Great Western Turnpike, carrying settlers west after the Revolutionary War, but the Erie Canal's opening in 1825 had ended the turnpike's traffic and Springfield had reverted to a mid-state rural backwater. It was home to a gristmill, a sawmill, two stores, and fifteen dwellings. The same year Richard and Catherine had moved to Springfield, James Fenimore Cooper (who set his *Leatherstocking Tales* in the area) had returned after a decade in Europe to his family home in Cooperstown, ten miles away. In *Home as Found* (1838), Cooper satirized the area as a pit of vulgarity, demagoguery, and hypocrisy.

Theodore's father was the type of man Cooper would have disliked; a famous fire-breathing evangelist approvingly recalled Reverend Davis's preaching at an 1836 revival meeting as "bordering on the verge of insanity."[23] The climate in the Davis household had been one of godliness, temperance, and abolitionism. Reverend Davis had been one of the leaders of the "New School" antislavery Presbyterians when the issue split the church in 1837; the Springfield congregation, along with another sixty thousand "radicals," had been expelled by the church's general assembly. The reverend had died at forty-one; a friend recalled that he "killed himself through his loud, high toned preaching." He had lived his entire life within 150 miles of his birthplace and was buried under a handsome marble tombstone donated by the church.

That night, after the children were asleep, Catherine sat in silence and considered her future. Born in Berne (twenty miles from Albany), Catherine Hubbell had married at nineteen in 1832. Arthur had been born in 1835 and the family's situation had improved enough by the following year that Reverend Davis had borrowed $200 to buy a few head of cattle from a Springfield farmer. When Theodore was born on May 7, 1838, New York City banks had just resumed making payments to depositors after the financial Panic of 1837, Queen Victoria was about to be crowned in London, Samuel Morse had just demonstrated his new invention called the telegraph, and a slave named Frederick Douglass would soon escape from his owner in Maryland to New York City. Such events were little noted in Springfield, however; the farmers paid scant attention to the outside world as they raised their corn, cattle, and clover among rolling hills, lakes, and forests. By the time Gertrude Matilda Davis had been born in 1841, Reverend Davis's consumption had grown so serious that his church had hired a second minister to assist with his duties.

Left destitute with three small children, Catherine was forced to rely on charity. Family helped (she had a dozen aunts and uncles) and friends pitched in as well, but the next few years were difficult. Her sorrows increased when Arthur died in 1843 at age eight. Theodore, now five, returned with Catherine to the cemetery where his big brother was buried next to his father, under a much smaller tombstone. The early loss of his father and brother doubtless contributed to Theodore's fatalistic attitude, without the comforts of his father's religion. Years later he wrote to a bereaved friend, "Such is life, and all we poor mortals can do is to face the situation and work out of it as best we may."[24]

Catherine's years of money troubles also made a strong impression on the boy. A relentless drive to become wealthy clearly grew out of Theodore's childhood poverty, but Catherine managed to raise her son into a man without the bitterness or hardness their circumstances might have produced. She instilled him with a sense of self-confidence and optimism that developed into a cheerful personality; he was recalled by friends as constantly making jokes and quips. Catherine placed a high value on learning, and although he received no formal schooling in Springfield, self-education became a lifelong habit for him.

Catherine survived a half dozen years on the kindness of friends—a farmer and town supervisor who paid off the loan for Reverend Davis's cattle was never repaid. Other helpers included Jonas and Lucy Titus, who had been friends since Reverend Davis had led the Presbyterian church in Jonas Titus's hometown of Marshall in 1833. The Tituses raised seven children on their fifty-acre farm, and Catherine had maintained her friendship with them after the ambitious Jonas moved his family west to Detroit in the Michigan Territory in 1836, where he became auctioneer for Wayne County and bought an eighty-acre farm. In 1838 he traveled in a canoe with pioneer Douglass Houghton surveying Lake Superior and Michigan's Upper Peninsula. The following year his political connections won him the job of warden at the state prison in Jackson.

When the Titus family returned home to New York for a visit in 1846, they shared their excitement with Catherine about two locations in the Upper Peninsula that Titus had bought to mine for copper. A trip to New York City had produced financial backers who formed a company with him to start mining operations, and in addition to 20 percent of the stock in the company, Titus had received $4,500. He planned to use the money to start the first horse-drawn omnibus line in Detroit.

When Lucy visited again in the fall of 1847, she told Catherine that although the omnibus venture had failed, her hopes were high that the copper mines Jonas had found would soon start producing; the New York financiers had sent their own man to inspect the location and her husband had stayed in Detroit to help the New Yorkers buy another site that also looked promising. On her way home after the visit, Lucy fell overboard from the steamer *Hendrick Hudson* during a storm on Lake Erie and drowned a few miles west of Cleveland; her body was never recovered. Within a few months of Lucy's death Catherine's money problems were solved when she wed Jonas Titus. The marriage was providential for Catherine; it lasted more than twenty years and provided a comfortable, secure life.

She traveled with her children to their new home in Detroit—a fascinating trip for the curious, energetic ten-year-old Theodore. The journey entailed taking a wagon for twenty-five miles north to the Erie Canal, then gliding in a barge pulled by mules for two hundred miles along the canal to Buffalo and Lake Erie. Another two hundred miles by steamer across the lake brought them to the Detroit River, which took their boat north to Titus's farm in Wayne County.

Titus's other children had left home by now and the marriage was a new beginning for both partners, although the change from bucolic and relatively civilized Springfield to frontier Detroit must have been jarring for Catherine's children. Detroit's population had increased from 2,000 in 1830 to 21,000 by 1850, its growth fueled by the opportunities of the developing wilderness. A mile west of Detroit the forest started, stretching to the Pacific. An influx of immigrants caused the town to boom as settlers moved

west through Detroit while fish, lumber, and produce were transported east. The mineral wealth of the Upper Peninsula, where
Titus's copper mines were located, added to the boom; the first
iron furnace west of Pittsburgh fired up in Detroit the year Theodore Davis moved there.

The move allowed Davis to receive the only formal schooling
he ever had, in the Detroit public schools. Since Titus had to split
his time between the farm and his duties at the Jackson prison fifty
miles away, much of the farm labor fell to young Davis and the
nineteen-year-old African-American laborer who lived with them.
As schooling sharpened Davis's mind, brutal farmwork hardened
his body.

Shortly after Davis's arrival, in the summer of 1848, Titus received news from his lawyer that enraged him and made a strong
impression on his stepson. At dinner in the farmhouse, over vegetables and meat raised on the farm and cooked on a wood-burning
stove by Catherine, the flickering oil lamps and candles illuminated Titus's flushed face as he shared the story.

The New Yorkers who had bought his copper leases had
agreed they would develop Titus's mines and any others the
company bought. The man they had sent to the Upper Peninsula
had determined Titus's sites were worthless, but the new spot he
had found that Titus had helped purchase—"Location 98" it was
called—appeared to be worth the large investment required to
open a mine. The New Yorkers' lawyers had then formed a separate company to work the new site with ownership identical to
the old company—except for Jonas Titus. None of the profits from
Location 98, which proved to be enormous, would go to Titus;
he had been betrayed, robbed, and made a fool of by the eastern
sharpies. It is likely this was when ten-year-old Theodore decided
to be a lawyer.

. . .

Inside Yuya's tomb, Davis's reflections over Thuyu's body ended when he stood up, cried, "Oh my God!" and keeled over in a dead faint. The archaeologists carried him out of the tomb, up the stairway and the long ramp, to the entry, where they bathed his head and hands in water and gave him a drink of brandy. He came to and was helped to one of the carriages, where the young ladies attended to him.

Davis was fully recovered by four o'clock when His Royal Highness the Duke of Connaught, who was touring Egypt in his official capacity as inspector general of the army, arrived with full military escort. Traveling with the party was the crown prince of Sweden, who would marry the duke's daughter at Windsor Castle in four months. The duke, Maspero, and Weigall spent an hour in the tomb marveling at the treasures, including Thuyu's elegant coffin.

When they emerged, Emma records, the duke "strode over to the rocks where Theodore was and heartily congratulated him, and begged to present him to the Duchess." The artist Joe Smith recalled waiting for the duke to make a short speech thanking Davis for his contribution to archaeology; as he began speaking, Smith saw his "donkey boy" Hassan—who had not been fully paid for the animals he had provided the Smiths—burst through the line of distinguished foreigners and begin shouting in Arabic that he wanted his money. The duke, who spoke Arabic, stopped in midsentence and asked Hassan, "Who is it, my good man, that owes you so much money?" Hassan pointed to Smith's wife. The duke turned to the embarrassed woman, said "Madame, you should settle your donkey debts," and resumed his tribute to Davis.[25]

The world press lavished attention on the discovery. *The New York Times* called it "the greatest find in the whole history of

Egyptian research," with contents that "surpass in beauty and interest any previous discovery in the land of the Pharaohs." The paper noted with provincial pride that the discoverer was "an American, a New Yorker."[26] *The Illustrated London News* called it "Egypt's richest treasure trove,"[27] and other newspapers spoke of Egyptologists at Harvard "in a flutter over an archaeological discovery of the first magnitude in the land of the Nile."[28] *The Century Magazine* described the "surpassing splendor and significance"[29] of the find. The foremost Egyptologist at the British Museum, E. A. W. Budge, hailed it "the most envious and gorgeous funeral furniture which has ever been seen in an Egyptian tomb." Davis became an international celebrity; in different press accounts he was given the titles of professor, archaeologist, and Egyptologist (although he never claimed to be any of those things).

Publicity in the United States gave Americans a direct connection to Egyptian archaeology for the first time. Newspaperman William Randolph Hearst had written to his mother in 1900 that "In Egyptology as in everything else the great idea is to do something new and 'sensational' and not laboriously potter over what has been done before."[30] An ancient tomb full of gold was sensational, and the hero in America was the Yankee who had found it. The explorer was a distinct category of public hero in the early twentieth century, and Davis was the first American one in Egypt.

Yuya's tomb and treasures fueled an outbreak of "Egyptomania" worldwide. Newspaper coverage, magazine articles, and books found an eager reading public, and interest in the pharaohs increased so much that tourists visited Luxor in unprecedented numbers the following year. Davis's career kept Egypt in the limelight; when he was credited with discovering the tomb of Yuya's daughter Tiye two years later, she became the archetypical Egyptian queen (Nefertiti was still unknown) and a cigarette company that provided trading cards of celebrities to sell its products dedicated a card to her, endowing the ancient Egyptian with blue eyes and blond hair. When Davis later discovered what became known as the "Gold Tomb" it sparked an international craze for Egyptian-themed jewelry. Popular interest generated funds for more exploration; from 1905 the Museum of Fine Arts in Boston began paying for digs in Egypt, followed by the Metropolitan Museum in New York, the Brooklyn Museum, and the Universities of Chicago and Pennsylvania.

The discovery also proved to be a pivotal point in the practice of archaeology. Explorers in the valley had previously scrambled for treasure in spots where they thought finding a tomb was likely; as Davis put it, "exploring hither and thither where I supposed the greatest probability existed." However, after Davis's find in such an "unpromising" spot, he realized he was leaving the intervening areas unexplored, and conducted his digs for the next nine years in a methodical, exhaustive search of every inch of the valley. "I commenced at the south end of the valley," he wrote, "and cleared every foot of the mountains and foot-hills of all the deposits of stone and debris, and continued this manner of search by following the rock down as long as it was vertical and until it flattened."[31]

Years later it was suggested Davis's search policy had been Maspero's or Howard Carter's idea. It seems likely; the plan of inspecting every foot of bedrock for tomb entries is not an especially complicated concept, but Davis was the first digger in Egypt to commit himself to the years of effort the task would require and who was willing to pay the considerable costs for doing it. It resulted in Davis's setting an all-time record for discoveries in the valley. By the time he was through he had found eighteen tombs (almost a third of the valley's total) and immeasurably increased knowledge about the valley, the royals who were entombed there, and their world.

He remained relatively modest about his achievements, however; toward the end of his life he told Joe Smith that "what he would always remember with pride was that his work was merely a clearing job, and he had never searched for loot on a 'likely' site."[32]

The only flaw in Davis's policy was his belief that the ancients had known the valley was sometimes a watercourse; he and the Egyptologists assumed no one would dig a tomb into the flat floor where it would be vulnerable to vast floods of water on the rare occasions of rainfall. When he concluded his work, Davis believed he had found every tomb left in the valley.

He was close to correct. In the hundred years since, only three more tombs have been found. To keep things straight, the tombs in the valley are given numbers; Davis's last find was KV (for "Kings' Valley") 61, and Tutankhamen's tomb is KV 62. In 2006 American archaeologist Otto Schaden discovered the curious cache of coffins, jars, and pillows in the chamber known as KV 63, and a tiny, undecorated, and thoroughly looted chamber designated KV 64—usurped for an "intrusive" (later than the original) Twenty-second Dynasty chantress of Amun's mummy—was discovered in 2011 by Susanne Bickel and Elina Paulin-Grothe. The splendor of Tutankhamen's treasures, however, erased the public's memory of Davis's accomplishment; he was the most famous Egyptian explorer in the world in his day, but the discovery by his ex-employee Carter (seven years after the American's death) has overshadowed everything else ever found in Egypt and made Davis virtually unknown.

Even the blockbuster exhibition that showcased Thuyu's coffin in the twenty-first century was titled "Tutankhamun and the Golden Age of the Pharaohs," although a quarter of the show's artifacts were dug up by Davis. His only mention in the catalog is "a rich American businessman . . . Not an easy man to work for."[33]

Like the pharaohs he resurrected, Davis had hoped that his works would preserve his name, but he has been forgotten. His methods transformed archaeology from grave robbing into a science, but today he is scorned by the archaeological community. He stole the fortune that allowed him to indulge in hunting ancient treasures and gave away everything he found to museums. Those who came up against him while he was amassing his wealth would have been surprised he ever shared anything with anyone; those who knew of him when he was born would have been surprised he ever had anything to share at all. The tens of millions who have gazed in awe at Thuyu's coffin since Davis discovered it would be surprised to know the first man to contemplate its beauty in modern times followed a path to Yuya's tomb almost as dramatic as any of his discoveries.

Bronze flower bowl, presented to Davis by Percy Newberry, 1901. Reproduced with permission of the Metropolitan Museum of Art, New York.

Two

REKHMIRE'S BRONZE BOWL

One of the minor treasures of the Metropolitan Museum of Art in New York is a small bronze bowl[1] probably created in the workshops of Pharaoh Thutmose III during Egypt's Eighteenth Dynasty (ca. 1450 B.C.). The delicate piece was a votive offering, presented by the otherwise unknown Lady Nefrether to the goddess Hathor. It was intended to hold flowers and includes an exquisite miniature depiction of the goddess in the form of a cow, wearing a plumed headdress and sun disk, on a slightly elevated platform that allows the goddess to peek out through the lilies when the bowl is filled (a likely allusion to a mythological episode in which the god Horus was nursed in a marshy thicket). The lovely little bowl combines purity of design with superb technical execution. Only nine inches in diameter, it is not on display but secured in the Metropolitan's storerooms.

. . .

Four years before Davis peered into the glittering gloom of Yuya's tomb, he was just another rich tourist visiting Egypt. Aboard the *Beduin,* he and Emma spent their winters sailing up and down the river, socializing with other wealthy Westerners, visiting dig sites, and enjoying the ancient monuments. Their travel was leisurely, the boat tying up to shore every evening. "We are happy on this wonderful Nile," he wrote of his winter vacations, "with its warm, certain and hospitable sun and mild, sweet airs. We eat, drink, sleep, read, study, write, talk and sing."[2] On the evening of January 19, 1901, he was expecting a visitor who would turn out to change his life forever.

Percy Newberry fretted to himself as he walked through the Luxor twilight and up the gangplank of the *Beduin.* A very precise, particular individual who tended to fret and preferred things to go smoothly, Newberry was worried how Mr. Davis might respond to the news—and the gift—he had in store.

Newberry would have to wait before his anxiety would be allayed. He joined Davis on deck, where the American and his entourage were enjoying the Egyptian sunset, and took one of the thickly cushioned chairs at the card table. Bridge, whist, euchre, solitaire, chess, and dominoes occupied much of the time of the *Beduin's* passengers (three female friends had joined Davis and Emma this year). Davis greeted Newberry cheerfully, put down his cigar, and called one of the crew to fetch the guest a drink before dinner.

They made an odd pair; Davis was talkative, roughly humorous, and extremely competitive, even at whist and dominoes. Newberry was kind, considerate, and thoroughly decent, but reserved. He was also one of the most experienced archaeologists in Egypt, and when they had first met him two years before, Davis and Emma had been charmed by the Englishman. "We found him more interesting than we thought," Emma had written in her journal. "Knows everybody and everything. We fraternized at once over our mutual tastes in gardening and architecture."[3]

Newberry, for his part, was experienced at getting money for his excavations. After graduating from King's College in London he had first come to Egypt in 1888 and worked with the legendary William Matthew Flinders Petrie (the "father of Egyptian archaeology") for the Egypt Exploration Fund (EEF), a British fundraising group formed by novelist Amelia Edwards. (Davis was a member of the board of the American branch of the EEF and Emma was the honorary treasurer for Newport.) Newberry had dug on his own with money provided by Lord Amherst and the marquis of Northampton, but funding was always short, and Newberry and the other diggers made a regular habit of cultivating potential patrons; three months after they had first met, Newberry had presented Emma with a box of three-thousand-year-old flowers from a tomb he had excavated in Hawara (250 miles north of Luxor, site of the Twelfth-Dynasty pyramid of Amenemhet III).

Sitting together now on the *Beduin,* the two exchanged the usual pleasantries shared by acquaintances after a year's separation— Davis mentioned his mother had passed away the previous September, at age eighty-eight—and then Newberry got to the point of his visit. Five months earlier he had sent a letter to Davis at his Newport mansion. "I remember that you mentioned to me when we visited the Theban necropolis two years ago," Newberry had written, "that if I ever wanted to clear the tomb of Rekhmara you would like to join me in the expenses of the work."[4] He had asked for £250 and offered to undertake the work in Davis's name. The American had instantly cabled him the money.

Sitting at the card table with Davis, Newberry described the ten "tombs of the Nobles" he had spent the past two months clearing. His nervousness grew as they talked; in the intervening months he had told Davis it was likely they would find the mummy and an undisturbed burial in the tomb of Eighteenth-Dynasty vizier Rekhmire, and he had sent the American a note that he had discovered three golden bowls buried in the courtyard of the vizier's tomb chapel. He worried now that he had raised Davis's expectations too high.

Rekhmire's burial shaft had proven to be empty. What Newberry thought was Rekhmire's tomb was actually a chapel where offerings were made to his spirit; his tomb was elsewhere. However, Newberry put the best face he could on the season's results and before the group adjourned to the dining room below for dinner, Newberry unveiled the parcel he had brought. It was the usual procedure at the time for archaeological finds to be shared between the digger and the Egyptian government, and Newberry had been allotted one of the bowls—bronze, not gold—which he now presented to Davis. In fact, the artifact had nothing to do with Rekhmire; the three bowls had been stolen from some other location and stashed by robbers who never returned to pick them up. They were found with three large scarabs, Newberry explained, which he had recognized as modern forgeries made by a local Egyptian he knew. The bowls were indisputably genuine, however, and from the time of pharaoh Thutmose III.

The Englishman need not have worried; Davis was delighted with the bowl and accepted it with exaggerated gratitude. After the group finished its five-course meal with wine, served by the uniformed staff on fine china, crystal, and silverware, they moved to the *Beduin*'s salon, where Davis set his gift on display on top of the grand piano. They all talked, some played cards, and others read. Davis's eyes returned more than once to his ancient bronze bowl; it was his first reward for his first dig. The provenance of the

find did not disturb him; he had been involved with thieves before. He had been robbed in 1853 and it had nearly killed him.

By age fifteen, Davis had realized there was no future for him on
Jonas Titus's farm. Titus had seven children from his first marriage
and two more since marrying Catherine (Kate had been born in
1849 and Isabella in 1853), and a stepson would have to make his
own way. The unending farmwork was not to Davis's liking in any
case; James Hagerman, a Davis business partner in years to come,
worked on a Michigan farm at the same time and wrote, "Plowing,
mowing with a scythe, hauling manure, pitching hay, laying up
rail fence and pressing hay with a rude machine nearly killed
me . . . I detested it."[5] Davis undertook his first self-transformation
when he left home forever to seek his fortune, although such pre-
cocious maturity was not unusual in 1853.

Jonas Titus influenced the boy's development considerably. He
was not a soft or mild man; the prison he ran routinely inflicted
floggings, the ball and chain, and solitary confinement with bread
and water rations as punishment on the inmates. He was also ambitious, if frequently unsuccessful. In addition to his farm, Titus
had chased a number of schemes to become rich besides the copper mines and the omnibus line. He had operated a failed "temperance inn" in New York (the bar served no alcohol) and tried to
found a town and built a water mill in Lakeport, Michigan, that
also came to nothing. Titus's urge to hit it big was his legacy to his
stepson, and his connections helped get the boy on his way.

When Davis left home the St. Mary's Falls Ship Canal Company was building a canal to bypass the twenty-two-foot waterfall
that blocked access from the other Great Lakes to Lake Superior
at Sault Ste. Marie. The company's payoff for building the "Soo"

canal and completing a waterway that would extend from New York City to Minnesota was to be 750,000 acres of federally owned land in Michigan (although Henry Clay, arguing in Congress against the land grant, had criticized the canal as "beyond the remotest settlement in the United States, if not in the moon"). The company could select which acres they wanted, and land commissioner George S. Frost had the job of picking the parcels the company would take when the canal was finished. The problem was that much of Michigan was almost completely unexplored.

Frost, an elder in the First Presbyterian Church of Detroit, was a friend of Titus's, and when Titus mentioned his stepson was hoping to leave the farm, Frost offered the fifteen-year-old the chance to become a "landlooker"—one of a crew of prospectors hired to explore the unknown territory, gauge its value, and report back to Frost—thus guaranteeing the richest reward possible to the canal company owners. Davis leaped at the chance and struck out on his own. His relations with his family and his feelings on leaving them are largely unrecorded. He remained a dutiful son and responsible brother for the rest of his life and maintained polite connections with his relatives, but years later he cryptically referred to unspecified "qualities I have fought against, hated and *endured* in people of my own blood since I have been old enough to think."[6]

As a neophyte woodsman, Davis's job was to carry a hundred-pound pack containing some of the supplies the crew of four men needed. Flour, beans, dried pork, tents, blankets, cooking pans, knives, guns, and axes all had to be carried, as well as surveying tools.

The winter of 1853–54 was particularly harsh in Michigan. Temperatures reportedly reached thirty degrees below zero and snow lay sixteen feet deep. Davis's crew remained in the field, however, because the canal was due to be completed in eighteen months and their surveys had to be done by then. Exploring south of Cheboygan, the men traveled part of their way in a canoe and trudged on snowshoes into the woods to make their explorations.

When they reached the point where they needed to leave the river, the men pulled their canoe ashore, started a fire, and built their camp for the night. The next morning they stored enough food to get back to their starting point under their overturned canoe and set off into the forest. After several days tramping through the untracked wilderness, mapping the timber and mineral deposits, Davis and his partners were surprised to come across two men who claimed to be lost. They were actually independent prospectors seeking land to buy for themselves, and wanted to mislead the canal company crew about where they had been. After giving the two men directions back to the river, Davis and his partners moved on.

They continued their mapping, judging the country's value acre by acre, until their supplies ran out. Returning to the river, they were horrified to find the "lost" men had stolen their canoe and taken most of the food the landlookers had left behind. With no supplies or transportation, the four were confronted with a desperate challenge: Hungry, frozen, and footsore they snowshoed for a week to cover the fifty miles back to Saginaw, the nearest source of shelter and food, enduring subzero temperatures and sometimes blinded by blizzards. The trek was a major feat of physical endurance and a formative event for the young Davis. "Such experiences may be severely trying and even exhausting at the time," another landlooker wrote, "but you gain a sense of strength and self-confidence that can be obtained in no other way."[7] After surviving the trek through conditions as hostile as any the planet could produce, Davis was seldom intimidated by anything for the rest of his life.

The experience also provided the teenager with a valuable lesson in the world of business. On their safe arrival, the landlookers learned that the thieves, benefiting from the canoe, had beaten them to the land office and filed claim to some rich forest property the Davis group had found. "Our 'hooking' the canoe is what saved my land purchase," one of the thieves wrote fifty years later. "To 'hook' a canoe, pushed and driven as we were, seemed then a merit."[8] The merit of taking what you wanted and ignoring the niceties was a teaching that stayed with Davis.

After the ordeal in the wilderness Davis returned to the family farm for a rest. Following his stepson's advice, Titus bought a few acres in the newly explored area. The boy's value as a landlooker had increased; a quick study, he had picked up the routines and learned how to navigate the woods and map the territory. He could tell the difference between a good common, fair common, or poor common pine tree and estimate how many feet of sixteen-foot lumber a tree would provide. In the spring of 1854 he was sent with a crew farther afield, assigned to work in the extreme northwestern end of the unexplored Upper Peninsula.

Just getting to his starting point was an adventure; after taking a steamer 250 miles north from Detroit as far as the Soo canal construction site, Davis got off the boat and walked up past the falls to the shores of Lake Superior. He watched as large masses of copper that had been blasted from the Upper Peninsula's earth with black powder (some of the ore doubtless from Titus's ill-fated Location 98) were unloaded from boats on Lake Superior and portaged down past the waterfall in wagons to boats on Lake Huron for the trip to smelters farther east. When the canal was finished, boats would sail from one lake into the other without interruption, but in 1854 Davis boarded another ship on Lake Superior and traveled northwest for another 300 miles. He sailed around the Keweenaw Peninsula—a hook of land that extends 70 miles into Superior's waters—until he went ashore at the western end of the Upper Peninsula. The area he was to explore stretched 100 miles, from the Wisconsin border east across the Keweenaw to the town of Houghton (named after Titus's 1838 canoe mate) on Portage Lake.

It was a wild land, even wilder than Lower Michigan. Almost impenetrable forest alternated with areas nature had created bare and blasted. The trail Davis blazed along the base of the Keweenaw Peninsula was strewn with swamps, burned-over plains, rocky wastelands, and lakes. It was a country "beyond the boundaries appointed for the residence of man," according to an early explorer.[9]

Landlooking in the summer was as dangerous as in the winter and provided torments of its own. Swarms of mosquitoes and black flies covered the men with itchy, swelling sores; gnats clogged their eyes, ears, noses, and mouths. Tramping for miles carrying hundred-pound packs caused even the most experienced men's feet to swell painfully; boots took a terrible beating. Campsites had to be selected on high ground to avoid flooding in the sudden squalls and among trees to minimize the danger of windstorms. Getting lost in the forest that stretched from shore to shore was easy, and accidents were frequently fatal; stories around the fire told of many landlookers who had left camp in the morning and disappeared forever.

Living with the frontiersmen taught Davis more than just how to survive in the wilderness. He learned to play cards (forbidden in his mother's home) and for the rest of his life played poker with men, bridge with women, and euchre and whist with anyone available. He was also weaned from the habit of temperance; years later a visitor to his yacht on the Nile wondered where the wine cellar on the boat might be, since it was so well stocked.

The Soo canal finished on schedule in June 1855, the company claimed its land, and Davis was out of a job. Most of his companions continued to work as landlookers for other outfits, but two years of brutal conditions and low pay spurred Davis to seek a more rewarding profession. Again, Jonas Titus provided an opportunity.

While Davis had been tramping across the wilderness in 1854, Titus had traveled to Pittsburgh to inspect the prison there and at the same time pursue his political interests by attending the national convention of the American Party, called the "Know Nothings" for their reluctance to discuss the party with outsiders. The participants were a motley assortment of men, opposed to Catholics and foreigners but also against slavery. Titus met a lawyer from Iowa City named William Penn Clarke, a staunch abolitionist who had been a Whig and then joined the Free Soil party before he became a Know Nothing to "divide and disrupt the Democratic Party."[10] Both Titus and Clarke would soon join the fledgling Republicans.

In a Pittsburgh hotel, late in the evening after the day's debates, Clarke and Titus shared nonalcoholic beverages and became acquainted. Clarke boasted of the progress he was helping Iowa City achieve; he had represented the city in offering the Mississippi and Missouri Railroad the most money of the competing towns to run their line there, and won. It would make Iowa City the farthest point west any railroad had reached yet. When Titus mentioned that his stepson hoped to become a lawyer, Clarke suggested Iowa City as a good place to start. Back at the farm in Michigan, Titus shared Clarke's advice with the seventeen-year-old Davis. The youth had saved his landlooker wages and seized the opportunity for his next self-transformation.

. . .

The five-hundred-mile train trip from Detroit took Davis across four states. He took a ferry across the Mississippi River (the first bridge to span the river, at Davenport, Iowa, would not be finished until the following year). He walked the final fifty miles west to Iowa City, took a room in Trusdell's Boarding House, and presented himself the next day at William Penn Clarke's office—where he learned there were no positions available. Clarke complained his office was already full of young men.

Many attorneys in 1855—especially in the west—never attended law school. Instead, the aspirant would work in a sort of apprenticeship for an established attorney until the local bar association saw fit to admit him to the fraternity. Davis looked further and was taken on by a lawyer named George W. Clark (no relation to Clarke) who had come to Iowa from Pennsylvania three years before. Davis began reading the law and assisting his new mentor in preparing briefs and arguing cases.

On the last night of 1855 Davis was part of a large crowd of volunteers (many of them drunk, despite the state law prohibiting liquor) laying the final thousand feet of railroad track into Iowa City. By the light of torches, lanterns, and bonfires the crowd led horse- and mule-drawn scrapers to elevate and smooth the roadbed to the newly built depot. Ties were placed at measured intervals and rails quickly laid on them, bolted together, aligned, and spiked down. The cheering crowd then shoved a stalled locomotive down the rails through the freezing weather to the depot; the railroad company, for finishing on schedule, won a $50,000 bonus and Iowa City was connected to the rest of the world.

Three days later, Davis attended the "Grand Railroad Festival" celebrating Iowa City's connection by rail to the Atlantic Ocean. Thousands of residents (and notables from around the country who had been given free railroad tickets) attended the festivities in the state capitol building, which concluded with a feast and ball. Davis hurried up the steps of the Greek Revival–style stone building, past the stately columns (due to construction budget cuts, the capitals were made of hand-carved white pine), across the portico, and through the eight-foot-high double doors. The evening gala was lit by candles and oil lamps; gas lighting would not come to town for another year. Davis chatted with his new lawyer friends, including Samuel Kirkwood from Ohio, who with Penn Clarke was forming the Iowa Republican Party.

The railroad brought prosperity to Iowa City. When Davis arrived it was a place of unpaved roads and wood-framed buildings; the city of five thousand was trying to enforce a new ordinance prohibiting pigs from running loose in the streets. The only industries were grist and lumber mills, powered by the currents of the Iowa River, but over the next five years the population would more than double as the railroad turned the town from a frontier outpost to a jumping-off point for western expansion. A financial panic, and then the Civil War, stopped railroad construction at Iowa City, and it remained the end of the line until Davis left in 1865. Settlers headed farther west arrived by train, bought the provisions to continue their trek by wagon, and Iowa City business boomed. Property values soared and legal disputes multiplied.

Davis accomplished much of his self-education in Iowa. A voracious reader, he acquainted himself with the classics, picked up a smattering of French, and learned about technological matters in addition to his legal work. He attended theatrical and musical performances in the third-floor auditorium of Market Hall, which opened the year after he arrived. He spent two years clerking for

G. W. Clark (their friendship lasted the rest of his life), and was admitted to the Bar of the Iowa Supreme Court on June 7, 1857, at the age of nineteen.

Davis had ambitions different from those of his peers. Politics, writing, and public life were paths for most of his colleagues, but for Davis the only goal was financial. In his entire life he never served on a committee, made a speech, or worked for any party. James Grant, a Davenport lawyer (and founding president of the Rock Island Railroad) who traveled the circuit of state courts with him regarded Davis as "more cunning than learned,"[11] and more astute than profound. Devoting himself to his work, his education, and his income, Davis began investing in Iowa real estate while still living at Trusdell's Boarding House.

After joining the bar Davis returned to William Penn Clarke's office with better results than on his first visit, getting added to Clarke's staff as an attorney. He also moved out of the boarding-house and into Clarke's home, where Clarke's wife, son, law partner, and one of their clerks also lived.

Joining Penn Clarke was a profitable move. Davis's boss was one of the most prominent attorneys in Iowa, and Clarke introduced the young lawyer to the important men in the suddenly ascendant Republican Party. Clarke was an ardent abolitionist; his home was a station on the Underground Railroad for escaped slaves and his office was a regular stopping point for the militant firebrand John Brown. Fugitive slaves moved north through Iowa with Brown, who then returned south, taking guns and men to the fight raging in "Bleeding Kansas" between pro- and antislavery factions. When Clarke first met him in 1856, Brown and his men were on the run after hacking five Kansas slave owners to death with swords.

In 1858 Davis argued his first case before the Iowa Supreme Court. He took the daily stagecoach the hundred miles to Des

Moines (the new state capital) and entered the three-story brick capitol building topped by its stately square-framed cupola. Davis's client was a Chicago merchant who had not been paid after selling a shipment of liquor to an Iowa bootlegger. Iowa's temperance law held that such contracts were illegal but Davis argued that the law violated the U.S. Constitution and would allow Iowans to defraud innocent parties in other states.

"It can be readily seen what this would lead to," the twenty-year-old argued. "It would open a door to the citizens of this state to commit the greatest frauds with impunity. Not only would the wheels of commerce be blocked, but the credit of this State would be ruined. There are plenty of men residing in this State who would take advantage of this act, and in so doing would not only rob innocent men of foreign States, but deprive us all of our characters for honesty."[12] Davis had achieved a rough degree of eloquence and learned to steer a case toward his objective, and his brief against the morality of a law designed to preserve morality rejected the temperance convictions of his father and stepfather. The court disagreed with him on the legal issues, however, and his client went unpaid. Davis continued to handle ordinary cases— property disputes and unpaid debts—for Clarke's firm and devoted his spare time to increasing his connections in town and buying real estate.

Clarke (who had founded the Iowa City Sons of Temperance) was a man of courage and lofty principles. In February 1859 John Brown crept into the city after dark, leaving a dozen escaped slaves hidden fifteen miles east of town (their former owner lay dead in Kansas). A $3,000 reward had been posted for the escapees, a federal warrant had been issued for Brown's arrest, and a mob of proslavery men assembled under the new gas streetlights outside the house where the heavily armed abolitionist was holed up, planning to capture him in the morning. Clarke managed to slip his guest past the mob before dawn, however, and as attorney for the Mississippi and Missouri Railroad he secured a boxcar that took the fugitives to Chicago. At their last dinner together, Clarke gave Brown $10 and advised him to go home and rest; instead, Brown proceeded to Harper's Ferry, Virginia, where he led an abortive slave revolt and was captured by U.S. troops led by Robert E. Lee. Brown was hanged that December in front of a crowd that included Stonewall Jackson and John Wilkes Booth.

Clarke also had a tremendous ability to antagonize people. By 1859 he had run for office six times and won only once, as a city alderman. In 1860 he was named chairman of the Iowa delegation to the Republican National Convention (where he supported William Seward for president against Lincoln); Davis's friend Samuel Kirkwood supported Lincoln and was elected governor. Davis limited himself to joining the Freemasons; he became a Master Mason and senior deacon in the Iowa City lodge that year, but quit masonry forever after he left Iowa.

Davis's next opportunity arose in July 1860. When Clarke and his partner had a bitter argument and dissolved the firm, Davis became the junior partner in the new firm of Clarke & Davis, handling the office work while Clarke pursued other interests, including running for Congress that year. He was again defeated.

As Davis rode over the city's still unpaved streets in Clarke's carriage with his partner on August 21, 1860, they could take satisfaction in the progress Iowa City had made. The small wooden structures that had made up the city five years before were gradually being replaced by buildings of brick and stone; the new Gothic Revival–style county courthouse had just been completed, and at the corner of Dubuque and College Street the three-story Mendenhall Block building housed the Burrows Variety Store, selling dry goods, hats, boots, shoes, and groceries. The old state capitol building now housed the University of Iowa.

Their carriage was headed to the imposing house on College Street that had been built the year before by "Judge" Joel Benoni Buttles, a prominent businessman. Judge Buttles had never been a judge, but he had been a lawyer ("judge" was a common honorific for lawyers at the time), a newspaper editor, and a prison warden in Warren, Ohio. In 1857 he had moved with his five daughters to Iowa City amid charges he had embezzled $8,000 from the prison (the governor's salary was $1,400 that year). Davis was well acquainted with the two-story, wood-framed house, the front porch with its square wooden columns topped with Corinthian capitals, its elegant floor-to-ceiling windows, and its sumptuous, gaslit interior; he had been courting one of the judge's daughters there for more than a year. Today was his wedding day.

They were met at the door by Judge Buttles, a rotund, severe, clean-shaven man with a mane of white hair combed straight back. Preparations for the wedding ceremony were fussed over by his five daughters; their mother had died six years before and the judge had never remarried. The eldest girl, Mary, helped her sister Annie adjust her wedding gown and finish fixing her hair. Sister Sarah, a pinched, birdlike woman, adjusted her spectacles as she finished preparing refreshments in the kitchen. (Sarah was the only sister Davis never got along with.)

Younger sister Malvina helped her father greet the visitors, and the youngest daughter, eighteen-year-old Julia, rearranged the seats in the crowded parlor. More seats were needed when Davis's first Iowa mentor, G. W. Clark, arrived with his wife, Nancy, and her brother from Pennsylvania, George Boal, now a partner in Clark's firm. Boal flirted discreetly with the Buttles girl he was courting, Malvina. The wedding party was rounded out by Davis's sister, Gertrude, with her new husband; Gertrude Davis Galloway had surprisingly married one of the partners in the copper mining company that defrauded Jonas Titus.

Theodore's bride, at twenty-four, was two years older than he was. Always described as gentle and kindhearted, Annie Buttles seemed a good match for the shrewd and aggressive lawyer. She was a conventional woman of her time, raised by a dominating father, subservient to the men around her, and ambitious only to be a good wife and mother. Dark haired, brown-eyed, and rather plain, Annie was no match for Theodore intellectually or physically;

Theodore Montgomery Davis, around thirty years of age. Reproduced courtesy of the Columbus Chapel and Boal Mansion Museum, Boalsburg, Pennsylvania.

her husband, with his wiry, muscular body, strong jaw, high forehead, and bushy muttonchop sideburns, was a stylish dresser as
well, sporting a tailed jacket, high stiff collar, and a fancy cravat.

The ceremony was performed by the Episcopal minister, in def-
erence to Annie's wishes. Theodore saw the choice as inconsequential; his personal religious feelings were minimal. He observed the
proprieties of the day but never joined, or even attended, any
church. The wedding celebration was a joyful occasion; Davis's
outgoing, jocular style added laughs and good feelings to the gathering. When it was over, the newlyweds borrowed Clarke's carriage
and drove to the house Davis had rented for their married life.
The poor minister's son, who had arrived in Iowa City five years
before just out of the woods, was a property owner, had married
the daughter of an influential man, and was partner with one of the
most prominent attorneys in the state. His future looked bright,
with the prospect of someday owning a home as fine as Judge
Buttles's. It might have seemed, at the time, to be enough.

Davis traveled a great deal his entire life, and on their honeymoon Theodore and Annie took a grand tour, stopping in Chicago, Niagara Falls, Boston, and New York City. The trip expanded
the young lawyer's horizons considerably, but the most lasting im-
pact of the trip was a stop on the way home in Columbus, Ohio, to
visit more of Annie's family.

Judge Buttles's cousin, also named Joel, had lived in Columbus
since 1803, when his father had brought his family there as pio-
neers from Connecticut. Joel had worked as a teacher, a farmer,
a newspaper editor, a storekeeper, and a postmaster and owned a
pork-packing business, a bank, a hotel, and an insurance company.
By the time he died in 1850 he owned property in four different
states and was one of the wealthiest men in Ohio. Theodore and
Annie stopped to visit Joel's children, whom Annie referred to as

her cousins (terms of relationship in the family were more often used with affection rather than with accuracy). Cousin Albert had graduated from Yale, was a lawyer and a member of the city council; Cousin Lucian had also served on the council, ran the hotel, and was a general in the state militia. Most significant, Davis met Joel's youngest daughter, Emma Buttles Andrews.

Cousin Emma was also a newlywed, and pregnant. She was everything Annie was not; educated and cultured, Emma was a confident, intelligent woman curious about the wider world. A year older than Davis, she was a tiny woman, only five foot one. There was a significant gulf between them; while Davis was still hoping to make his fortune, Emma's was already secure, having married the boy next door, Abner Lord Andrews, whose father was even richer than Joel Buttles and president of the State Bank of Ohio. Abner had graduated from Marietta College and was also a lawyer, practicing in Cincinnati before returning home to marry Emma the day after Christmas in 1859. Whether any sparks flew when Theo and Emma first met is unrecorded, but Theodore would visit Columbus every year from then on and his friendship with Emma grew into the great love affair of his life; twenty years later Theodore and Emma had become permanent partners.

Perhaps still thinking of Emma, Theodore returned with Annie to Iowa City in September. They set up housekeeping in their rented home and invited Annie's older sister, Mary, to move in with them. For their entire married lives Theodore and Annie never lived alone, not an uncommon situation for the time.

Two days after Davis accepted Rekhmire's bowl from him, on January 21, 1901, Percy Newberry invited Theodore and Emma to his house for the opening of a mummy case he had just found at nearby Deir al-Bahri. Along with its occupant, the case held a *Book of the Dead* scroll and a heart scarab that went to the Cairo Museum. "[H]aving robbed this ancient Egyptian of his spiritual equipment," Emma wrote that evening in her journal, "his body was consigned to a decent burial in the sand." The mummy case was given to Newberry and Davis bought it, shipped it to America, and gave it to the Semitic Museum at Harvard.[13]

On February 1 Davis was invited to another unwrapping by another archaeologist (Emma found it "a very ordinary mummy"). Their host was the antiquities service's inspector for Upper (southern) Egypt, a young Englishman named Howard Carter. Davis had met Carter in 1899; Carter had been Newberry's protégé and first worked with him in Egypt in 1891 copying tomb paintings in Beni Hassan with money from the Egypt Exploration Fund. Carter had learned archaeology from William M. F. Petrie at Tel el-Amarna, the city built by the "heretic pharaoh" Akhenaten, and then taken a job copying the wall paintings in the mortuary temple of the female pharaoh Hatshepsut on the west bank at Luxor. He was working there when he first met Davis, and Emma had hired him to paint two pictures of scenes from the temple. It was the first time Carter had taken a private painting job, and he appreciated the extra money; he had sent Newberry a note thanking him for the introduction to "Mrs. Davies."[14]

Emma had not approved when the twenty-six-year-old Carter was appointed inspector (a decision "which no one with a sense of fitness can understand") because she thought Newberry should have gotten the job, but she and Davis soon formed a close friendship with Carter as he began currying the Americans' favor. By 1900 Carter was a regular visitor to the *Beduin,* and he had taken the pair for a private visit in January that year to the newly discovered tomb of Amenhotep II in the Valley of the Kings. The undisturbed mummy still lay in its coffin, "probably protected, Mr. Carter told us," Emma wrote, "by the curse pronounced in the band of hieroglyphs" around the top of the stone sarcophagus. Carter was trying to impress the visitors or add drama to the moment; there is no curse on Amenhotep's box, an ironic note considering the difficulties the equally nonexistent "curse of King Tut" would cause for Carter two decades later.

The unwrapping was performed by Carter at the house the Service des Antiquities provided at Medinet Habu. "His taste for all natural things is so charming to me," Emma had written the year before. "We admired the pretty house and the little garden within the enclosing walls. There was a real avenue of scent trees." Two days later Carter invited the couple for dinner, and he mentioned that two local men he had permitted to dig where they thought a tomb was located in the valley had discovered an undecorated, completely plundered chamber (now designated KV 42), but also come across a fragmentary *shabti* (literally "answerer," a small statue of a workman intended to serve its dead owner in the afterlife) inscribed with the name of pharaoh Thutmose IV. Carter was sure, he enthused, that Thutmose's lost tomb was nearby. After dinner Carter treated his guests to a private visit to the tomb of the thirteenth-century B.C. craftsman Sennedjem at Deir al-Medina, a special privilege since the tomb was closed to the public. "An excellent dinner," Emma recorded. "Brilliant little tomb."

A few days later a column and part of the ceiling collapsed in the burial chamber of the magnificent tomb of Seti I in the valley. Carter shored up the ceiling with wooden beams, but the damage illustrated the problems confronting the antiquities service; preservation of the tombs was crucial to keep them from deteriorating. Barriers needed to be built in front of the entrances to keep out floods and boulders, electric lighting and handrails were needed inside, pathways through the valley had to be made, and Carter proposed cementing cracks in the hillside that channeled water into the tombs. The service's budget was inadequate to do even the preservation work, so exploration was a luxury Egypt could not afford. Though Carter was sure he was on the verge of discovering Thutmose IV, crews and supplies for any digging would have to be paid for by a patron.

Howard Carter felt slightly defensive as he crossed the gangplank onto the *Beduin* on a mild spring evening in 1901. Newberry had told him how pleased Davis had been two months before with the gift of the bronze bowl (which Inspector Carter had allotted to Newberry for his work). Part of Carter's unease was simple—and familiar—anticipation of what his meeting with Davis would produce. The old man was frequently cantankerous and nothing near a gentleman, as Carter well knew, but the millionaire was also consistently honest and direct, if a bit tactless. The two men were accustomed to talking plainly to each other.

The affinity between Carter and Davis might have had something to do with their similarly deprived backgrounds. Carter's father had been an artist who painted the pet dogs of the local gentry in Norfolk; Howard had inherited his father's talent and, like Davis, learned his trade on the job when he was enlisted by Newberry to copy tomb paintings. Unlike Davis, however, Carter retained an element of resentment against those who considered themselves his social betters, and he compensated by frequently acting in an aggressive manner. Such a self-concept would have been inconceivable for Davis, who never felt inferior to anyone, but the two men found each other kindred spirits. The archaeologist had charmed Emma as well: "Always so pleasant," she wrote, "in spite of his dominant personality."

Seated on the deck of the *dahabiyeh,* enjoying another brilliant Egyptian sunset, Carter made his pitch to Davis. "The Egyptian government would be willing," Carter recalled, "when my duties permitted, for me to carry out researches in the Valley of the tombs of the Kings on his behalf, if he would be willing on his part to cover the costs thereof. The Egyptian Government in return for his generosity would be pleased, whenever it was possible, to give him any duplicate antiquities resulting from these researches." To close the deal, Carter told him of "my conjecture regarding the possibility of discovering the tomb of Tuthmosis IV."[15]

It is impossible to know how much courting the needy archaeologist had to do of his potential patron. Exclusive invitations to closed tombs and mummy unwrappings were Carter's inducements to entice Davis's help; Davis doubtless realized he was being primed for a proposal and was probably ready to agree as soon as the offer was extended. In any case, Davis did accept and it was a noteworthy achievement for Carter; a secure source of continuing funds eliminated the need to seek new money constantly and put valley explorations, for the first time, on a predictable footing. Most of Carter's work to date had been on an ad hoc basis; he had installed electric lights in the Abu Simbel temple with money from Thomas Cook's Tours, Lord Amherst's daughter paid for a few weeks of excavations at Aswan, and a Mrs. Goff (whom Emma found "charming") had paid £10 to put a door on the tomb of Seti II in the valley.

For Davis, the pitch was irresistible. It meant his future winters in Egypt would be far more interesting; Rudyard Kipling once said that archaeology "furnishes a scholarly pursuit with all the excitement of a gold prospector's life,"[16] and Davis soon wrote a friend that "I am hot on the trail of a royal mummy, which if I find will be an event as its contribution to history and its certain charms and ornaments will be of great value."[17] Their verbal agreement set, Davis and his entourage moved north for their usual tour through Europe on their way home. In Venice a few weeks later, Davis paid $10,000 for Vincenzo Catena's "Portrait of a Venetian Senator,"[18] an amount far greater than Carter's digging would cost.

On January 15, 1902, Davis was back in Luxor. The *Beduin*'s luncheon guests were Carter and his boss, Maspero. The Frenchman had charmed Emma when they first met in 1900: "He is so interesting—simple, and agreeable . . . He talks well on every subject," she had written. After two years of socializing with him and taking Davis's measure, Maspero had approved Carter's idea of enlisting him to fund the valley excavations and he appreciated the American's largesse: "He undertook the task in no egotistical spirit," Maspero later wrote. "He paid the workmen and made the excavations, but we retain all that he found . . . and it is a great merit on his part to be contented with so little."[19]

The three men agreed to meet in the valley the next day. When Davis and Emma arrived, the valley was filled with tourists and Carter unlocked the closed tomb of Rameses IV to eat the lunch the crew had prepared. After lunch they walked through the valley and picked the site where Carter would start digging.

The Valley of the Kings is actually several different waterways that have formed winding paths between the limestone hills of the ancient cemetery, where pharaohs of the New Kingdom (ca. 1550 to 1069 B.C.) dug their tombs in hopes of escaping the robbers who had plundered the older kings' pyramids. The valley had been sporadically explored since Napoleon's invading savants had seen it in 1799; some tombs had been open since antiquity and more had been found by explorers like the Italian adventurer Giovanni Belzoni, who had discovered the extraordinary tomb of Seti I in 1817. By 1902 some forty tombs had been found by diggers who looked wherever they thought something might be found.

Carter tried to pick a location that might produce something to excite his new patron while also improving the site overall. He proposed excavating along the sides of the access road into the valley, which needed to be widened to handle the increasing numbers of tourists. Davis approved; as in his American business ventures, he had no difficulty deferring to people he considered reliable.

As with Newberry, complete responsibility for conducting the work lay with the professionals; there was no real question of Davis participating in their decisions. Although it was how Davis operated his entire time in Egypt, it was by no means a universal practice. Employing professional archaeologists was seldom a requirement for excavating at the beginning of the twentieth century.

The pattern had been set in Turkey thirty years before by Heinrich Schliemann, another millionaire dilettante. Schliemann, a German businessman later lauded as the "father of Mediterranean archaeology," had studied the *Iliad,* dishonestly gained access to private property, hired local laborers to bring their shovels, and torn down a hill. At the bottom, after untold destruction was done to the site, he found what he believed was Homer's Troy and became world famous. The treasure he found—and smuggled out of the country illegally—proved a trained archaeologist was not necessary to find wonderful things. The first woman to excavate in Egypt, Margaret Benson, had no experience beyond a brief chat with Petrie before she began digging in the temple of Mut at Karnak in 1895; she supervised the workers herself with no tools more specialized than a lacy parasol.

In 1902 approval to explore—or despoil—the ancient sites was granted based on Maspero's judgment and might or might not include an archaeologist. When the Earl of Carnarvon asked for a site to explore in 1906—which Maspero approved after a gentle suggestion from Consul General Cromer—he built a screened tent near the excavation to protect himself from dust and flies and sat watching his workers dig. Without professional assistance he found two tombs and the "Carnarvon Tablet," an important account from the Seventeenth Dynasty that was damaged due to improper treatment. "A sadder instance of the sin of allowing amateurs to dig could not be found," Inspector Weigall wrote.[20]

Davis's excavations, in contrast, were always conducted by trained professionals. Some were genuine scholars—like Newberry—and some had learned by watching and doing, like Carter. Employing an archaeologist was convenient for Davis, who preferred to spend most of his time visiting with other elite tourists, but he always hired the best people available, always for a top salary, and always in consultation with Maspero. Davis set an example and a standard that, during his time in Egypt, became universal. Scientific archaeology in Egypt was transformed during Davis's time there from brilliant improvisations by a self-trained pioneer like Petrie to a defined discipline with a body of practices, a philosophy, and a tradition. Davis fostered that change by very publicly endorsing the professionals, allowing them to demonstrate their worth and (in most cases) deferring to their judgment.

The domination of archaeology by archaeologists was one of Davis's legacies. Following his example, Lord Carnarvon gave up his tent in 1909 and hired Carter to do the digging. A dozen years later they discovered Tutankhamen—and erased Davis from popular memory.

. . .

By late January 1902, Carter had hired a crew of sixty men and was clearing the hundred yards of hillside between the tombs of Rameses II and Rameses IV, removing heaps of ancient chippings. He cleared the entrance to KV 5, a completely filled-in tomb that appeared to be a single undecorated chamber first seen eighty years before. Carter considered it inconsequential and moved on; twenty years later he used the hillside in front of KV 5 to dump the debris from his excavation of Tutankhamen's tomb. In 1989 American archaeologist Kent Weeks (accompanied by his patron, a California land developer named Bruce Ludwig) dug through twelve feet of Carter's debris, rediscovered the entrance, and astonished the world by finding that KV 5 was the largest tomb ever dug in the valley; intended for the sons of Rameses II, it includes at least 150 chambers.

Davis visited the dig from time to time (between lunches, teas, and dinners with other foreigners) as Carter's men cleared the sides of the gully down to bedrock, ensuring no tomb entry would be missed. The debris that was excavated was tossed behind the diggers, filling in their previous work and giving the appearance of a trench slowly crawling down the valley. When Davis sailed south to Aswan, Carter kept the work going in between his other duties (such as guiding the visiting crown prince of Siam). When Davis returned to Luxor on February 20, Carter came to dinner and excitedly reported that in clearing the hundred feet between KV 4 and KV 21 he had found the doorway of a sealed pit tomb, which he had covered over to await Davis's arrival. Carter also reported that he had found another clue in his continuing quest: a fragment of a fine calcite vessel with the name of Thutmose IV. They set the tomb opening for the twenty-fifth.

Carter's enthusiasm was contagious. The night of the twenty-fourth Davis began a letter to a friend at Harvard by quoting Shakespeare: "I am so pleased with myself I cry, 'Shine out, fair sun, till I have bought a glass / That I may see my shadow as I pass.' We have found a tomb in the Valley of the Kings, so you can see that we are somewhat excited!"[21] He closed by saying they were sure they were near Thutmose IV.

The next morning Davis traveled to the valley with one of his guests, Emma's forty-year-old Ohio niece, Janet "Nettie" Buttles. They joined Carter and Newberry at the site with another friend, a British painter named John Varley Jr., and ate a lunch catered by the *Beduin*'s crew as Carter's workmen dug out the ten-foot shaft in the valley floor. After lunch the foreigners peered from the edge of the hole as Carter descended into it to find that the shaft opened into an undecorated single chamber (designated KV 45) that was one-third filled with flood debris.

The mud was removed to reveal contents severely damaged by the water; Carter first came upon an intrusive burial from the Twenty-second Dynasty with two double coffins so ruined they were impossible to remove. "[E]verything went to dust when we touched them,"[22] Davis wrote home. Beneath the coffins Carter came upon fragments of three canopic jars (which held the embalmed organs of a mummy) inscribed for an Eighteenth Dynasty overseer of the fields of Amen named Userhet, apparently the original owner of the tomb.

If Carter was unimpressed by the find, his audience waiting above was enthralled by the objects he sent up. From the deteriorated coffins he salvaged a heart scarab and a wooden face piece, or "mummy mask," which Nettie Buttles described as "finely carved and painted. Eyes and eyebrows are inlaid." They were quickly disappointed. "When first taken out of the tomb, the mask was entire and highly colored," Nettie continued. "It afterwards fell to pieces, one bronze eyebrow dropped out and was lost, and the brilliant blue of the beard and much of the coloring has disappeared."[23] KV 45 was reexcavated in 1991 by American archaeologist Donald Ryan, who was appalled by Carter's technique. "There was no visible sense of any archaeological care . . . The whole scene was dreadful."[24] Ryan found fragments of eighty *shabti*s Carter had overlooked, pieces of five different bodies, the damaged face from the second coffin, and the lost bronze eyebrow from Nettie's mask.

The day in 1902 was memorialized by a photo, likely taken by Carter, of the patron and his entourage next to the excavation, Nettie holding the mask that had not yet fallen to pieces. The group is suitably attired for the Egyptian desert: Davis carries a walking stick and wears a jacket and bow tie, Nettie a floor-length skirt and flowered hat.

If the tomb was a disappointment to the diggers ("a great deal had been expected from this tomb" Emma wrote, although she had stayed on the boat that day), Carter and Maspero were generous to their patron in disposing of the finds. What was left of the mummy mask found its way to Nettie's collection in the villa she and her sister shared in Florence, Italy; Davis sent Userhet's canopic jars to the Semitic Museum at Harvard.[25] An otherwise undocumented piece also stayed with Davis; he wrote to a friend that he was bringing home a skull "in good condition, and has a wonderful set of teeth." At his Newport mansion it was put on display, "associated with the head of a man who died 3000 B.C."[26]

KV 45 increased Davis's enthusiasm and he authorized Carter to hire another forty workmen. He wrote that "we are quite well satisfied that Thotmes 4 will be found . . . All good things come to those who dig long and deep enough; in any event I am having great pleasure and doing some good in showing where there are no tombs!"[27] He left Carter to continue work with his enlarged crew when the *Beduin* headed north a week later.

In Cairo, Maspero gave Theodore and Emma a sneak advance tour of the almost-completed Egyptian Museum on Ismailia (now Tahrir) Square. Emma was not impressed; she wrote "it looks more like a goods station than a Museum—a hideous failure."

At home in Newport with his new skull, Davis wrote that summer to Professor David G. Lyon at Harvard of the "hankering for Egypt" that had possessed him. "All countries seem youthful in comparison with Egypt," he wrote. "The works of man give a meaning to a country, and a personal touch which is peculiar to Egypt; and there it being, as it were, the childhood of the world, makes it uniquely interesting . . . Intensely interesting dear old peaceful Egypt is, it soothes one's perturbed spirit and leads him in ways of harmony, free from the turbulent spirit of the present age."[28] He was inspired by the timeless atmosphere of Egypt, with its intimations of mortality; to another friend he wrote, "I live just now so much with the evidences of the great that have gone, leaving behind their works, deeds and characters, it seems most natural that all should go and almost unnatural that any should be here."[29]

Davis and Emma were back in Cairo on December 12, 1902, and as always they checked into Shepheard's Hotel while the *Beduin* was readied to sail. They had stayed at Shepheard's, the ultimate digs for the elite, since their first visit to Egypt in 1887. Remodeled from a palace in 1850, the hotel offered a view of the pyramids from its roof and its courtyard held "Kleber's tree," where Jean Baptiste Kleber—the general left in charge when Napoleon abandoned his Egyptian campaign—had been assassinated in 1800. Luxurious rooms, fine dining, evening orchestra concerts, and an expansive balcony had made Shepheard's a world-famous institution; wealthy visitors to Cairo would stay nowhere else.

In 1890 the building had been expanded, adding a generating plant that made it the first hotel in the Middle East with electric lights. The balcony had been replaced by a terrace that became synonymous with Shepheard's. Native guides (called "dragomen"), donkey boys, antiquities peddlers, and the rest of Egypt congregated in front of the eight-step staircase leading to the terrace, where the foreigners dined and passed their time in countless meetings and encounters. In 1900 a newly arrived American tourist had been sent to the terrace's marble floor by one punch from Sir Thomas Lipton, founder of the tea company and a perennial competitor in the America's Cup yacht race, after the American had mistaken him for the hotel pimp.

In 1897 Shepheard's had added the "Moorish Hall" by roofing over the courtyard; topped with a great glass dome, the roof was supported by vaults covered in Arabic-style mosaics and arches painted with stripes. The bronze chandeliers were accented by alabaster tables and red Persian carpets. Upon arriving in December 1902, Emma noted with disappointment that the hotel was empty; a cholera epidemic had just ended and scared away less courageous travelers.

Arrivals in Cairo were always elaborate for Davis; a friend traveling with him recalled that when their train arrived from Alexandria "three or four of cousin Theodore's native servants were waiting to welcome us with kissing of hands and those touching of the forehead and the breast that somehow look so theatrical. At the hotel the manager met us at the door and conducted us at once to a gorgeous suite of rooms, while all our traveling companions were waiting and writhing at the desk . . . We are a sort of Royal Party here."[30]

Davis was anxious to get to Luxor and traveled there more speedily than usual, but the *Beduin* did stop in Girga on the way south to visit Albert Lythgoe, a professor at Harvard whom Davis had met through his Newport friends. Lythgoe had been working in Egypt for several years and just been hired as the first curator of Egyptian art at Boston's Museum of Fine Arts. The two Americans discussed possible homes for Davis's "gifts" from the antiquities service; their chat soon had major results for U.S. museums.

In Luxor on January 10, 1903, Theodore and Emma joined Carter for tea at the archaeologist's house. Davis was presented with more fruits of Carter's labors; above the entrance to the tomb of Maiherpri (an Eighteenth-Dynasty courtier of Nubian descent), which had been discovered in the valley in 1899, Carter had come across a hollow in the rock holding a yellow painted wooden box with Maiherpri's name (it is assumed the box was placed there by ancient robbers who failed to return for it). Inside were two loincloths of exceptionally fine quality, each cut from a single piece of gazelle skin into an extremely fine mesh by the ancient craftsmen. "The most wonderful work I have seen in Egypt," Emma enthused. Davis presented the box and one of the cloths to Lythgoe for the Museum of Fine Arts.[31] The other was given to the Field Museum in Chicago where it was imaginatively displayed as the earliest example ever found of a Freemason's apron. The Chicago loincloth was later stolen and has never been seen again ($5,000 worth of Egyptian jewelry had been stolen from the Field Museum in 1895).

While Carter continued his search for Thutmose IV, moving his trench past KV 21, Davis did his usual socializing. E. A. Wallis Budge of the British Museum came to tea on the boat and described for Emma his first meeting with the great Petrie: "He was dirty, verminous and, saving your presence, Madame, as odiferous as a pole cat."

A few days later the *Beduin* set off for Aswan. While en route Davis wrote a letter to Eleanor "Nellie" Salome Wilson, the daughter of his friend and business partner Nathaniel. "I have not found my dead king, for whom I have been looking for now two winters, but as I left Luxor yesterday I was told that the 'dig' was showing many signs of being near the tomb of some king," Davis wrote. "The keen content one takes in finding, or trying to find such a tomb cannot be understood except by one who is a seeker such as I am." He concluded by asking Nellie to tell her unmarried sister that "Carter is finer than ever and still needs a wife!"[32]

A few days after Davis left, Carter's men were clearing the entryway to the long known KV 19 (the tomb of the Twentieth-Dynasty prince Montuhirkopeshef) when they came upon a shaft that led down a stairway to a two-chambered, uninscribed tomb. Carter and Newberry entered the tomb and found the contents "much destroyed and rifled" with "two much denuded mummies of women."[33] The diggers found the tomb of no importance, recovered the entry, and moved on.

The tomb (later designated KV 60) was visited four years later by another Davis archaeologist who sent one of the mummies to Cairo. In 1989 the tomb was rediscovered by Donald Ryan, who took the second mummy off the floor and placed it in a wooden box. In 2007, after CAT scans were done on the mummies, Supreme Council of Antiquities secretary general Zahi Hawass announced with great fanfare that the mummy Carter had left on the floor had been proven to be the body of none other than female pharaoh Hatshepsut. As in most mummy matters, the conclusion was not universally accepted.[34]

While Carter's crew continued their hunt in the valley, Davis visited the new Aswan dam, which the British had built across the Nile and opened the month before (now known as the "old" Aswan dam). At the time it was the largest dam ever built, and while protecting Egypt from flooding during the annual inundation and preserving water so two or even three crops could be grown each year, it also caused the flooding of the Isis temple at Philae. "Utilitarian vandalism," the French novelist Pierre Loti had called it. "What an effect of gross and imbecile profanation this bellowing of English joy produces!"[35] Emma was less disturbed, and wrote only of the "wonderful metamorphosis" it had created at the temple.

Davis was still lounging in Aswan on January 22 when the *Beduin* received a surprise visitor with a startling announcement. "Carter appeared unexpectedly while we were at breakfast," Emma wrote, "and announced the thrilling news that he had found the tomb of Thothmes IV—finding a splendid sarcophagus, beautiful wall decorations and floor strewn with blue pottery more or less broken, etc. This is a fine success both for Theo and for Carter." Davis had found his dead king at last. As Carter took the train back, the *Beduin* embarked for Luxor.

Carter had discovered buried foundation deposits (ritual objects, often models of tools, buried near monuments during construction) naming Thutmose IV on January 18; the next day his men had found a stairway that led to the tomb's entrance. When the stairway was cleared Carter had entered and seen wall decorations of Thutmose being presented to various gods and goddesses, "which, as you may conceive," he wrote, "gave me a considerable degree of satisfaction."[36] Carter closed the tomb, sent word to Maspero, and left immediately for Aswan to share the excitement with his patron.

Davis arrived in Luxor on February 1. The next day, even before visiting Thutmose IV, Carter showed him another astonishing find. The day before, a few of Carter's men had been clearing in front of the entry to KV 20 (a completely blocked tomb that had been known since the French savants had seen it in 1799 but never excavated—Davis knew it as the "Napoleon tomb"), and had uncovered more foundation deposits: bronze tools and alabaster vases. The archaeologist excitedly pointed out to Davis that they were inscribed with the name of Pharaoh Hatshepsut. Davis was ecstatic; he had a special affinity for the Egyptian queens and Hatshepsut was a "particular favorite," according to Carter. What appeared to be her tomb, however, would have to wait until the beckoning Thutmose IV had been finished.

Carter spent the night of February 2 sleeping in front of the tomb; he had set the next day for the official opening and at 4:00 A.M. descended inside to prepare for his distinguished visitors. First to arrive in the deserted valley were Maspero and Newberry; next came Davis riding his donkey and Emma traveling in her "chair" (a device Davis's valet Daniel Jones had improvised for her that could be drawn by donkeys). They brought with them their American friend Robb de Peyster Tytus, a wealthy twenty-four-year-old Yale graduate who had first come to Egypt in 1899. A frequent visitor to the *Beduin,* he was working with Newberry at Malkata Palace (and paying most of the costs) and had entered the tomb the first time with Carter.

Carter was still underground when they arrived. "[W]e waited about half an hour, when he emerged looking like a ghost," Emma wrote. After a drink of water and a cigarette, Carter took Newberry and Tytus into the tomb with him for another half hour, extending electric lights. When they came up Carter invited Davis, Maspero, and Emma to enter the tomb of Thutmose IV; Davis's valet went along as well to help Emma down the passages.

At the bottom of the twenty-four steps was a steep corridor thirty-six feet long. The explorers made their way down hanging on to a rope with the workmen outside holding the other end. The incline was so steep that Maspero had to lay his considerable body down flat on the floor, bracing his feet against Carter's shoulders. Another fourteen-step stairway was followed by another ramp; at the bottom of that ramp was a "well," a thirty-foot-deep perpendicular shaft (most likely placed in tombs for religious purposes, although wells could also have been intended to deter robbers, divert flood waters, or even assess the depth of rock formation). The well had failed as a theft prevention device, since an ancient robbers' rope was still hanging down the side. Carter had rigged a bridge over the well for the visitors to cross.

"Then we emerged into a hall supported by two pillars," Emma recorded. "There was a beautiful decoration of gods and goddesses and emblems around the top of the walls of the well, quite fresh and perfect." From the hall the tomb made a sharp left turn. "[W]e scrambled down another steep shaft and came into a small hall partially choked with debris, the walls beautifully painted," Emma wrote. Around another left turn they entered the six-pillared burial chamber. The floors were littered with broken grave goods; Carter wrote it looked more like "the scene of a riot than a hallowed shrine of the illustrious dead . . . The tomb plunderers had held an orgy here. The floor of the hall was literally strewn from end to end with splinters from the original funerary equipment. Everything had been broken to bits and thrown helter-skelter by those ruthless vandals, who in their thirst for gold had spared nothing."

Carter had arranged a series of planks on the floor to keep the visitors from stepping on the fragments of pottery and other objects. Maspero described the attitude of the explorers: "The dread of the tomb, so lately shut up, and whence the visits of tourists has not banished the impression of death, has invaded them without their knowledge. They speak in whispers, moderate their gestures, walk or rather glide along as noiselessly as possible. Occasionally they stoop to pick up an object, or group themselves around a pillar, remaining motionless for a moment, then they resume their silent rounds."[37]

From Emma's depiction of the scene of ancient chaos, she seems to have been almost overwhelmed. "It was astounding to look at the mass of things—statuettes, figures of animals, fragments of embroideries, leatherwork and countless bottles and ornaments of heavenly blue color . . . A charming alabaster face looked up smilingly at me, as if to welcome our coming." A magnificent inscribed quartzite sarcophagus drew their attention. Its lid had been removed and placed at the side by the thieves, one corner supported by a wooden cow's head.[38] The box was empty; Thutmose's mummy had already been discovered, in a cache of royal mummies found together in another tomb in 1898. "The crowning object of interest," Emma decided, "was the dash board of a war chariot, of leather, beautifully embossed and painted on both sides. Maspero was delighted with this as it is absolutely unique."[39] The tomb was spellbinding, but the visitors ended their tour to make room for the others still waiting outside. For Emma, "the getting up was worse than the going down," as valet Jones carried her and Carter pushed Maspero. After the inspection the group had a joyous lunch in a nearby tomb.

The find (designated KV 43) was Carter's first royal tomb and the first important discovery Davis was involved in. Thutmose IV reigned for around ten years, ca. 1400 B.C., and is best known for the stele he placed in front of the Great Sphinx at Giza recounting a dream in which the god appeared to him and promised him the throne if he cleared away the sand that had covered the monument. He dedicated the tallest extant Egyptian obelisk. The 105-foot column was originally placed in Karnak temple and today fronts the basilica of Saint John Lateran in Rome. He commenced a fifty-year era of peace by marrying a Mittanian princess and began the elevation of the god Aten; two generations later Aten was decreed the supreme god of Egypt.

The tomb shed light on Eighteenth-Dynasty art, architecture, burial customs, and tomb robbery. A graffito left during the reign of King Horemheb, eighty years after the burial, is the oldest known instance of a "renewal" (rewrapping of a mummy after a robbery) in the valley. The tomb is significant for the perfection of its construction; every line is straight, every corner perfect, every corridor and doorjamb carefully designed and carved out of the rock. The wall paintings are equally noteworthy; the hot yellow background causes the colors of the characters to almost glow, and has been likened to the work of Monet. The characters are the first in the valley to be painted in the "normal" Egyptian mode, noticeably more full-bodied than the stick figures found in earlier tombs.

Despite the destruction by the ancient robbers, the objects left in the tomb were a treasure trove of artistic and scholarly value. Pieces of a royal throne, canopic jars, boxes, statuettes, small shrines, *shabti*s, magical bricks (inscribed with spells for the dead), model boats, throw sticks, amulets, jars, a wooden game board, and an ivory mirror handle were all recovered. Many of the amulets were made of a striking blue faience (earthenware coated with an opaque glaze) and they were joined by a splendid carved wooden panther depicted in mid-stride. An embroidered piece of a robe carrying the name of Thutmose's father, Amenhotep II,[40] established for the first time that the pharaohs had worn colorful, elaborately woven shirts and robes. The sarcophagus, stained red and shaped like a cartouche (the oval hieroglyphic indicator of a royal name), was carved in sunken relief with deities painted in yellow, blue, white, and black.

At lunch that day Davis likely made some quip about another find in the tomb; a mummy, perhaps a son of the king, was found propped up against the wall of one of the side chambers. Its abdomen had been slashed open and left to flap outward. The disturbing corpse was left in the tomb until 2005, when the tomb was reopened for public inspection.

It had been the most outstanding day for Davis in Egypt so far. The group was back on the *Beduin* by five o'clock. "[W]e tumbled out of our dusty garments and were glad enough to have tea," Emma concluded.

Carter and Newberry spent ten days clearing the tomb of its treasures. It took seventy-three men and boys to move the packed finds to Carter's government house. "They are the delight of all who have seen them,"[41] Davis wrote a friend. The discovery increased his enthusiasm for continued work and justified his faith in Carter; the archaeologist had discovered exactly what he had predicted he would.

Carter's crew next began digging into the rock-hard fill blocking KV 20, where the men hoped to find Hatshepsut. "Though we say nothing about this to the people here," Davis wrote, "we are very much excited . . . Doubtless the tomb was robbed thousands of years ago, and probably the body was carried away, but likewise doubtless we shall find some beautiful things." The work proved harder than anyone had anticipated, however, and with summer coming on the diggers decided to close the entry for the season. There were already a few minor rewards; as they started digging four alabaster jars with Hatshepsut's name on them were found and Emma wrote, "It looks encouraging."

Thutmose's things were transported to Cairo, some of the most fragile aboard the *Beduin*. The discovery was the talk of Egypt; at a dinner party in Cairo a young lady asked Carter if he had heard of the wonderful discovery by Mr. Davis in Luxor. Typically, Carter feigned ignorance and the girl explained that on her Cook's tour she herself had witnessed three white camels emerge from the tomb carrying the king's chariot. "Oh, Madame!" Carter enthusiastically replied. "I must indeed congratulate you!"[42]

On March 26, 1903, Theo and Emma took a carriage to the new Egyptian Museum from Shepheard's (where Emma now found "the crowd and noise were insufferable"). They had been invited to another event for the elite, the unwrapping of the mummy of Thutmose IV, which had lain untouched in storage since its 1898 discovery. The museum had officially opened the previous November, and as the Americans entered they observed the façade of the building, which saluted the giants of Egyptology to date—all Europeans. The only Egyptian immortalized on the building was Khedive Abbas Himli II, the puppet ruler the British had installed; his inscription was written in Latin.

Inside the museum, in a small room holding an audience of around thirty, Theo and Emma were presented to Lord and Lady Cromer for the first time. Maspero gave a short speech and then commenced the unrolling, which revealed "a fine, agreeable, well-preserved face," according to Emma. Dr. Grafton Elliot Smith, an Australian anatomist, afterward proposed a new type of examination for the mummy; he and Carter bundled Thutmose into a carriage and traveled to the private nursing home that housed the only X-ray machine in Cairo. It was the first time a mummy was subjected to such a device, although Thutmose's innards revealed no secrets.

Maspero was generous to the patron in dividing up Thutmose's spoils. He made gifts to Davis of 84 of the 612 objects cataloged by the museum, including vases, faience ankhs (the hieroglyphic symbol of life), amulets, canopic jars, and the side panels from the king's throne. Davis presented 54 of the items to Lythgoe for the Museum of Fine Arts in Boston, including 45 of the faience porcelains, the carved panther,[43] 1 of the throne panels, and 2 of the canopic jars.[44] The rest, which Davis displayed with his personal collection, eventually went to the Metropolitan.

The day Davis left for Italy, *The New York Times* ran an article about the discovery. "Mr. Theodore Davis of Newport, a collector of old masters," the paper announced, "has just reaped a rich reward for his trouble and outlay, having discovered the tomb of Thotmes IV, one of the pharaohs of the eighteenth dynasty." The treasures "prove of the highest interest for those who study the arts and religious ideas of the epoch. A unique find is the body of the war chariot of the king,"[45] the paper enthused.

The article made no mention of Davis's earlier career in New York, although he had been the subject of many earlier pieces in the *Times* that were far less flattering. Davis had not been content to remain a prosperous lawyer in Iowa City, but had been pushed on by his youthful ambition. The relentless drive that had compelled him to become wealthy was now mirrored in his determination to uncover all the secrets that remained in the valley. He had no intention of abandoning Egypt after finding his first king; he was having the time of his life.

"The Sarcophagus of Thoutmosis I" (*recarved after initially being made for Hatshepsut*). *From Davis,* The Tomb of Hatshopsitu.

Three

HATSHEPSUT'S QUARTZITE SARCOPHAGUS

The first Egyptian to be interred in the Valley of the Kings in a stone sarcophagus was the female pharaoh Hatshepsut. Her first sarcophagus, made for her when she was only a king's wife, was a copy in stone of the square wooden boxes used to hold coffins during the Middle Kingdom. Cut from yellow quartzite and painted red, it stretches seven and a half feet long by thirty-two inches high and thirty-four inches wide. After Hatshepsut became pharaoh (around 1480 B.C.) she ordered a new box for herself; the older one was recarved with beautiful images of gods and hieroglyphs for her father, Thutmose I. It is the only royal sarcophagus to find a home in the Western Hemisphere and is displayed at the Museum of Fine Arts, Boston.

"It was one of the most irksome pieces of work I ever supervised,"[1] Howard Carter later wrote, understating the case. He had resumed

digging in what he believed was the tomb of the pharaoh Hatshepsut in October 1903, and the struggle to clear out the tomb was
physically miserable and seemingly endless. The tomb was filled
with rubble washed in by floods over the millennia and cemented
into a solid mass that had to be smashed with pickaxes, then carried out in baskets by a continuous chain of workmen. The rock
the roughly hewn tomb was carved into became so unstable as the
tunnel descended into the earth that there was a constant danger
of the ceilings collapsing, and the air was extremely bad.

One hundred fifty feet into the tomb a rectangular chamber,
filled with stones and sections of the fallen ceiling, had been
reached. Carter assumed there was an entry to the next passage concealed under the rocks but hoped to avoid clearing the entire room.
"We agreed to toss a penny," Davis explained, "with the understanding that if 'heads' came up we were to make for the right-hand
corner. Fortunately it came 'heads,' and when we had tunneled
through the debris to the designated corner we found the mouth
of the descending corridor."[2]

Conditions grew worse the deeper the explorers went. Candles
melted in the heat so Davis installed electric lights. The tomb had
been occupied by bats for centuries, Davis noted, "and their ex-
crement had become so dry that the least stir of the air filled the
corridors with a fluffy black stuff, which choked the noses and
mouths of the men, rendering it most difficult for them to breathe."
The archaeologists installed an air pump at the mouth of the tomb,
connected to a zinc pipe to bring in fresh oxygen. The heat had
forced the work to stop the previous April 15, a month after Davis
left Luxor, and Carter had returned to the job six months later.

By January 2, 1904—when Davis and Emma arrived—Carter's
crew had penetrated more than five hundred feet into the hillside,
with no end in sight. Davis later recognized "the long, patient,

tiresome and dangerous work executed by Mr. Carter, the difficulties which he overcame, and the physical discomforts which he suffered . . . The serious danger of caving ceilings throughout the entire length of the corridors and chambers was a daily anxiety."[3]

Davis spent his time socializing on the *Beduin*, hosting lunches, teas, and dinners for archaeologists and friends, including the season's guest—twenty-one-year-old Jean Hardy from Columbus, another member of Emma's extended family. The Americans spent their time visiting other excavations and inspecting the construction of the girls' school in Luxor that Davis was paying for. He was persuaded to change the plans and add a second floor.

The morning of February 12, Davis joined Carter and Newberry at the tomb. Carter's men had reached a doorway at the end of the corridor they had been chiseling through; the archaeologist was anxious to see what lay beyond, but the entry was almost too much for him. Carter and Newberry each tried the descent, but Emma was told when Davis returned to the *Beduin* that Newberry had been overcome by foul air and "emerged after a time looking very ill. Carter went on to the end and found the room into which the door opened choked with rubbish to within two feet of the ceiling.

"Theo said that when Carter emerged from the tomb he was a horrid object—dripping and wet from the heat, with a black dust over his face and hands—he was very sick, too, and had to lie down for sometime."[4] The archaeologist saw they had reached a large room—the burial chamber, as it turned out—but it was so filled with rubble that much more work lay ahead. Disappointed that a grand entry with Maspero was impossible, Davis decided to sail south to Aswan. The *Beduin* was still there on February 28 when a message arrived from Carter: The burial chamber had been cleared and two magnificent sarcophagi had been uncovered. Davis set sail for Luxor.

The excavation had been miserable but the tomb—designated KV 20—proved to be of great importance. Twice as long as the tomb of Thutmose IV, KV 20 was burrowed some seven hundred feet into the hillside, the longest and deepest in the valley. Rough hewn and meandering, with none of the smooth walls or clearly cut angles in other sepulchers, the tomb, Egyptologists now agree, was started by Hatshepsut's father, Thutmose I, and enlarged by his daughter when she decided they should be entombed together. It is the oldest tomb in the valley, dating to around 1480 B.C.

It had been thoroughly looted in antiquity, but when the clearing was finally finished on March 10 a canopic chest carved from red sandstone inscribed with Hatshepsut's name was recovered (although the jars it had held, containing the queen's embalmed organs, were missing). Most imposing were the two empty sarcophagi; in addition to the recarved square box for her father, the cartouche-shaped lid of Hatshepsut's own box set the style followed by kings from then on. On the floor were fifteen blocks of limestone, apparently installed as wall coverings, which were inscribed with the oldest known form of the *amduat*—the ancient "book of what is in the Netherworld," describing the sun god's twelve-hour journey of regeneration every night. The *amduat* became the primary royal tomb decoration in the valley after Hatshepsut set the example. The square sarcophagus was given to Davis by Maspero; Davis presented it to Boston's Museum of Fine Arts, and it became the only royal sarcophagus in the New World.

The find drew more publicity for Davis the explorer and also for his guest that season. "Miss Jean Hardy, a Columbus girl, will be among the first persons to gaze upon the tomb," the *Columbus State Journal* reported, and imaginatively added, "There is supposed to be a large treasure in the tomb, and though the object of the trip was purely scientific it is probable that the members of the party will also benefit financially."[5]

Davis was generous in his praise for Carter's work; he wrote later that while the excavation went on, "Braving all these dangers and discomforts, Mr. Carter made two or three descents every week and professed to enjoy it." It seems a bit embarrassing, therefore, that Davis barely mentioned the people who actually did the work; the Egyptian crew were in the miserable hole all day, six days per week, smashing rock with picks and dragging baskets of rubble up the ever-lengthening tunnel through the heat and bat dung. Davis was insulated from the workers, however; his decision to trust the professionals ensured there were at least two levels of bosses between him and the men with the picks.

Throughout his time in Egypt, Davis treated his archaeologist-in-charge as the chief of the excavation. Each of the archaeologists, in turn, left management of the laborers to an Egyptian *reis,* a native who enlisted, directed, paid, and disciplined the work crew through an elaborate web of family and village relationships, favors, kickbacks, and feuds. The workers all knew who Davis was; one of his guests wrote that when she visited a dig "the children who were carrying off the dirt were all singing some sort of chant. 'Have they been singing like that all day?' I asked. 'Oh, no,' said Harry [Burton, the archaeologist at the time]; 'they are simply singing "the boss has come, the boss has come.' "[6] The work was hard and the wages low (except for the *reis,* who collected a fee from each worker each payday), but the money was dear to the impoverished villagers. An American observer had noted a few years before that excavation pay had fallen to seven and one-half cents per day, and unlike times past the workers were required to provide their own food and tools. "This shows that English civilization is working,"[7] he noted sarcastically. The situation for the workers depended on the attitude of the *reis,* unless the archaeologist saw fit to interfere. Harry Burton, running Davis's dig in 1911, took away the whip the overseer had carried after he saw him "cut a piece out of a boy's leg with the lash."[8]

The archaeologists were almost daily visitors for tea or dinner on the *Beduin,* but no *reis,* let alone a lowly digger, was ever invited. The American's interest in the local people was colored by a combination of a culturally imperialist attitude, racism, and religious prejudice—factors that were the basis of the occupying British administration's psychology and the beginning efforts of the United States to engage with Egypt. Emma wrote that the Egyptians were "very superstitious. They seem entirely lacking in independence—and have absolutely no initiative . . . They are devoted to Islamism—and under evil influences are ready to burst into fanaticism . . . Their perceptions and sensibilities are not keen—they seem almost indifferent to pain and physical discomfort. I think they are like children and animals—they do not suffer from imagination, which makes half of our suffering." Emma noted the "personal dignity" of their Nubian crew, but "Theodore is so unkind as to suggest that the noble indifference of manner is sometimes the result of hashish." An 1890 account, in fact, estimated that one in four men in Cairo used the drug and "thus lower themselves below the beasts."[9]

Theodore's and Emma's attitudes were shared by their countrymen. When former President Theodore Roosevelt visited Egypt in 1910 (after he had visited Davis in the valley and toured the Egyptian Museum in Cairo with him) he made a speech at the University of Cairo that soundly endorsed Britain's imperial policies and predicted "it will be years, perhaps generations, before Egypt is able to govern itself." Following the speech several hundred nationalists gathered outside Shepheard's for the first anti-American demonstration ever seen in the Middle East.

The Westerners simply believed the gap between themselves and the Egyptian peasants was unbridgeable. "However friendly we may be as individuals, we cannot understand each other," Emma wrote in 1890. Continued exposure, however, resulted in changed attitudes to individuals they came to know. By 1895, Emma records that Davis arranged for "our two faithful Mohommedan boys, Mahomet and Hassan," to attend school and learn English. He gave money to cover their tuition and living expenses to the manager of Shepheard's, who doled it out to them each month. Emma adopted a young girl she named "Nubia" and in 1902 enrolled her at the girls' school Davis paid for in Luxor, although she worried it was "almost as though I should take a wild colt out of the fields and expect it to be satisfied and interested." Two years later Emma was pleased with the girl's progress: "What a change in that little savage!" she wrote affectionately. Nubia eventually converted to Christianity, changed her name to "Freda," and married a teacher in Aswan.

Davis was especially generous, if paternalistic, to the crew of the *Beduin*. Before Davis left Egypt in 1904 he paid for the extended hospital care for a crew member named Abdul, who had become seriously ill. When they returned the next season, Emma wrote, they checked on Abdul and found he had "recovered remarkably and seems stronger than he has been for three years—but we found he had been drinking a good deal." They took it upon themselves to send Abdul, his wife, and their child home to Dongola. "We decided it was better for him to go back to his own people—and to a warmer climate where he will be free from temptation . . . It seems a happy solution to the condition which has given us a good deal of anxiety lately," Emma cheerfully concluded.

Christmas on the *Beduin* was always a festive occasion; one of Davis's guests described the observances in 1912. After breakfast the dining room table was cleared and gifts were presented to the twenty-two crew members. "The crew and inside servants came in one by one, kissed our hands, and each received a white shawl, a box of cigarettes, a bag with candy and nuts and some money, and departed beaming. When they all had had their presents they gathered on the deck and shouted 'Hip, Hip, Hip Hooray! T'ank you, t'ank you, t'ank you,' and we retired to our several apartments and washed our hands in dioxygen."[10] "Dioxygen" was a chemical disinfectant of the time.

Davis's most sizable gift to the Egyptian people was the girls' school he funded, likely at Emma's urging. Theodore's mistress was not easy to please; in 1893 they had visited the American Missionaries' School in Aswan and Emma found the staff "too narrow in their teachings and of too distinctly a religious type." In Luxor, however, they were both charmed in 1901 by Miss Carrie Buchanan, a Presbyterian missionary from Indiana. Buchanan had been sent to establish the American Missionary School for Girls and by 1902 the school had around 130 students; one-quarter were Egyptian Muslims and the rest Arabs, Turks, and Christian Copts. Davis bought the site for a permanent school and then paid to build it.

Carrie spoke fluent Arabic and taught her charges reading and writing as well as sewing and other useful skills. She became a regular guest on the *Beduin,* and Theodore and Emma visited the school every year. By 1905, the school had expanded to more than two hundred girls with fifty of them boarding there, some with their children. In 1916, Emma recalled, "When we went out there they were the only people who ever did anything for the benefit of the common children."[11] The Americans' feelings may have been condescending, but they were sincere; Emma wrote, "I think the work she is doing is about the biggest in Egypt. Each one of her girls as they marry and have homes and children will form a leaven for succeeding generations." When Davis died he left today's equivalent of $1 million to Buchanan, suggesting she might use it to benefit the school further.

Of course, relations between Davis and the average Egyptian were similar to his relations with everyone else—determined by his wealth and their desire for a small bit of it. The obsequiousness the locals displayed was described by a Davis guest in Luxor in 1912; as he rode to Karnak temple on his donkey, "along the waterfront of Luxor Cousin Theodore had an ovation. Lines of dragomans and humble folk rose to their feet and beamingly shouted a welcome to him. As his own donkey boy said, kissing his hand, 'All the world is thankables that Mr. Davis are come back!' " It is unlikely he was impressed by the praise, and his guest's claim "he is known up and down the Nile as 'the friend of the poor,' "[12] is the hardest to believe of all—at least, unless he was there to hear it.

Nobody in Iowa City in 1860 would have confused Davis with "a friend of the poor." An example of the esteem his profession held arose shortly after his return with Annie from their honeymoon. The records of all county tax sales since the establishment of the Iowa Territory had mysteriously disappeared from the courthouse and an observer suspected "snide lawyers did it, because the loss would make oceans of tax-title litigation, whereby they might profit."[13] Although there is no indication Davis himself was involved, such was the common opinion of lawyers' ethics—and not without cause. Davis learned the ways of greasing the wheels of legal and business deals while greasing his own palm as well; like the canoe thief a few years before, he had come to recognize the merit of hooking what might be hooked. Years later, an Iowa attorney repeatedly refused to discuss any of Davis's business transactions with congressional investigators.

Davis closed the Clarke & Davis office early the afternoon of April 18, 1861, to join the parade moving through downtown Iowa City (avoiding the block that had burned down three weeks before). The crowd of several thousand, many waving flags, moved past Capitol Square while the university band (led by William Penn Clarke's son) played patriotic music. The march came to a halt in front of the Clinton House, the finest hotel in town. The mass rally was to demonstrate support for the Union; federal troops had been fired upon at Fort Sumter in South Carolina six days earlier to begin the Civil War. An impromptu speakers' platform was erected in front of the hotel and stirring speeches were delivered by Davis's mentor, G. W. Clark—who had been elected mayor two weeks earlier—and Davis's father-in-law, Judge Buttles, who assured the crowd that the Union would triumph quickly in a short war.

Davis sat out the war. He might have felt an obligation to stay with his wife and provide for his mother; the possibilities that he was a pacifist, a Southern sympathizer, or a coward are all unlikely. The best explanation is he probably did not consider the war important enough to interrupt his business. John D. Rockefeller, Jay Gould, Andrew Carnegie, and J. P. Morgan—future tycoons all—paid the $300 fee required to opt out of the army ($300 was also the exact amount budgeted for cigars in Morgan's office that year), but since Iowa always met its quota of recruits through volunteers Davis never had to pay the fee to avoid being drafted. Whatever their supposed reasons, Davis and the other tycoons did not fight to save the Union or to end slavery because, ultimately, they simply did not wish to.

His lawyer friend George Boal stayed home as well and married Annie's sister Malvina shortly after the war started. The marriage linked Davis to the Boal family for the rest of his life. George's younger brother John rode off to war, a captain in the Ninth Pennsylvania Cavalry, from the family home in Boalsburg and most of Davis's other friends answered the call as well. G. W. Clark left Iowa in August as captain of the Twenty-second Iowa Volunteers (he was succeeded as mayor in 1863 by Judge Buttles); Penn Clarke's son gave up the university band to serve as a sergeant in the regiment. Gov. Sam Kirkwood was reelected and became known as "Iowa's War Governor" (as his tombstone states); his son was adjutant of the Twenty-fifth Regiment of the Iowa Infantry. Davis's stepbrother, Jonas Titus Jr., gave up his life as a printer and semi-professional baseball player in Detroit to become a lieutenant in the Michigan Sharpshooters.

Penn Clarke's Republican connections produced him an appointment as a paymaster in the army, with the rank of major and a salary of $3,000. He left Davis in charge of their practice, with the understanding that Clarke would continue to receive his full partner's share of the firm's profits. Davis spent the war litigating unpaid debts and property disputes and buying real estate.

Theodore and Annie visited Columbus and Emma Andrews every summer; the baby girl Emma had carried when she first met Theodore in 1860 had died, but in 1862 she had a son named Charles. (The child died a few years later.) At almost the same time, Emma's husband, Abner, was struck by an affliction severe enough to force him to retire from work for the rest of his life. The particulars of Abner's illness are unrecorded (gossip had him losing his mind, committed to an insane asylum); in 1865 his father's will provided Emma with a separate bequest because her husband was "an invalid" who could not provide for her. Whatever it was,

Abner's illness doomed him to a slow decline. The relationship between Theodore and Emma developed in the shadow of her lingering, increasingly fragile husband.

Visits to Ohio brought Davis into Emma's circle of friends, members of other pioneer families who had prospered. Hiland Hulburd was ten years older than Davis and the son of a Presbyterian minister; he had grown up in Warren when Judge Buttles had edited the newspaper there. After an adventure in the California gold fields and a stint as a deputy sheriff in San Francisco, Hulburd had gone to Washington and become deputy comptroller of the currency (hired by another Columbus native, Secretary of the Treasury Salmon P. Chase). Nathaniel Wilson, two years older than Davis and destined to be his closest friend for the rest of his life, was a lawyer from Zanesville who had also gone to Washington; in 1861 he was named assistant U.S. Attorney and in 1862 was made the first solicitor general of the navy. Emma's Ohio friends— and their descriptions of life in the larger world—stoked Davis's ambitions; after a few years of managing Clarke & Davis alone, the junior partner resolved to follow them east.

In 1864, Davis began cashing in the Iowa land he had bought; in two years he sold six properties, saving for his next move. By the beginning of 1865 the end of the war was in sight and his connections with the dominant Republican Party would be valuable. The cost of victory had been high; among the war's six hundred thousand casualties was the beau of Annie's sister Sarah, Kirkwood's son (killed in Arkansas), and John Boal (killed in North Carolina). G. W. Clark was severely wounded in Virginia in 1864 and returned home shattered, unable to work ever again. He began selling pieces of his farm to support his family.

When Maj. William Penn Clarke returned to Iowa City in January 1865, it was for only a brief visit. He was on his way from his previous posting in Mississippi to his new assignment with General Sherman's forces in the East. It was a rare chance to see his wife, although his son—now a captain—was with his troop in Alabama.

Iowa City was a depressing place compared to the boomtown Penn Clarke had helped build before the war. Most males on the street were either old men or boys; the war had drawn away most of the labor force and in 1864 a regiment formed of students from the university was sent to join the attack on Memphis. With no factories to profit from war contracts, Iowa City business had stalled; construction had come to a standstill and currency was in such short supply that stores issued their own vouchers for making change.

The bad business climate was the prime topic of conversation when Penn Clarke visited his partner in their office. Penn Clarke launched into a series of accusations; he thought the amounts Davis had turned over to him as the senior partner's share were smaller than they should have been. Davis replied that the war had ruined the law business in Iowa and offered to go over the account books with the older man, but Penn Clarke's temper erupted and he accused Davis of cheating him. Davis became equally enraged at Clarke's aspersions and a loud argument followed. The fight was not resolved when Penn Clarke stalked out of the office, and it had not been settled when the paymaster left to join General Sherman.

In February Davis placed advertisements in the local papers announcing the dissolution of Clarke & Davis, listing a new office address and stating he would retain the old firm's clients and cases. Penn Clarke responded with a lawsuit charging Davis with fraud and demanding an accounting; Davis hired Governor Kirkwood for his defense. Kirkwood pointed out to Davis that Clarke's temperament prevented him from seeing "any evil in a friend, or any good in an enemy, especially if as in your case that enemy was formerly a friend."[14]

Their partnership likely would have collapsed earlier if the hotheaded, temperamental Clarke had stayed home; Davis lasted longer with him than any of his other partners. The two had differences beyond their professional ambitions; Clarke had been a founding member of the Iowa City Sons of Temperance and secretary of the Iowa Anti-Capital Punishment and Prison Discipline Society. Coupled with his militant abolitionism, he was much more in the mold of Davis's father than Davis was. The outcome of the lawsuit is not clear, and whether Davis really did cheat Clarke will never be known; ten years later Davis stated, "I had a lawsuit with him and I beat him," but in December 1865 Davis quietly transferred ownership of one of his Iowa properties to Clarke, implying some kind of settlement.

President Lincoln was assassinated on April 14, five days after Lee surrendered to Grant in Virginia. When Lincoln's funeral train passed through Columbus, Emma's brother Albert was on the local decorations committee and her father-in-law was an honorary pallbearer. In Iowa City, Davis and Annie joined a march through town to the university on the day of Lincoln's funeral. All businesses and saloons were closed and draped in mourning, flags were flown at half-staff and upside down, and the climactic oration at the ceremony was delivered by Sam Kirkwood.

Davis's decade in Iowa was over. The end of the war meant the time was right for him to make his next move; he later admitted he was already a man of means when he moved to New York City, where his political connections would allow him to secure a portion of the spoils among the powerful. Iowa City was no longer sufficient for what Davis wanted to accomplish, and his passion to compete and triumph in the world drew him to the high-stakes arena of New York, the place for men of ambition to be.

He was surprisingly well prepared to take on the challenges and opportunities he would find there. His native intelligence had been honed by his legal experience, he had developed a capacity for intense periods of concentrated work, and he had learned how politicians behaved and what motivated their decisions. The self-confidence fostered by two years in the wilderness had increased as he discovered how to prevail over human and societal obstacles as successfully as the physical ones he had faced as a boy in the Upper Peninsula.

Davis's personality was the product of his experience, and he would always retain a bit of a rough-edged, frontier persona. His intellectual curiosity and continual self-education overcame his lack of formal schooling, but although he became an extremely sophisticated individual he was never what eastern society considered polished. He was "eccentric" and "brusque," and known for "wisecracks and tactless sayings." When the Duke of Devonshire visited him in Egypt years later and declined Davis's offer of a cigar, "to the horror of the English Davis said jocosely, 'Duke, with one foot in the grave you'd better take a good cigar while you can.' "[15] While Davis was building a railroad in Colorado in 1890 the mayor of Leadville took him to the town's premier brothel, where Davis was attracted to the proprietress but was warned she had retired from her old profession. "I see," Davis replied wistfully. *"Hors de concours"*[16] ("Out of the competition," a term frequently used in horse shows).

Davis could have remained in Iowa the rest of his life and prospered, but he was not content to be a big fish in a provincial pond. Instead he chose to enter the most intense competition in post–Civil War America. He was not a particularly reflective man, and if spiritual or philosophical matters did not concern him much it was because the world had rewarded the pragmatic, materialistic traits his youth and young manhood had developed. The brutal, corrupt, every-man-for-himself regime that would frame the industrial transformation of the United States into an empire was the perfect stage for a man of Davis's talents and drive.

When Davis arrived in New York City in 1865 the tallest buildings in the city were four or five stories; the streets were paved with cobblestones (except Wall Street, with its newly installed granite slabs). Forty thousand horses plodded through the streets, producing four hundred tons of manure and two hundred carcasses every day and a mat of brown matter that carpeted the thoroughfares and raised a stench above the forest of telegraph lines that were beginning to block the sky. The city was about to experience a boom as the financial center of the postwar development that settled the West and turned the country into an industrial superpower. City rents doubled the first year after the war and the population increased 20 percent, to 950,000, by 1870.

Davis came to New York alone. Annie stayed with her father in Iowa City, although she frequently joined her husband for extended visits. Davis moved in with another lawyer named Henry Knox (who in 1883 was forced to resign from the Southern District Court of New York for stealing public funds) and a mysterious "Mr. Gilman," who later helped Davis rig auction sales.

The city was in tune with Davis's ambitions; a contemporary account noted, "All the world over, poverty is a misfortune. In New York, it is a crime." Joining the bar was easier than in Iowa, but competition was fierce: "The most accomplished city barrister finds success a slow and uncertain thing," the same account observed.[17] Esteemed lawyer George Templeton Strong noted that the profession ranked "next below that of patent-medicine mongering"[18] in public opinion; Davis's closest business associate within a few years was the biggest patent-medicine peddler in the country.

The first known photograph of Davis is from around this time. He appears a bit of a dandy, wearing a coat with a velvet collar and sporting a mustache and muttonchop sideburns that appear extreme even for the time; he continued to wear the style until it was long out of fashion. Most striking about the portrait is the extraordinarily cool, appraising expression Davis wears. The eyes, below slightly raised brows, are clear and direct and the chin is firmly set, less an irresistible force than an immovable object. His friend Nathaniel Wilson recalled his chief characteristics as "strength of will, adherence to his purpose and perseverance in carrying out and doing whatever he undertook to do . . . He was very quick and arbitrary and sometimes impatient, and he was absolutely unchanging in his fidelity to those to whom he thought fidelity was due."[19]

He formed a partnership with a silk-stocking New York aristocrat, Thomas Henry Edsall (Edsall Avenue in the Bronx is named after his family), and the firm of Davis & Edsall located their office on Pine Street. With Edsall's connections and Davis's charm and hard work drawing clients to the firm, the pair made money quickly. Their first case before the state supreme court won their client $4,000 worth of disputed bonds.

In May 1866, Davis visited Washington, D.C. He rode in one of the horse-drawn carriages operated by the Metropolitan Railroad Company, along tracks set in the middle of the street, to the home of Nathaniel Wilson, Emma's friend and one of the company's founders. Wilson combined private business and his law practice with public service; in 1865, as assistant U.S. Attorney, he had prosecuted one of the most sensational murder trials in Washington history, the case of a woman who had shot her errant lover in the Treasury Building. The accused was so sympathetic to the public (Mary Lincoln had sent a bouquet to her prison cell) that she was acquitted by the jury after five minutes' deliberation. Wilson was more successful that year in defending himself against the charge he had solicited a $25,000 bribe to secure the release of a federal prisoner.

When Davis joined Wilson and his wife for dinner, the center of attention was Wilson's newborn son, Charles. What the men discussed at greater length, however, was the meeting Davis had held earlier that day with the board of the Bank of the Metropolis, a meeting that set the stage for Davis's first major financial coup.

The National Banking Act, passed by Congress in 1863, had been intended to finance the war and provide currency to keep the U.S. economy from collapsing; part of the act had established national banks under the supervision of the comptroller of the currency. The first national bank in the country had opened in Davenport while Davis was in Iowa. Oversight of the banks was so loose—and the authorization to print money so attractive—that hundreds of banks had converted to national bank status. The first institution to go bankrupt had failed in Attica, New York, the day Lincoln was shot. The Bank of the Metropolis had been a venerable Washington institution that helped finance the rebuilding of the White House after the War of 1812; by 1866 it had converted to a national bank and its board members, unable to resist the ample temptation, had looted it into insolvency.

The law called for the comptroller of the currency to close a broken bank and appoint a receiver to liquidate its assets and pay its creditors. The matter of the Bank of the Metropolis, however, was in the hands of the deputy comptroller, Davis's Ohio friend Hiland Hulburd. Hulburd arranged with Davis and the bank's board to handle the failure as a "private suspension," keeping the insolvency secret from depositors and, if successful, allowing the board members to hang on to some of their ill-gotten gains and avoid prison. Despite the law, the bankrupt bank continued operating. Hulburd was widely suspected of taking bribes from those he regulated (winning a national bank charter cost $5,000, paid to Hulburd's brother Lew), and his selection of Davis to handle the lucrative affair—which if done legitimately would have netted him some $35,000, equivalent to around $750,000 today—doubtless involved some compensation for the deputy comptroller.

"I was attorney for the bank to close up its affairs," Davis later testified. "I was employed by the officers of the bank. The bank owed some $700,000. Its assets consisted of about $400,000."[20] One of the ways Davis covered the debt was later revealed: A month after Davis was hired, the Metropolis received $618,000 in bonds issued by the State of Tennessee from a bank in Memphis operated by a crony of the Metropolis board member named George Rutter. (Rutter later testified he had received the bond deposit by bribing the Tennessee legislature: "It was a common thing," he explained).[21] The loan of the bonds was ostensibly to help the Metropolis inflate its asset sheet, and Rutter had been promised that when the Metropolis solved its problems the bonds would be returned. Davis, however, promptly cashed the bonds. The Memphis bank then failed, but Davis paid the Memphis receiver $5,000 to forget the debt owed by the Metropolis. Tennessee eventually sued Davis for fraud, but he was acquitted for lack of evidence.

There are few surviving records of the closing of the Bank of the Metropolis, and corruption in New York and Washington was so widespread that bribes, kickbacks, and gifts covered much of the process. A 1980 reconstruction of Davis's transactions, however, determined that $227,000 unaccountably disappeared, "as if evaporated,"[22] and went to Davis. The equivalent of some $5 million today, much of the pile had to have been distributed to other conspirators, but it was Davis's first major financial score; by 1871 his personal net worth was around $150,000. No matter how profitable his Iowa real estate dealings had been, Davis prospered more after he moved east and joined the ranks of the New York lawyers like those who had lied to Jonas Titus. In 1867, Hulburd was rewarded for his good work and appointed comptroller of the currency; Davis & Edsall moved to more prestigious offices on Wall Street in 1868.

Davis & Edsall needed to be sensitive to the local politics that governed the courts, and by 1868 all New York politics revolved around William M. Tweed, known to history as "Boss" Tweed and arguably the most corrupt politician in American history. As wealthy Republicans the two partners would have been natural enemies of Tweed's Democratic machine, but Davis was never one to let politics get in the way of business. He and Tweed became friends; recollections of Tweed as a man with a swaggering style who used slang and coarse humor are similar to remembrances of Davis. In 1868 Tweed controlled several banks, and hired Davis as attorney for the Ocean National Bank, the largest national bank in the city.

As he explored the circumstances of his new client, Davis learned of its rather unusual transactions. Ocean Bank officers would routinely remove $20,000 or $50,000 from the bank's cash drawers and replace the money with their personal notes, which were entered on the books as cash. In 1867 the bank had loaned Tweed the money to buy the *New York Transcript,* a newspaper that published legal decisions and court calendars and printed fewer than one hundred copies per week. Government official Tweed began approving payment for advertising bills submitted to the city by the *Transcript*'s new Tweed-picked editor, Charles Wilbour (later a prominent figure in archaeology circles in Egypt). For space in fewer than a hundred papers per week, the bills were in excess of half a million dollars per year; the payments approved by official Tweed were paid to owner Tweed. In 1868 Davis oversaw a loan to Tweed and Wilbour to organize the New York Printing Company, which instantly began to receive all of the city's printing business; in its first year the firm paid its owners—which also included the principal stockholder in *The New York Times*—a $75,000 return on their $10,000 investments. Soon Wilbour was operating six facilities around the city and employing two thousand people.

In 1869, Tweed borrowed money from the Ocean Bank and bought an entire block of the city, between Fourth and Madison avenues and Sixty-eighth and Sixty-ninth streets. The next morning he ordered the public works department to extend water mains to his block, increasing its value tenfold. By one estimate Tweed was now stealing $1 million per month from the city, including the $40,000 bribe he received for cooperating with the company that was about to build the Brooklyn Bridge.

Another interesting discovery Davis made was the tie between the bank and the Lake Superior Ship Canal Company, which had its offices on the second floor of the bank building. The company had been formed by two brothers, Perez and William Avery, to build a canal across the Keweenaw Peninsula that Davis had surveyed in 1854. The Averys were confidence men with a long trail of illegalities behind them; when Davis had arrived in Iowa in 1855, Perez Avery had been stealing negotiable notes from the safe

of a New York insurance company that had fired him, which he
ransomed back to the company for $25,000. The Averys had fleeced
no less a person than Henry Wells, founder of Wells Fargo, in a
fraudulent scheme to build a canal in South America.

The Averys had persuaded Congress and the Michigan legislature in 1865 to allocate four hundred thousand acres of federal
property to finance construction of the Keweenaw canal, the
land to be awarded when the canal was completed in 1867. The
brothers issued $500,000 in bonds to finance building the canal,
swearing the bonds were secured by the Michigan property—
notwithstanding the inconvenient requirement that the canal be
completed before the land was theirs. The Ocean Bank bought
$150,000 worth. The bank president received $50,000 cash (borrowed by the Averys from the bank) and the cashier $100,000 worth
of stock in the canal in return for the favor.

In July 1868 Congress granted an extension for the completion
of the canal—which hadn't been started—until 1870, and Davis
supervised the Ocean Bank's issue of another half million dollars
in bonds. The Averys had now mortgaged the Michigan land
twice and still did not own it. The prospectus for the sale, nonetheless, guaranteed the bond buyers an unconditional title to the
four hundred thousand acres. The federal examiner whom Comptroller Hulburd had assigned to the Ocean Bank, a man named
Charles Callender, began touting the canal bonds to other banks
he examined; the Averys paid him $100,000 in canal stock for his
efforts, which Callender put up as security for loans to himself
from the Ocean Bank ("a mere cloak to cover the bribe," as Davis
later put it).

Davis traveled west every year, either with Annie or meeting
her in Iowa City. In Columbus he visited with Emma Andrews. In
Detroit he visited his mother; his half-sister Isabella, now fifteen,

Wall Street during Davis's time. The offices of Davis & Edsall were at no. 38, the small three-story building at the center of the photo. Reproduced by permission of the New-York Historical Society.

was attending the Convent of the Sacred Heart. His old boss George Frost, the real estate man, provided valuable information on the Averys' lack of progress in starting their canal. In Iowa City, where Judge Buttles was building a new house with a bedroom designed for Annie, Davis visited the first child named after him; in 1867 George and Malvina Boal had named their first son Theodore Davis Boal.

Davis and Annie never had children and it was one of the tragedies of their lives. Davis was extremely fond of young people and later went to great lengths to include other people's children in his home. If the problem was medical it was not present in Annie's sisters, and it is possible Davis was sterile due to smallpox; the disease plagued America his entire life, there had been a major outbreak in Michigan in 1853, and another swept New York in 1865. What little evidence survives indicates he was heterosexually active as an adult; his lack of offspring was a permanent sadness and doubtless contributed to his gradual estrangement from Annie. Their marriage never appears to have been especially passionate, and as he grew intellectually and his interests broadened she failed to follow him.

After less than five years in New York, Davis had made himself a wealthy man; his net worth was the equivalent of around $3 million today. He was widely known as an effective and discreet, if not overly scrupulous, attorney. His friends from Emma's Ohio circle had provided the access and credibility crucial to his schemes, and allies such as Tweed and Nathaniel Wilson (now retired from government work after losing his prosecution of John Surratt for the murder of President Lincoln) offered the means to even more ambitious ends. Davis was not finished chasing wealth; a few years later, he explained that "I was not so anxious to make all the money I wanted at once."[23] His patience and foresight complemented his pragmatism; he made the comment while negotiating a bribe.

The discovery of Hatshepsut's sarcophagi in 1904 was the last Davis and Carter made together. The excavation season over, they were all in Cairo on April 1; Emma and guest Jean Hardy toured the zoo with Carter that morning, and Davis joined them for lunch and an afternoon playing bridge at Shepheard's. There was a great deal to discuss over the cards.

Hatshepsut's tomb was not the only remarkable discovery that year; the group chatted about the find by Italian archaeologist

Ernesto Schiaparelli of the magnificent tomb of Nefertari in the Valley of the Queens (Carter had escorted H. Ryder Haggard, author of the quintessential "lost world" novel, *She,* through the tomb when he had visited Luxor the month before). Britain and France had just reached an agreement on the Entente Cordiale, which gave Morocco over to exclusive French control and made Britain the sole power in Egypt; the agreement retained the earlier understanding that France would continue to oversee the Service des Antiquities, however, specifying that the director would always be French.

The most pressing item they talked about between bids and trumps was the change Maspero had announced in the service's personnel structure. He had decided the time was right to rotate his inspectors; Carter had been in charge of Upper Egypt, which included the Valley of the Kings, but he was now to switch jobs with the inspector for Lower Egypt, another English digger named James E. Quibell. Carter was unhappy about the move and had briefly considered resigning when his request to stay in Luxor had been turned down. Although Davis and Carter were friends, the change was not one Davis minded; he had known Quibell for six years.

It was understood that Davis would continue paying for excavation in the valley, with Quibell taking over from Carter. Quibell was unavailable to discuss the coming season, however; he and his wife, also named Annie, were in St. Louis mounting the Egyptian exhibit at the upcoming World's Fair, which featured an entire reconstructed tomb with mummies and mummy cases. The fair, according to its organizers, was intended to contrast the "barbarous and semi-barbarous peoples of the world" with the "enlightenment of America." When some white St. Louis schoolteachers invited some Filipino men who were part of the exhibition to stroll with them through the fairgrounds, the Filipinos were taunted with shouts of "nigger," attacked by the fair's police force, and shot at by a group of marines. Fortunately, a lynching by the enlightened Americans was avoided.

Davis and Emma returned to Egypt on December 9, 1904. They always traveled in the finest style; a friend describing a trip on an ocean liner with Davis noted "the luxuries with which we are surrounded, and everybody kowtowing, from the Captain who looks like Santa Claus to the least of the stewards."[24] On some voyages Emma was given the captain's cabin; she called her quarters on the bridge of the S.S. *Koenig Albert* "my little sky apartment." When the ship docked in Naples, a guest recalled, "the Grand Hotel had sent a special carriage for us and away we drove, unencumbered by anything except a small black bag with cousin Emma's jewels, while Jones and Amelie" (Theodore's valet and Emma's maid) "looked after the forty odd pieces of luggage."[25]

In Cairo, they ensconced themselves at Shepheard's while the *Beduin* was readied to sail. Quibell was back from St. Louis and had assumed his new duties in Luxor; in November he had supervised the removal of the two gigantic stone sarcophagi from Hatshepsut's tomb and readied them for shipment to Cairo. Davis sent him a message confirming his continued support for valley exploration and (probably unnecessarily) asking Quibell to begin excavating without waiting for his arrival. The archaeologist finished clearing the sides of the gully where Hatshepsut's tomb was and moved on to a small side valley.

On December 16 the Americans were reunited with Carter, meeting him for lunch at the Mena House hotel by the Giza plateau with its spectacular view of the pyramids. The Mena House had been a favorite lunch location for them since 1899, when the converted royal hunting lodge had opened as a hotel with marvelous carved *mashrabia* wooden screens surrounding the veranda, blue tile mosaics on the floor, and carved wooden doors embossed with medieval brass. As they talked amid the furniture inlaid with mother-of-pearl and the antique brass Islamic lamps, Emma concluded Carter looked "better and happier" than he had eight months before. He had adjusted to his new job; by one account he had enlarged his office in the museum to twice the size of Maspero's and was proposing a scheme to create a position for Quibell at the museum and place all of Egypt's excavations under his own supervision. There were indeed changes coming, but not what Carter proposed.

James Quibell was a bit preoccupied as he helped his wife, Annie, cross the gangplank onto the *Beduin* for dinner on January 16, 1905. Davis and his entourage had arrived in Luxor the day before after a leisurely sail south from Cairo, and Davis would want a report on the past two months' digging. Nothing of interest had been found since he had moved Hatshepsut's sarcophagi. Quibell was more concerned about the new job he would be starting shortly— and the task of telling Davis about it.

The most experienced and qualified archaeologist to yet work in the valley, Quibell had graduated from Oxford and come to work in Egypt in 1893, excavating with William M. F. Petrie at digs in Coptos, Ballas, and Naqada. At Hierakonpolis (twenty-five miles north of Luxor) in 1898, Quibell had discovered the famous Narmer Palette and a spectacular statue of a golden-headed falcon. He had fallen in love with Annie Pirie when they were both working for Petrie and recovering together from ptomaine poisoning caused by Petrie's parsimonious expedition techniques; in Petrie's camp, buried caches of the previous season's canned goods were dug up and tested for freshness by throwing the cans at a stone wall. If a can did not explode, the contents were deemed fit to eat. James and Annie Quibell had become regular visitors to the *Beduin*; Davis's dinners were considerably superior to Petrie's. In 1902, Annie Quibell had traveled with Davis from Aswan to Cairo.

The Quibells joined the group on deck. Davis had two extra young women with him this season: Jean Hardy had come again from Columbus and Davis had picked up Alice Wilson (Nathaniel's daughter) in Florence; she had been visiting her sister Nellie in Dresden and after Egypt would return home to Washington with "Uncle" Theodore and "Aunt" Emma.

After greetings had been effusively exchanged and drinks served, Quibell delivered the news Maspero had announced after Davis had set sail from Cairo almost a month before. (Sailing the Nile in 1905 was still a relaxing experience; the quiet of the journey and the ever-changing panorama of seemingly eternal village life gliding by on the shore was uninterrupted by messages from the outside world.) While the *Beduin* traveled south, Maspero had decided that Quibell would move north to a new job created to supervise operations at the ancient cemetery of Saqqara, near Cairo.[26] Another inspector would be hired to take charge of Upper Egypt—and of Davis. Quibell was now waiting to move north; his replacement's identity was only a topic of speculation and rumor.

The news of Quibell's transfer disappointed Davis, and as he puffed a cigar he considered what it meant for his excavations in the valley. The crew Quibell had set working in a small gully would be finished soon. Neither man knew when the next inspector would take over—Maspero was now far to the south on an inspection tour in Nubia—and Quibell had no inclination to begin any ambitious project in the valley since he knew he would be leaving almost as soon as it began.

Davis brought out a rough map of the valley and spread it over the card table. He knew Quibell would be more concerned with his move to Saqqara for the rest of his time in Luxor, but the American did not want the work to stop. After the men had glanced over the map for a few minutes, Davis pointed to a spot in another of the side gullies. Between KV 3 (the tomb of a son of Rameses III) and KV 4 (Rameses XI), he had noticed a large, untouched mound of chippings. Quibell explained the chips were from the mining of the two Ramesside tombs. The rest of the gully had been explored; Davis wondered if the earth under the mound should be cleared as well.

Quibell was unenthusiastic about the spot; there was small chance of finding a tomb there, he said, because the space between the two known tombs was too narrow for another to have been crammed in. Quibell—and Maspero, when he arrived—also believed that even if there was a tomb there, the workers involved in making the two flanking tombs in ancient times would certainly have looted it thoroughly. Davis was not deterred. The experts were probably right, he acknowledged, "but I knew every yard of the lateral valley, except as described," Davis later wrote, "and I decided that good exploration justified its investigation and that it would be a satisfaction to know the entire valley, even if it yielded nothing."[27] Quibell saw no reason to argue with the patron's foibles. They agreed that as soon as the crew was finished where Quibell had them, work would move to the spot Davis suggested.

The dinner on January 16, 1905, marked a major change in Davis's involvement in the valley excavations; Newberry, Maspero, and Carter had selected the places they would dig with Davis's money. With no archaeologist in effective command, however, Davis now started making decisions himself. Having assumed responsibility for the diggers' location, Davis would never relinquish it. His new attention to the work kept the *Beduin* moored in Luxor for the entire season, without the usual cruise to Aswan. He visited the worksite every day.

When the Quibells dropped by for dinner again on January 21, there was plenty of news to discuss. Carter was in trouble; while Davis had been sailing south, a party of drunken French tourists had visited Saqqara and gotten into a fight with the guards, whom Carter had ordered to defend themselves. The floor of the antiquities service's rest house was stained by blood at the end of the fight, which involved fists, chairs, walking sticks, and rocks. The political implications of Egyptians striking Frenchmen at the orders of an English bureaucrat were serious, and Maspero was attempting to calm the firestorm it caused in the press by working with Lord Cromer and the French consul. Carter was certain he had behaved properly, but the French were adamantly demanding official action over the "attack."

Quibell also shared the news Davis had been waiting for: He had received word that the next inspector for Upper Egypt would be yet another English archaeologist, Arthur Weigall. Davis had first met Weigall three years before; "so nice and amusing," Emma had judged. Weigall's father had been a captain in the British army and died in Kandahar, Afghanistan, the year Arthur was born. He had left school at sixteen and, fascinated by Egypt, had been introduced to Petrie by Percy Newberry. In 1901 he had come to Egypt as Petrie's assistant at Abydos and then took a job copying inscriptions at Saqqara. He had visited Davis regularly on the *Beduin* and at Shepheard's. Carter had urged him to apply for the inspector's job, possibly because Carter did not see him as a serious competitor. It was unclear when the appointment would become official, or when Weigall would arrive.

Four days later the work crew finished the gully where Quibell had placed them, having found nothing, and reported to the spot Davis had picked. They were confronted by a huge bank of limestone chippings 30 feet high, stretching for 120 feet against the hillside. As Davis watched, a trench was started down through the chips, which still bore the chisel marks of the ancient workmen who had quarried them from the neighboring royal tombs. The sides of the trench inevitably caved in as the diggers made their way down to bedrock. The hot and dusty work proceeded slowly, since the chips each needed to be checked for ancient inscriptions or drawings. The work plodded forward, spurred by Davis's daily visits.

Socializing on the boat continued; on January 29 artist Joseph Lindon Smith and his wife, Corinna, moored their rented *dahabiyeh* next to the *Beduin* and came to dinner. Maspero's boat arrived two days later, and at dinner on February 3 the Frenchman agreed with Quibell that Davis's site was unlikely to produce anything, although he had no objection to thoroughness.

He shared the solution he and Cromer had reached regarding Carter's "Saqqara Incident": Carter and Maspero would formally express their regrets to the French consul general (who seems to have been none too sympathetic to his intoxicated countrymen), and the whole thing would blow over. To Maspero's amazement, however, Carter had refused to go along, insisting that the French should apologize instead. It was a troublesome inconvenience for the director.

The next day Davis visited the excavation and found it "most discouraging." He returned to the *Beduin* and sent Carter a telegram advising him to do as Maspero asked. "Sacrifice your rights for the benefit of the government," he urged. "Don't hesitate."[28]

After breakfast on February 6, Davis took Jean and Alice with him on donkeys to visit the worksite. When they arrived, Davis recalled, "I was greeted by my *reis* and workmen with great acclamation. I quickly made my way to the spot, where I saw a few inches of the top of a well-cut stone step, which promised steps below and the possible existence of a tomb."[29] There was much work to be done before a tomb would be revealed, if one was there; the stairway into the hillside was choked with the chips and cemented rubble the workmen had been fighting since the digging began. The mound had to be completely cleared back to the hillside to expose the stairway, and the danger of collapse was real; Smith recalled at least one avalanche as the entryway was cleared. Nonetheless, it was "very encouraging," as Emma wrote that night, and Davis enjoyed a bit of self-righteous vindication.

The next morning, as the crew worked on clearing the stairway, Davis decided to celebrate by visiting an antiquities dealer on the east side of the river in Luxor. He returned with a wonderful purchase, an exquisite solid silver statuette of a graceful standing woman. Maspero dated it to the Twenty-sixth Dynasty (664–525 B.C.), and after Davis had given it to the Metropolitan it was finally studied (in 1986) and cartouches of Necho II, second king of the dynasty, were revealed.[30] In 2012 it was loaned to the Jacquemart-André Museum in Paris for a special exhibition.

Weigall arrived in Luxor and joined Davis and Emma for lunch that afternoon. Weigall was not yet the new inspector—his appointment still waiting for formal paperwork to be finished—but he was naturally excited to learn of the staircase; after lunch he, Davis, and Joe Smith rode their donkeys to the site, where the workmen were slowly cutting back the mound and revealing more of the stairs. The fill was so hard the men's pickaxes had difficulty breaking it up.

The next day Maspero sent Quibell away on an important mission; the Duke of Connaught, the King of England's younger brother and inspector general of the army, was touring Egypt and required the best guide the service could provide. Quibell departed for Edfu to lead His Royal Highness and his entourage through the temple there.

Friday, February 10, was the workmen's day off. The weather was cold and windy, and Davis stayed on the boat and wrote a long letter of advice to the recalcitrant Carter. "You are so entirely wrong, and in danger of a crushing blow," the American warned, but in a kindly manner, addressing Carter as "my poor boy." He wrote of "the *astounding* fatherly advice of M. Maspero . . . There is only one manly, upright and gentlemanly thing to do, and that is to express your regrets. Contemplate the harm of being dismissed from the service 'for disobedience.' It will stick to you as long as you live, and all your justification will be forgotten. I have written as a true friend should, however much you may dislike it." He signed the letter "Always your friend."[31]

The following day, Davis and Weigall visited the excavation and were excited to see that in clearing the stairway the top of a doorway had been revealed. Davis called upon the Egyptian police on his way back to the boat and requested a guard be posted overnight at the site. After tea with Emma he went next door to Maspero's boat, the *Miriam,* and told the Frenchman the doorway would probably be cleared the next day. Maspero authorized Davis to open the tomb, Quibell's absence notwithstanding. "Mr. Weigall will look after it," he told the patron. Davis sent a note to Annie Quibell, explaining the decision.

The next day Weigall came to lunch on the *Beduin* and brought an acquaintance, "a handsome, agreeable little fellow," according to Emma, who had ridden from the Red Sea to Luxor on a camel. After lunch Davis and Weigall left on their donkeys for the valley to inspect the day's progress, and rode into archaeological history.

The discovery of the tomb of Yuya and Thuyu (described in chapter one) was a landmark in Egyptology. The information the tomb provided was a windfall for scholars; objects that had been seen before only in paintings on the walls of looted chambers filled the tomb, including furniture, statues, jewelry, amulets, chests, and even the tomb owners' sandals. Yuya's beautifully illustrated *Book of the Dead* contained a chapter never seen before, and the mummies were among the best examples ever found of the ancient embalmer's art. Annie Quibell called it "the greatest find of funerary furniture that has ever come to light."[32] Worldwide publicity increased public interest in Egypt and made Davis an international celebrity. A *New York Times* article was typical, using the words "magnificent," "astonishing," "dazzling," and "gorgeous." It was "beyond the wildest dreams of the archaeologist."[33]

The find also changed Davis's approach to excavating and raised expectations about what else rested beneath the valley floor. *The Century Magazine* predicted "the Valley will be searched with a new energy and thoroughness that should receive a superb reward."[34] Explorers as early as the Italian strongman/engineer Giovanni Belzoni in 1820 had concluded there were no more tombs to be found in the valley, but the 1905 discovery created a momentum that would carry along Maspero, Davis, and their hired archaeologists until all possible nooks and crannies had been investigated.

The American had filled the breach when the professionals had dithered in administrative confusion, had decided where to dig, had monitored the workmen every day—and had discovered the richest tomb in history. The success reinforced his self-confidence; from now on, the Davis explorations would have a great deal more Davis in them.

The afternoon of the discovery some of the most precious and delicate objects were packed up and loaded onto the *Beduin*; Maspero wanted to avoid the jolting a railroad trip would have caused them. Quibell had arrived back in Luxor late that day ("very much disgruntled to find the tomb had been opened in his absence," according to Emma), and Maspero, concerned about robbers, ordered the tomb to be emptied as quickly as possible, putting Quibell in charge with assistance from Weigall. Yet another young English archaeologist working nearby, Edward Ayrton, was enlisted and the group, along with artist Joe Smith, inventoried, cataloged, photographed, and packed the treasures. They were stored in the tomb of Rameses XI until they were ready for the trip to Cairo.

The archaeologists' work was frequently interrupted by visitors; Prince Gustaf, the Duke of Connaught, and the Duke and Duchess of Devonshire dropped by more than once. Toward the end of the clearing, Joe Smith was in the tomb preparing to pack the last remaining object, a superb wood and gilt chair that had been presented to Thuyu by her granddaughter, Princess Sitamon. While Quibell swept the dust from the empty floor one last time, the men heard voices outside the tomb, an elderly woman speaking French and a male companion who addressed her as "your Highness." Without any invitation the two entered the tomb and the woman asked to be told about the discovery. As Smith recalled it, Quibell cordially agreed but regretted he could not offer her a seat. "Why, here is a chair which will do for me nicely," the old lady said. "Before our horrified eyes she stepped down onto the floor of the chamber," Smith wrote, "and seated herself in a chair which had not been sat in for three-thousand years! But the anticipated catastrophe did not take place."[35] The woman proved to be Empress Eugenie, the widow of Napoleon III (a "very hot, cross old lady," according to Weigall). The first bottom to grace Sitamon's chair after three and a half millennia was an imperial one.

The Duke and Duchess of Connaught came to tea on the *Beduin* before they left Luxor ("I never met simpler, pleasanter people," Emma noted) and Davis presented his new chum with a copy of the book he had just published about his first royal find, *The Tomb of Thoutmosis IV.* It was the first in a series of seven books he would pay to have written and printed about his excavations, and marks another improvement Davis provided for Egyptian archaeology. Discoveries were one thing; making them available to scholars and the reading public was another, and publications in the field (due to lack of money) were few, far between, and seldom appeared promptly. Davis published his Thutmose IV book just a year after the find (after Carter began digging with Lord Carnarvon's money in 1909, it was three years before their first report appeared).

Aside from brief acknowledgments or occasional self-congratulatory introductions, Davis wrote none of the books he published. In the Thutmose book Carter described the excavation, Maspero contributed a biography of the king, Percy Newberry wrote a chapter on the tomb and its sarcophagus, a doctor discussed the king's mummy, and Carter and Newberry compiled a catalog of the tomb's contents. Davis's other books similarly called upon the experts to create the reports. Like all Davis's publications, it was richly illustrated, with drawings and paintings by Carter as well as photographs of the tomb and the objects. The series was published by the respected London house of Archibald Constable & Company under the title *Mr. Theodore M. Davis' Excavations: Biban El Moluk* (using the Arabic name for the valley), and later reprinted in the United States.

Although today the Davis books are seen as lacking in the improvements a century of scholarship and technology has provided, they were seen at the time as remarkably well done. Davis's 1910 book, titled *The Tomb of Queen Tiyi,* was reviewed as "sumptuously illustrated . . . To all who care about the history of ancient art and the story of old Egypt, its memorials and mythology it will be an invaluable possession."[36] Eighty years later the book was not so highly thought of, called a "mix of fact, assumption, error and omission."[37] The book's chapters were written by three archaeologists and a medical doctor.

At the time, however, scholarly reviewers like the American Egyptologist James Henry Breasted (whose work was partially funded by Davis) also found the Davis books "sumptuous" and "stately," and popular reviewers raved about the books even more enthusiastically. Davis's books advanced the science's documentation to a new level, and increased interest in Egypt among the general public as much as the more sensational newspaper accounts of his exploits.

On March 3, 1905, 120 men and camels started at sunup to move the heavy cases holding Yuya's treasure from the valley to the river, where they were put on a train to Cairo under a police guard. The weather was so hot that by midday 70 of the men had quit; the remaining crew worked until 9:00 P.M. to finish the job. According to Quibell's report, only a few items were stolen during the transfer. Davis and Emma remained in Luxor a few more days to attend the dedication of Carrie Buchanan's new school building before the *Beduin* sailed north.

They arrived in Cairo on March 17. Four days later Emma noted, "the things from the tomb are now pretty well unpacked. A whole large room [in the museum] has been given to them." Located on the second floor, Maspero had the room named the Salle Theodore M. Davis, the only time such an honor has ever been bestowed. The room kept the name until 1915; eventually, the space was rededicated to housing the treasures of Tutankhamen.

Although their informal agreement guaranteed none of the treasure for Davis, Maspero offered the American a share of the spoils. "I confess that it was a most attractive offer," Davis wrote, "but on consideration I could not bring myself to break up the collection which I thought ought to be exhibited where it could be seen and studied by probably the greatest number of appreciative visitors."[38] The sentiment is lovely, but Maspero did prevail upon the patron to accept something from the find as "keepsakes"; that summer Boston's Museum of Fine Arts displayed three of Yuya's *shabti*s lent by Davis, "the only fruits of this excavation which have been taken away from Egypt" according to the MFA *Bulletin*. Ten years later, however, Davis gave the *shabti*s, the two boxes they were found in, a pair of Yuya's sandals, and two large jars from the tomb to the Metropolitan.[39] Two small scraps of linen, said to be from the outer wrappings of Thuyu's mummy, were donated by Emma.[40]

Maspero had good reason to press keepsakes on the patron and name a room after him; before Davis left Cairo they negotiated a written agreement to define Davis's future work in the valley. The document was unusual for a Davis contract in that its language was distinctly clear and un-lawyerly. The American was authorized to "carry out scientific excavations in the Valley of the Kings,"[41] and a clause Weigall had suggested required the patron to hire a qualified archaeologist—specifying young Ayrton—to conduct the digs. Davis agreed, already having recognized the wisdom and personal convenience a professional provided him ("I know that you will be glad to escape the bother of looking after my work," Davis wrote to Weigall; it "certainly will make life more harmonious!"),[42] but it did change the tone at the worksite. The digger would now be an employee of the American rather than an independent partner.

Davis also agreed to continue producing reports, including drawings and photographs, on any discoveries. Unlike the other permissions granted by the antiquities service, the Davis deal specifically denied the patron any of the objects found, reserving them for Egypt (although it was understood that "gifts" and "keepsakes" were Maspero's prerogative to grant). This aspect was distinctly ahead of its time; when Carnarvon was granted permission to dig in the valley in 1914, his agreement with the government called for an even division of the spoils (except in the highly unlikely event that an unrobbed tomb was found, a provision that caused distinct difficulties in 1922).

Davis was not given an exclusive right to work in the valley, although in fact few other permits were issued while he was there (the French Institute in Cairo was granted permission to dig there in 1906). The antiquities service reserved the right to "correct" the process if it saw fit, and Ayrton would be required to notify Inspector Weigall immediately if anything of interest was found. Davis was granted the right to be first to enter any new tomb.

Although the 1905 agreement was extremely generous to Egypt, it clearly placed Davis in charge of the work. His attitude was primarily that of a patron who wanted the explorations done for the benefit of science—and his own amusement and aggrandizement—but Weigall wrote later that Davis "identified himself more closely with the work" after 1905 and "was inclined at length, very understandably, to resent government supervision" (although the inspector also noted Davis's "good nature").[43] Not part of the written agreement, but discussed at the time, was Davis's newfound determination to "exhaust every foot-hill and mountain in the Valley," thoroughly and methodically looking at every foot of the cliff sides in search of tombs. "When I stated to M. Maspero my proposed manner of exploration," Davis recalled, "he replied 'It will require money, perseverance and patience. I am not sure about the latter.' I accept M. Maspero's requirements, but I would add 'Hope' to his catalog."[44]

Most important for Davis, the agreement offered the chance to achieve great things. The American was sixty-seven; his father had died at forty-two, and Theodore had already lived half again as long. Finding another Yuya was unlikely, but the thrill of future finds still beckoned. Davis was positioned to indulge in the ultimate treasure hunt, the type of task he had followed since his landlooker days. His fortune had been based, after completing his nefarious business schemes, on taking iron and silver out of America's earth; at the end of his life he would make one more try to pull what he wanted out of the ground—this time, Egypt's.

On March 23 Emma and Theodore made the short walk from Shepheard's down Kamel (now Republic) Street to the Continental Hotel, on the edge of Opera Square and the Ezbekiyah Gardens. They approached the block-square building with its elaborate façade, topped by three enormous flags carrying the Ottoman Empire's crescent and star (which would remain atop the hotel until the British ended the charade of Ottoman rule in 1914). The Continental was Shepheard's only real rival for upscale visitors; Lord Carnarvon died in his suite there in 1923. The Americans passed through the columns that supported the oversized pediment and proceeded to a ballroom where a fund-raising event for the Cairo YWCA was about to begin; the attraction was the first public lecture on Yuya's tomb, given by Maspero. One attendee reported that Maspero "rendered well-merited praise to the rich foreigners who, like Mr. Davis, with their time and money lent aid to his Department." According to Maspero, the discovery "took place in a corner of the Valley of the Kings where the majority of Egyptologists did not consider that anything interesting would be found. Destiny decreed that just there Mr. Davis should make one of the most interesting and important discoveries of our time."[45] Davis was still basking in the glow when he left Egypt for home on April 7.

The trip home was eventful. In Venice, Davis and Newberry met to discuss the chapter Newberry would write for the new book Davis was planning; in Milan, Theo and Emma attended a performance of *Don Pasquale* at La Scala. "Theo and I went to the back of the box," Emma wrote, "piled the cushions behind us and took a nap . . . How strange to discover that so many people live who can take Italian Opera seriously!" In Paris, Davis purchased Rembrandt's *The Sybil,* a life-sized painting of a seated young woman, for £6,000 (around sixty times what the excavation of Yuya's tomb had cost). Also known as *Young Woman in Fancy Dress with a Book,*[46] the painting is now attributed to one of Rembrandt's pupils, Willem Drost by some scholars, but others (as Davis and Bernard Berenson did) believe it is a late Rembrandt. In London, the couple stayed awake for the premier performance of George Bernard Shaw's *Man and Superman.*

Back at Shepheard's on November 24 (again accompanied by Jean Hardy), Davis had dinner with the American Egyptologist James Henry Breasted. The two had been friends for some time; Breasted had stayed at Davis's mansion for a week in 1903. In late 1905 Breasted had just published one of his most important works, *A History of Egypt*; an autographed copy was part of the library on the *Beduin*. Breasted, with money from John D. Rockefeller, planned to move south to the first cataract and record the inscriptions on ancient sites during the coming season, where he would develop what became known as the "Chicago Method" of copying ancient wall inscriptions using photographic blueprints that were hand corrected and enhanced at the site. The process is still considered the most perfect and reliable methodology for the task.

The Americans also dined with Carter, who was now unemployed. His refusal to express his regrets over the Saqqara incident had forced Maspero to reassign him to the obscure backwater of Tanta, which had so insulted the Englishman that he had quit his job in October. "He is going to devote himself to painting—a thing he should have done years ago," Emma opined. His first commission was from Davis, who hired him to paint fourteen of the items from Yuya's tomb for the upcoming book. The fee of £15 per painting was generous and much needed by Carter, who would receive considerable help from Davis during his period of poverty.

Edward Russell Ayrton bounded up the *Beduin*'s gangplank on December 11, 1905, feeling pleased with the world and pleased with himself. The athletic twenty-three-year-old tended to bound rather than walk; he was an energetic, strapping young man. He had been working for Mr. Davis since October, and his salary—£250 per year, with a two-year contract—had bettered his situation considerably (the amount is equivalent to around $50,000 today, when a full-time postdoctoral fellow in Egyptology at Yale receives $39,000). The previous season he had been excavating and recording graves at the Mentuhotep temple discovered at Deir el-Bahri, but the money from the Egypt Exploration Fund had run short and Davis had saved their season by giving the diggers £100.

Born to a British diplomat stationed in Wuhu, China, Ayrton had been educated at St. Paul's School in London and come to Egypt in 1902, working for Petrie at Abydos for two years. He was not popular in excavation camps at bedtime; according to Joe Smith he had dreadful nightmares in which he shrieked in fluent Chinese, although he could not speak the language when awake. He was recalled by a friend as "a man of strong character and sterling worth . . . a hater of all forms of humbug and pretense; he had a very short way with fools."[47] He had been a regular visitor to the *Beduin,* and his work helping clear Yuya's tomb had impressed Weigall enough for him to propose Ayrton for the Davis job. The inspector knew he was conscientious and capable, and expected him to be cooperative as well.

As the crew served lunch on deck to the Davis entourage, Jean and Davis finished their game of dominoes and turned to Ayrton for his report. Ayrton understood Davis's new method of exploring every inch of the valley, and had busied himself until his patron arrived by spending three days digging at the entrance to the West Valley. He had found nothing but had determined the spot was suitable for the project he pitched to Davis: a "dig house" built in the valley. Ayrton needed a place to sleep (he was currently living in a tent), and a house would be a better place to store and work on objects they discovered than in neighboring tombs, as had been done in the past. Davis agreed and a building of stone and mud was constructed at the entrance to the West Valley next to a cliff that shaded and directed breezes in—and where it would not be visible to visitors to the main valley but only a five-minute walk to the worksites. The building also featured a double-skinned wooden roof to help keep it cool. Originally a four-bedroom affair with ten-foot square rooms, "Davis House" was expanded over the coming years and—restored—still stands today.

Having won his first goal, Ayrton summarized the past two months spent finishing areas already explored. He had moved to the extreme eastern end of the valley, clearing up around Thutmose IV, and finished the gully by Yuya, finding a few ostraca (stone chippings written or drawn upon by the ancients) and *shabti*s. The cleanup done, he and Davis decided to move to the northwestern end of the valley, near the entry of KV 12.

Ayrton brought an organization and sophistication to the Davis excavations that had been lacking. Previously the inspector had supervised the digs between other duties and Davis dropped by only sporadically; Ayrton arrived at the worksite at 6:00 A.M. every day and Davis gave up his daily visits of the season before. When the American came by a few days later, however, his attention was attracted to a large rock tilted to one side. "For some mysterious reason I felt interested in it," he wrote, "and on being carefully examined and dug about by my assistant, Mr. Ayrton, with the hands, the beautiful blue cup was found."[48] Located twelve feet below ground level and carefully sheltered by the rock, the blue-glazed cup they found bore the cartouche of a little-known king of the Eighteenth Dynasty named Tutankhamen. "From what cause it made such a perilous journey is, of course, unknown," Davis wrote,[49] and there is still no explanation of how the cup came to be there, but it was the first time King Tut's name had been found in the valley.

They moved to the extreme southwestern end of the valley, with a crew of two hundred moving the piles of chips and heaps of stone as the trench moved north. In mid-December Davis had a discussion with the *reis,* who claimed "he had thoroughly explored, some years ago, the same hill, and he knew there was no tomb in it."[50] Davis was skeptical and the crew pressed on, and on December 18 at the northern end of the hill a flight of rock-cut steps was revealed. Ayrton put every man on the task of clearing the stairway.

James Breasted happened to be in the valley that day, having just arrived on the train from Cairo with his crew and supplies for his expedition to the Sudan. It was his son Charles's first visit to the valley. "We saw in the distance a great cloud of dust," Charles wrote later, "and in the stillness heard the rhythmic minor chant of native workmen singing, and the shouts of their foreman upbraiding the laggards." They came upon "an old friend of my father's, a retired elderly American lawyer and financier named Theodore M. Davis . . . looking on with obvious excitement as his men dug at the entrance shaft of a tomb they had discovered only a few hours earlier. He was smoking cigarette after cigarette, intermittently leaving the group to pace nervously back and forth, oblivious to the white dust which lent an eerie quality to the twilight of the place."[51]

Just before nightfall the lintel of the doorway revealed the name of the tomb owner: Siptah, the next-to-last king of the Nineteenth Dynasty (ca. 1195 B.C.). Davis had found another pharaoh.

The tomb had been robbed long before; in clearing the stairwell the diggers had found *shabti*s, beads, and broken fragments tossed aside by the intruders. Siptah's mummy had been found in 1898 in a cache of royal mummies. Unwound just three months before (alone among the royal mummies the body had a deformity—a severely clubbed left foot, perhaps due to poliomyelitis or cerebral palsy), Siptah had been robbed of his jewelry in ancient times.

After photographing the entry, Ayrton began clearing the tomb (designated KV 47). Floods had washed in considerable debris, but past the entry they found two corridors coated with stucco and covered with beautiful sunken relief paintings and texts with still-brilliant colors. Paintings of Siptah, gods and goddesses, and hieroglyphic inscriptions with the "Litany of Re" (describing the unification of the dead pharaoh and the sun god, and their nighttime journey beneath the earth) covered the walls. A fragment of a calcite sarcophagus was recovered, along with pieces of broken pots and vessels.

The end of the Nineteenth Dynasty is still unclear; Siptah was apparently still a teenager when he died,[52] and his cartouches had been cut out and then restored. The diggers progressed through a square chamber and came to a large hall originally supported by four columns. Only one still remained in place and Ayrton propped up the ceiling with wooden beams. Farther on they came to worse problems. "[T]here was another chamber in which the invading water had deposited a solid mass of debris many feet high," Ayrton wrote. "In most places the roof had fallen in, exposing a cavity quite two meters high, thereby rendering the chamber most unsafe to work in."[53]

Davis and Ayrton mulled the situation. The tomb had been looted, the piece of sarcophagus indicated it had been destroyed, and anything left further on in the tomb had likely been smashed by the collapsed ceiling. Davis decided not to risk the danger of proceeding and quit the excavation but commissioned Joe Smith to do three paintings of the walls ("very brilliant in color and unexpectedly beautiful in details for so late a period,")[54] and hired a young Welsh artist named Ernest Harold Jones (another friend of Newberry's) to do three more. As Davis put it, "If Siptah did no great deeds during his reign, he would seem to have possessed extremely good taste in the decoration of his tomb."

As 1906 began, Emma held court on the *Beduin.* "We had of course visitors all day long—from those at breakfast to lunch, tea and dinner. I spent a great part of my time waiting for people to go!" They crossed to the east bank to see the construction at the Winter Palace Hotel, which was expanding into the building (now called the "old" Winter Palace) familiar to tourists today; the foundation work had uncovered flint implements 15,000 years old. The addition of 220 rooms and splendid gardens made it another of the gems in Egypt's touristic crown and a meeting place for the elite. Not everyone was pleased with the hotel; French novelist Pierre Loti called it a "hasty modern production . . . sufficient to disfigure pitiably the whole of the surroundings."[55]

Finished with the area around Siptah, Davis moved the work crew to a gully extending west from KV 35 where the northern slope had been fully explored but the southern side barely touched. It was another difficult spot; the heaps of chippings were twelve feet deep. The first find was a small, unfinished tomb (designated KV 49) empty except for a few pieces of cloth and broken pottery. The diggers moved on. Twenty yards farther on, on January 31, a shaft was found beneath six feet of debris. When the twelve-foot shaft was emptied it revealed a single eight-foot square chamber carved into the rock.

"I went down the shaft and entered the chamber," Davis wrote, "which proved to be extremely hot and too low for comfort. I was startled by seeing very near me a yellow dog of ordinary size standing on his feet, his short tail curled over his back, and his eyes open. Within a few inches of his nose sat a monkey in quite perfect condition; for an instant I thought they were alive, but I soon saw that they had been mummified and that they had been unwrapped in ancient times by robbers . . . The attitude of the animals suggested that the monkey was saying, 'It's all over with me,' and the dog, with its bright eyes and manner, seemed to reply 'Have courage, it will end all right.' I am quite sure the robbers arranged the group for their amusement. However this may be, it can fairly be said to be a joke 3,000 years old."[56] Joe Smith's children were amused when they visited: "They both laughed in delight at the sight of a yellow dog . . . the animal looked alive,"[57] Smith wrote.

Before removing them from the tomb, Davis had artist Harold Jones draw the dog and monkey as they were found in the tomb. "Davis's dog"—and his companion monkey—is on display in the animal mummy room at the Egyptian Museum today, along with a copy of Jones's picture.

Three similar pit tombs were found nearby with animals inside (four monkeys, three ducks, an ibis, and a perfect specimen of a large ape wearing a necklace of small blue disc beads) and another holding only some stone fragments. The actual purpose of the "animal tombs" (numbered KV 50–53) has never been determined; since they were near the tomb of Amenhotep II, Davis guessed they had been the king's pets. They might have been sacred animals buried for religious reasons; biologists have determined they were well fed and lived lives of ease.

As the excavators moved eastward to the end of the gully one more find was made. A single-chambered undecorated tomb (KV 48) was badly plundered; on top of six inches of rubble Ayrton found a male mummy, coffin fragments, *shabti*s, pieces of broken pottery and furniture, and four "magical bricks" (inscribed with spells) owned by Amenemopet, a vizier of Amenhotep II. The entry was filled in again and lost to archaeology until 2008, when American archaeologist Donald Ryan reentered it and found the mummy missing. Ryan, taking more time than Ayrton, found pieces of eleven huge jars, faience beads, and a remarkable piece of cloth fourteen inches long, cut and painted to resemble a miniature leopard skin.

The season effectively over, Davis sailed south for Aswan on February 4. Part of the *dahabiyeh* life included visiting the hotels that lined the Nile; in Aswan the spot to meet other tourists was the luxurious Cataract Hotel. "We were delighted with it," Emma had written after it opened in 1900. Outfitted to the highest standards, it had elegant rooms designed in an "oriental" style, electric lights, and filtered water. Theo and Emma enjoyed the Cataract's large terrace overlooking the river with its dramatic view of boulders inscribed with ancient hieroglyphs. The grumpy Pierre Loti had noted the irony of the hotel opening just as the Aswan dam had eliminated the cataract it was named for: "Cataract Hotel—that gives the illusion still, does it not?—and looks remarkably well at the head of a sheet of notepaper."[58]

Back in Luxor on February 19, Davis and Ayrton agreed to finish the season clearing the tomb of Twentieth Dynasty prince Montuhirkopeshef (KV 19). The tomb had been found by Belzoni in 1817, but the exquisitely decorated entry was impassable and the tomb full of huge limestone blocks: "[W]e had to keep three strong men continually at work shifting and rolling them out,"[59] Ayrton wrote. The diggers recovered some unrelated fragments, including half a mummy, but none were of interest to the archaeologists. When finished, the tomb became accessible for the first time since antiquity.

Ayrton also apparently reentered KV 60, which Carter had found in 1903, and retrieved one of the mummies for the Egyptian Museum in Cairo. He left the body later touted as Hatshepsut's on the floor.

A few days later William F. Laffan, publisher of *The New York Sun* (considered the most reactionary paper in the United States) and a board member of the Metropolitan Museum, dropped by the *Beduin* and Davis took him and his wife (who borrowed Emma's "chair") to visit the valley. On their way back they visited another of Davis's friends, Swiss archaeologist Henri Edouard Naville, who was excavating the temple of Mentuhotep II at Deir al-Bahri. A rockslide a few days before had revealed a small shrine with a vaulted roof cut into the cliff face containing a life-sized statue of a Hathor cow being led by a man. The find, dating to the reign of Thutmose III, was the sensation of the season and is now one of the highlights of the Egyptian Museum (although an artist at the time noted the lining of the shrine set up around the statue in the museum creates "the unfortunate resemblance to a large dog kennel").[60]

At tea, after the visitors had viewed the cow, Naville complained that the Egypt Exploration Fund had notified him that their finances forced them to cut off his funding and asked him to close the site. (Emma suspected most of the EEF money was going to Petrie.) Laffan offered to come to the rescue, putting up £1,000 to continue the work if Naville would agree to donate a share of his finds to the Metropolitan. Thanks to Davis's introduction, Naville was able to complete his season.

The new chairman of the Metropolitan, J. P. Morgan, had given his friend Laffan another chore: to make the acquaintance of Albert Lythgoe. Davis strongly endorsed the archaeologist, and Laffan was favorably impressed when they met at Giza a week later. Lythgoe soon became the first curator of Egyptian art at the Metropolitan, and Davis's patronage followed his friend's move from Boston to New York; at home that summer, Davis revised his will and included the gift of his entire Egyptian collection (along with his old master paintings) to the Metropolitan.

Emma summed up the 1905–06 season as "Theo very busy with

his work. He unearthed 3–4 tombs. Only one having any special interest—that of Siptah, an unimportant king of the XIX dynasty." Yuya's tomb may have jaded the Americans' enthusiasm, but in fact the season had been important. Finding six tombs validated Davis's new policy of exploring every foothill, and publicity about Siptah contributed to his reputation for finding a new tomb every year. London's *Pall Mall Gazette* opined about Davis's work, "One really commences to wonder whether these discoveries will ever cease."[61]

Another famous American was staying at Shepheard's when Davis arrived after the trip north. L. Frank Baum, best known today as author of the Wizard of Oz books, was taking a grand tour of Egypt and spent several days at the museum. "One of the most interesting rooms in the museum contains the collection discovered by the American excavator, Davis," Baum's wife, Maud, wrote home. "He has been wonderfully successful in unearthing antiquities, and Americans may well be proud of his record."[62]

On the ship home Davis read Percy Newberry's new book. *Scarabs: An Introduction to the Study of Egyptian Seals and Signet Rings* was one of Newberry's most important works. It remains in print more than a century later and is still one of the most valuable resources on the subject. Among the 1,200 scarabs Newberry studied, 30 were from Davis's collection. The book is dedicated to "My friend, Mrs. E. B. Andrews, of The Beduin."

Davis arrived in Luxor again on December 16, 1906, and Ayrton reported to the *Beduin* for tea and planning their next dig location. "The central point and the meeting place of all the Wadis [gullies] at the southern end of the Valley of the Tombs of the Kings at Thebes is occupied by a large rock mound, in which Ramses IX excavated a great tomb for himself," Ayrton recalled. The eastern face had been explored already and some tombs found, but "the western face to the south of the tomb was covered with an immense heap of limestone chips . . . This had never been touched."[63] They began work there (near where the tourist rest house would later be built) on New Year's Day, 1907.

Davis was again pessimistic: "There was no sign of the probability of a tomb. On the contrary, it seemed to be a hopeless excavation, resulting in a waste of time and money."[64] Ayrton agreed: "We had but few hopes of finding a tomb there . . . since our pits were sunk so close to the tomb of Ramses IX that there scarcely seemed any room for another burial."[65] Davis stayed true to his plan, however: "Nevertheless, it had to be cleared, whatever the result . . . With a large gang of men we commenced clearing on the apex of the hill."[66] The rock face in the location was nearly vertical, and the trenches down to bedrock were nearly twenty feet deep.

Nettie Buttles, Emma's niece, arrived on January 3 from the villa she shared in Florence with her sister. She had not been in Egypt since 1902, when she had posed with the about-to-disintegrate mummy mask of Userhet that Carter had just dug up. Nettie was finishing work on her book, *The Queens of Egypt,* which was the first ever published on women in ancient Egypt (she received advice from Newberry and Maspero). A minor bestseller and one of the first efforts at what has become women's studies, it would include two paintings by Carter. Nettie was an amateur singer as well as a writer, and that evening her songs rang out over the river; she claimed her "Nile voice" was always her best.

The next evening, Emma recorded, "Mr. Ayrton sent a note to Theo this morning saying he had found a tomb." Davis went to the site but the situation was unclear; what Ayrton had come across proved to be a recess carved into the rock wall containing several large jars, possibly a cache of embalming materials. The next morning Ayrton sent another note "saying the tomb was not a tomb! Nettie was so disappointed." The trench had already reached the level of the entry to the neighboring tomb of Rameses IX and the archaeologist thought there was little likelihood going deeper would reveal anything, but he kept on and came to a flattened face on the hillside with squared corners on either side—indicating a tomb had at least been started there. To avoid unnecessary digging if it were an unfinished mistake, Ayrton guessed where the flight of steps descending to the tomb might lie and commenced to sink a pit there.

Davis spent all January 7, 1907, at the site, while Emma entertained Carter, Weigall, and Weigall's new American wife on the *Beduin*. "When he got back quite late," Emma noted, Davis "told us that Ayrton had this time found a real tomb."

Thus began the most confused and controversial episode in the history of Egyptian archaeology.

"Alabaster Portrait Head of Queen Tiyi" (now believed to be Kiya), photo probably by E. Harold Jones. From Davis, The Tomb of Queen Tiyi.

Four

KIYA'S
ALABASTER JAR

Among the most iconic and beautiful masterpieces to survive from ancient Egypt are four canopic jar heads associated with the burial of the "heretic pharaoh" Akhenaten (ca. 1360 B.C.). Elegantly carved in alabaster, the jar tops are exquisitely modeled in the likeness of a female head with a Nubian wig and a broad collar necklace. The faces, with their delicate features, full lips, and prominent chins, are inlaid with blue glass delineating almond-shaped eyes and arched brows; the irises are inlaid with obsidian. The identity of the owner has never been determined because the inscriptions on the jars were erased in ancient times, but they have been variously ascribed to a half dozen men and women. The current prevailing opinion is that they depict Kiya, a secondary wife of Akhenaten, who was possibly Tutankhamen's mother. Three of the jars are in the Egyptian Museum in Cairo; one is prominently displayed in the Metropolitan Museum of Art.[1]

• • •

On January 8, 1907, Davis brought Emma, Jean Hardy, Nettie Buttles, and valet Daniel Jones to the valley to watch Ayrton's crew clear the stairway dug into the hillside they had found the day before. They were joined on the dusty, sunny morning by the Weigalls (Ayrton had notified the inspector, as required) and the Smiths. The observers sat in carriages, on rocks, and on a few chairs or strolled about, the men smoking and the women chatting, as the workmen dug through water-cemented chippings to expose the steps carved into the valley floor. The work was slow and painstaking and required clearing the rubble mound back to avoid debris avalanching into the hole. After several hours they reached the eleventh step, and a floor of chippings ahead was so solid that Ayrton feared they had reached the bottom of the stairway. In front of them was a blank wall, a few feet beyond the step. It seemed the discovery was a false alarm, an unfinished start to a never-completed tomb. With considerable disappointment, the group adjourned for their midday meal to the "lunch tomb" (that of Amenmesse, KV 10), which had been equipped with tables and chairs and reserved by the antiquities service for the use of the privileged.

Lunch was provided by the *Beduin*'s crew and overseen by Davis's valet. Frequently called "Jones the Great" by Davis and "the faithful Jones" by Emma, Daniel Jones was an extraordinary individual, well suited to his master's needs. Leaving his wife and child behind in Newport for half of every year, Jones was an even more constant companion to his boss than Emma; he accompanied Davis on jaunts around Europe while Emma stayed in Florence with the Buttles ladies, and he traveled west to Colorado silver mines while she stayed home.

Born in 1859 in England, Daniel Jones had come to America in 1885; he worked for Davis for more than twenty years. His older brother, John, was Davis's butler and John's wife, Jane, was the cook. Jones had developed skills that made him invaluable to his boss; he spoke Arabic, wore native dress in Egypt, seemed to know every dragoman, hotel employee, and merchant in the country and had "a name to conjure with. He is certainly the most amazing man servant I ever heard of," one of Davis's guests judged. "In all my life I have known few men as worthy of admiration and affection as Jones."[2] As well as dragging Emma in and out of tombs, he wrestled the mountains of luggage they traveled with, guarded Emma's jewels, did carpentry jobs on the *Beduin,* and cared for Emma's pets. The two men were clearly friends as well as master and servant; in his will, Davis was more generous to Jones than to some of his relations.

The party was joined in the lunch tomb by David Erskine, a newly elected member of parliament whom Davis had met the day before. After his arrival and under Jones's watchful eye, the Egyptian *reis* interrupted the meal and spoke briefly to Ayrton, who got up and left the group. He had kept the men digging and they had found that the stairway had not ended; another nine steps down into the hillside the blank, smoothed wall had opened to a sealed doorway. They had found a tomb after all.

Every bit of the excavation of what became known as KV 55 has proven maddeningly unclear since that moment. Written accounts by Emma, Davis, Ayrton, Maspero, Weigall, Joe Smith, and archaeologists and artists who happened to be in the area at the time frequently contradict one another completely, and each author portrays himself to his own benefit. No one appears to have kept daily notes except Emma, who was the only witness not writing for publication. Smith's account, written fifty years after the fact, makes him the central character of the adventure and includes much thrilling—and imaginative—fiction.

According to Ayrton, he was confronted by a "loosely built wall" of limestone fragments blocking the door; a later reexcavation revealed mortar had been used. Ayrton makes no mention of photographing the entry, though Joe Smith says pictures were taken (and lost, if so). After dismantling the first wall Ayrton found a second, made of limestone blocks cemented together and coated with cement so hard "a knife could scarcely scratch it,"[3] bearing a seal of the guardians of the necropolis—a jackal crouching over nine captives. Weigall wrote that they also found a fragment of a seal of Tutankhamen[4] (which no one else mentions). Determining the number of entries in ancient times has bedeviled Egyptologists ever since.

Removal of the wall was time-consuming. Emma records that "a fine, broken alabaster vase and some bits of gold foil were found." Evening descended, work halted, guards and police arrived, and "we rode home, speculating as to whom the tomb had belonged." The mouth of the tomb was a crowded place that night; the Weigalls, the Smiths, and Jean and Nettie all camped out in front. "Theo and I had a quiet evening alone," Emma wrote, "a most unusual thing."

When Davis, Emma, Jones, and Emma's French maid Amelie Burgnon arrived at the site the next morning the doorway and staircase had been cleared and the tomb was ready for entering. The eight-foot-high, six-foot-wide doorway into the hillside opened into a seventy-foot corridor that was filled almost to the ceiling with limestone chips and rubble. Carrying electric lights, Ayrton, Davis, and Weigall wiggled and crawled over the fill into the corridor. At their entry point the gap between rubble and ceiling was around three feet; at the far end, the sloping mound provided a six-foot clearance. "Lying on this rubbish," Ayrton recorded, "at a few feet from the door by which we had entered, lay a large wooden object resembling a broad sled in shape. It was covered with gold leaf with a line of inscription running down each side. On it lay a wooden door with copper pivots still in place; this also was covered with gold leaf and ornamented with a scene in low relief of a queen worshipping the Sun-disk."[5]

What the explorers had found on top of the chips filling the corridor were later recognized to be parts of a shrine, a small house-like structure assembled around royal sarcophagi in burial chambers. No such object had ever been seen before (Tutankhamen was found with four internested shrines intact). The sections in the corridor were thought at the time to be doors; the following November Ayrton changed his guess to "the lid of a great square wooden coffin."

Beneath a large limestone block sitting on the shrine section they detected the edge of a cartouche; with great care the men lifted the block and peered at the inscription. "We were able to read the name of the wife of Amenhotep III and mother of Akhenaten— Queen Thyi," Ayrton wrote. Emma, sitting with the rest on rocks outside, described hearing the exclamations filter up from the tomb: "At last Mr. Davis's voice rang out, 'By Jove, Queen Tyi, and no mistake!' "

The apparent discovery of the tomb of Queen Tiye—variously spelled Thyi, Tyi, Tiyi, etc.—filled Davis and his companions with delight. "It is quite impossible to describe the surprise and joy," Davis wrote, "of finding the tomb of the great queen and her household gods, which for these 3,000 years had never been discovered."[6] Smith recalled, "Davis was almost inarticulate in his joy . . . He kept murmuring ecstatically, 'We've got queen Tiyi!' "[7] Weigall remembered that when the name was found, "glamour was added to the moment which will not easily be forgotten by any of the party."[8]

In 1907, Yuya and Thuyu's daughter was rivaled only by Cleopatra as a romantic and exotic ancient Egyptian figure; a commoner who was seen to have risen by her beauty and brains to become the most powerful woman in the land, her story of self-improvement was especially irresistible to Americans. In 1905 *The New York Times* had called her "one of the most fascinating figures of Egyptian history," a "beautiful woman of obscure origin."[9] In Nettie's book about the royal women, she described Tiye's husband as "so charmed by a daughter of the people" that he "erected monuments and carved on their walls the immortal story of his devotion to queen Thiy."[10] After the discovery, a "cigarette card" with Tiye's picture was issued with each pack by John Player & Co., which described her as "blue-eyed, and of very fair complexion."[11]

Their adrenaline renewed, the explorers proceeded deeper into the tomb. The first problem in negotiating the seventy feet to the end of the corridor was avoiding damage to the shrine pieces; the sections filled the space between the walls and the men recognized any movement or touching might damage them. Ayrton and the *reis* managed to slip a ten-inch-wide board between the pieces and the wall and started in. "I managed to crawl over, striking my head and most of my body," the sixty-eight-year-old Davis recalled, "but without damaging the doors."[12] At the far end of the corridor they came to another doorway, the entry to the burial chamber.

Extending their heads into the room, Weigall recalled that "the gold covered coffin and outer coffin, gleaming in the light of the electric lamps, formed a sight of surprising richness."[13] Maspero later waxed poetic about the scene he was not present for: "Mr. Davis might have thought himself transported to one of the marvelous treasure caves of the *Arabian Nights*. Gold shone upon the ground, gold upon the walls, gold in the furthest corner where the coffin leant up against the side, gold bright and polished as if it had just come freshly beaten from the goldsmith's hands, gold half-veiled by, and striving to free itself from, the dust of time. It seemed as if all the gold of ancient Egypt glittered and gleamed in the narrow space."[14]

Gold dazzled the explorer's eyes, but the chamber—an undecorated room about fifteen by eighteen feet—was a mess, "in a state of great confusion," Emma noted, "showing hasty burial, or robbery or desecration." They scrambled through the doorway (down another slope of rubble) into the room and found more sections of the shrine; the pieces lying horizontally still held their golden sheeting, but the gold leaf had fallen off pieces that had been leaned against the walls. A beautiful wooden coffin, covered with gold leaf and inlaid with carnelian and glass, had fallen from its pedestal and broken open; the mummy's head protruded through the gap. "A vulture headed diadem of gold could just be seen passing around her head," Weigall wrote, "and one could see here and there the shining sheets of gold in which the body was wrapped." Davis supposed "the coffin had either been dropped or fallen from some height, for the side had burst, exposing the head and neck of the mummy. On the head plainly appeared a gold crown, encircling the head, as doubtless it was worn in life."

Confronted by so much gold, the other notable objects in the tomb took second place. "In a small chamber or recess in the right-hand wall," Ayrton noted, "one could distinguish the four canopic jars."

After gazing in amazement at the chamber and wondering how it had come to such a state, the explorers laboriously crawled back up to sunlight and joined the rest of the group for another lunch provided by Jones, Amelie, and the *Beduin*'s crew. Smith, doubtless correctly, said everyone was too excited to eat much of it. After the meal the rest of the group crawled down to inspect the tomb; according to Emma, the men went first and then "Theo was determined Nettie should be the first one to see it, and she was the first woman to enter." Smith records that Maspero—who was not there—granted first female visitation to Smith's wife, Corinna.

The archaeologists recognized immediately the perilous condition of the find; after only a few hours' exposure to the air, the gold scenes and inscriptions on the shrine were falling to pieces. Ayrton judged the wood likely to crumble if touched and decided before any further work was done a thorough photographic record should be made. Davis telegraphed for a photographer from Cairo, Weigall notified Maspero, and additional guards were called for.

An artist working at Deir el-Bahri, a friend of Ayrton's named Walter Tyndale, recalled the rumors that were already circulating that afternoon; nothing could stop "a thousand native tongues from wagging," he wrote. "Ayrton was knee-deep in gold and precious stones, feverishly filling empty petroleum tins, pickle pots and cans from Chicago with the spoil," which would allow the finders "to retire, sip coffee and play backgammon for the rest of their lives."[15] Maspero heard the rumors that day as well: "The ingots of gold multiplied, the urns overflowed with heavy coins." The director judged the police were urgently needed "to prevent danger of an assault."

As the party adjourned from the valley, Ayrton rode to Deir el-Bahri to visit Tyndale. "His face bore the expression of a gentle angler," the artist noted, "who, having landed a big fish, joins his companions who have done no more than lose their tackle." On the *Beduin* that night Emma concluded her journal entry, judging it "A charming day."

. . .

Davis did not consider Monday, June 28, 1869, a charming day. Early that morning the messenger from the Ocean National Bank banged loudly and repeatedly on the heavy wooden door of the brownstone town house Davis shared with his housemates. Their manservant answered and carried the message to the lawyer, who was still in bed. There was an emergency at the bank, and Davis was needed immediately. Although he frequently walked to work, this time he took a horsecar to the bank's prestigious location at the corner of Greenwich and Fulton (later the location of the World Trade Center). He arrived at the bank an hour before the regular 9:00 A.M. opening.

The bank was housed on the first floor of a dignified four-story building. Still in front of the building thirty feet above the ground loomed the track that had carried the first elevated passenger cars in New York down Greenwich Street the year before. The experimental conveyance had transported people in a cart that looked much like an early automobile, pulled by cables powered by steam engines. It had been erected by Charles Harvey, the man who built the Soo canal. Although successful, the elevated had been declared a public nuisance and shut down by William M. Tweed, who feared it would interfere with the business of his own ground-level transit line.

The early morning sun shone down brightly as Davis rushed past the building next to the bank, Israel Minor's wholesale drug company, past the tobacco store with its sign advertising SEGARS. He hurried up the eight steps to the bank's stately corner entry, rushing past the two dark marble Corinthian capitol columns flanking the door. Inside the bank, the elegant wood paneling and furniture were undisturbed, but there was a strong smell of gunpowder in the air. The bank cashier, a friend of Davis's named Columbus Stevenson, hurriedly called the lawyer to the vault at the rear of the office.

A scene of chaos, discovered before dawn by the janitor, confronted them. Peering into the open vault they saw a fortune in bonds, currency, and gold coins scattered on the floor along with pieces of chipped iron, drills, chisels, jackscrews, lanterns, flasks of powder, fuses, and cigar butts. Tin safe-deposit boxes lay smashed. The "burglar-proof" vault had been burgled. Years later, when Davis discovered anciently plundered Egyptian tombs, he might have recalled the scene at the Ocean Bank that morning.

The bank's directors and employees began arriving and "as soon as they had recovered their senses," as one policeman recalled, the directors asked Davis to conduct the investigation. He proceeded to bank president Randolph Martin's office to summon detectives and saw how the burglars had entered the bank; they had cut a hole in the ceiling of offices in the subbasement and climbed through, popping up in front of Martin's desk. (The basement had previously been rented by an insurance company that the canal bond–selling Averys operated.) More bonds, currency, silverware, and some half-eaten sandwiches were discovered in the basement.

The police arrived around 9:00 A.M. As word spread, an angry crowd of depositors began gathering; in an era with no bank insurance, such a robbery meant depositors might bear the brunt of the losses. A squad of cops held the crowd at bay and a few select customers were allowed to enter. "The president, Mr. Martin, and the counsel, Mr. Davis, put on their blandest smiles [and] betrayed no sign of alarm,"[16] according to the newspapers. They assured the depositors the loss was between $20,000 and $25,000; by 4:00 P.M., Davis was telling reporters the amount was $300,000.

The bank later pegged its losses at $768,000, not including the contents of the safe-deposit boxes. The number was likely low, to conceal the bank's perilous condition; an informed guess set the loss at $2.75 million. When he learned of the robbery, Tweed was reported to have said he could not have done a better job himself. Either way, it was the largest bank robbery to date in U.S. history (the biggest haul Jesse James ever recorded was $40,000) and Davis, four years out of Iowa City, was assigned to handle it.

Catching the burglars was not Davis's concern; his object was to recover what had been stolen, and as was the common practice, he placed an advertisement to contact the robber. "He corresponded with me through the 'Personals' in the [New York] Herald first," Davis recalled, "and asked if I would negotiate for them, and I answered through the Herald that I would . . . I got acquainted with him in my office in Wall St."[17] Davis paid "a few thousand," and two days later a cop on his beat found a trunk sitting on the sidewalk addressed to an officer in the Sixth Precinct; it contained almost $600,000 worth of stolen bonds and paper (including $99,000 worth of checks cashed the day before the heist by the bank's president, Martin, and cashier, Stevenson). Davis offered a $25,000 reward for the rest of the loot but nothing else was ever recovered except a few notes mysteriously found on the body of a man who threw himself under a train in Liverpool, England, a month later.

The robbery actually plunged the Ocean Bank into insolvency, but Davis's bland assurances and the bank's size and reputation kept depositors from staging a run on its inadequate assets. Expressions of confidence (and juggling of accounts) allowed Davis to paper over the biggest bank job in history and the Ocean National to avoid collapse—for the time being, at least. Davis's rescue of the bank made him fully aware of how shaky it was, however.

He began thinking about opportunities that might arise if the Averys' canal company—and therefore the bank, with its hoard of canal bonds—both failed.

No one was ever arrested for the robbery, but popular opinion suspected the bank officers; one suit by a safe-deposit box holder alleged that Stevenson had accompanied the burglars into the vault and used bank funds to buy the robbers' tools. In 1907, ex-convict George Miles White claimed credit for the job in his memoirs and listed the bribes he had paid the police; the officer who picked up Davis's trunk received $17,000.

By his thirty-second birthday in May 1870, Davis had achieved grand success in New York. He was accepted that year into the Union League Club, an enclave for the city's wealthiest Republican power brokers, and he dropped by almost every afternoon. He was also a charter member of the Bar Association of the City of New York (organized to "sustain the profession in its proper position in the community"). He was rich, and getting richer.

All was not well for the "Tweed Ring" (as the papers called the Boss and his cohorts), however. The *New York Times* board member who had also been on the board of Tweed's printing company had died, and a new editor and new publisher decided an attack on the Boss might sell some papers. On September 20 the *Times* opened its barrage with an editorial charging that Tweed "now rules the State as Napoleon ruled France." With no proof, the paper could only lodge vague allegations of corruption.

William Avery was found guilty by the U.S. Senate in May of bribing senators the year before, handing out $10,000 bonds for a railroad he and his brother were supposed to build in Georgia (which went bankrupt). It does not seem to have inconvenienced the brothers, who sold another $1.25 million in bonds to build the Keweenaw canal in July (again claiming the Michigan land secured the paper). It was the third time they had mortgaged the property they did not own.

On December 13, 1870, a prosperous-looking man strode confidently down Wall Street to Davis's office, passing the U.S. Sub-Treasury building on the corner of Nassau Street with its eight Doric columns echoing the Parthenon, past the street peddlers displaying their wares on its steps, and past the oldest building on the street, the colonnaded Assay Office. The Davis & Edsall office at no. 38 was in a three-story building nestled between a more imposing five-story structure on the west and the stately Manhattan Company, with its figure of Neptune resting above the entrance on the east. (The second oldest bank in the city, it had incorporated in 1799 to supply the city with water.) Horse-drawn wagons and streetcars clogged the road, and amid the din of hawkers and horses and clanging bells, pedestrians' eyes were naturally drawn to the towering spire of Trinity Church at the west end of Wall; extending high above the five- or six-story office buildings, church steeples were the best guideposts for orienting the lost to city locations.

However, George Rutter was not lost nor was he going to church. He was out for blood, and had been directed to meet with Davis by Comptroller of the Currency Hiland Hulburd. The conversation that day in New York was reconstructed in testimony by both men during a congressional investigation two years later.

Rutter had been president of the bank in Memphis that failed when Davis and the Bank of the Metropolis cashed bonds Rutter had loaned them in 1866. Hulburd's inspectors had recommended shutting down the Memphis bank (as the law required), but Rutter had a private meeting with the comptroller in his Washington office and afterward they visited a carriage maker together. After Hulburd left, Rutter paid $625 for a new carriage and ordered it delivered to Hulburd's home. Hulburd let the insolvent Memphis bank stay open.

Now, four years later, Rutter had sent Hulburd a letter declaring that since his bank's final collapse he had been ruined and that he intended to "collect every dollar from persons who have blackmailed me."[18] He claimed his family had no clothing to keep them warm and demanded Hulburd pay him $500 for the carriage he had bought or he would "let the public know." Hulburd had directed Rutter to meet his friend Theodore Davis in New York.

"I don't know whether to arrest you or give you money," Davis said as Rutter sat down in his office. "I am inclined to think you are trying to blackmail the Comptroller." Rutter replied that the carriage had been a gift, purchased when he was rich. "When you *thought* you was rich," Davis interrupted. "Rutter, do you know how mean a thing, and how contemptible a thing it is to give a present and then come and ask pay for it?" Davis recalled, "I got excited and called him everything I could think of. I gave him a cursing and told him to leave the office. I told him he ought to be in the penitentiary." Before Rutter left, however, Davis offered him $100 for the carriage.

Rutter accepted and Davis insisted he sign a statement certifying he had no further claims against Hulburd. Rutter resisted. "My word is as good as my oath," he claimed, and Davis replied, "I think it is," demanding the signed statement. "I gave him a check for $100," Davis concluded. "I said, 'Take it and go.' I did not want to lay eyes on him again." Davis's hope was not fulfilled.

• • •

As 1871 began, *The New York Times* continued to make unspecified charges against the Tweed Ring. Tweed himself was formally voted onto the board of the Ocean Bank that year. The Averys bought another extension from Congress for the Keweenaw canal, changed the company's name to the Lake Superior Ship Canal, Iron and Railway Company, and sold yet another $1.3 million in bonds.

On May 31, 1871, Theodore and Annie left the corruption of the city behind and set off in the steamship *Wyoming* for Liverpool. Travel to Europe was a new perquisite for the financial elite. Davis's first trip there might have included some business (no records survive of where the couple went or what they did), but Davis certainly enjoyed his vacation; fine hotels, restaurants, theaters, art galleries, and museums gave him a glimpse of the life available to a truly wealthy man. Their tour lasted a leisurely four months, and when Davis returned in October his desire to become truly wealthy was even stronger. His chance was about to arrive.

Davis had timed his return from Europe to coincide with a payment due in November on the now $600,000 worth of Avery bonds the bank held. Davis had concluded the Averys would miss the payment, causing the bonds' value to collapse and the bank's apparent solvency to evaporate. He had not, however, anticipated the destruction of the Tweed Ring.

While Davis was still in Europe, the *Times* had received documents from a disgruntled ring insider detailing Tweed's enormous thefts of public funds. After they were published, indignation mounted steadily and citizens' committees and Republicans (led by Union League Club members) began moving for Tweed's ouster.

In September, a judge had blocked any further payouts of public funds by Tweed, specifically prohibiting any money for Tweed's New York Printing Company. As the Boss's troubles mounted Ocean Bank depositors—who all knew it was a Tweed operation—became nervous about their money. Hoping to calm the customers, a board member requested a report from the federal bank examiner on its condition; the examiner, Hulburd's employee Charles Callender, first cashed $76,000 in worthless checks at the bank and then submitted a glowing report completely neglecting to mention the canal bond exposure. He predicted the bank would soon be "a grand success."

Shortly after Davis's return home from Europe, his partner, Thomas Edsall, was enlisted by his mentor Charles O'Conor to join the attack team that was developing the case against Tweed. Edsall had assisted O'Conor before in defending Confederate president Jefferson Davis against treason charges. Their brief succeeded and on October 28, 1871, Tweed was arrested for "fraud and deceit." The Boss had spent the day transferring the titles to $750,000 in New York property to his son and burning his papers in his office fireplace.

After Tweed's arrest the canal company defaulted on their scheduled bond payments. Combined with Tweed's troubles, Ocean Bank depositors panicked and began a run on the bank. By December 8, the bank could not provide the cash to cover checks written by its depositors, but Columbus Stevenson (now president of the bank) showed Callender's glowing October report to the chairman of the Clearing House Association, which managed transfers between New York banks, and won loans to keep the bank open a few more days.

December 12, 1871, was the most important day in Davis's entire business life. A Tuesday, it began around 9:00 A.M. with bank president Stevenson calling and asking Davis to walk with him to the bank. A loan payment of $109,000 was due that day to the bank from Tweed's New York Printing Company, which had been cut off from its inflated city payouts by the courts. As the men strolled downtown, Davis recalled Stevenson told him that "if they did not have it there would be trouble. He wanted me to go to the office of the lawyer of the New York Printing Company and as soon as he came in make a desperate effort to get the money." Davis testified he tried but could not find the lawyer; scarcely surprising, since many Tweed henchmen (including Charles Wilbour, president of the printing company) had fled the state to avoid arrest. About half past eleven, "I returned to the bank and, to my utter surprise, it was announced to me that the bank had been suspended from the Clearing House."

In fact, Davis knew exactly what was about to happen. He had gone over the bank's books the day before with the chairman of the Clearing House, who had determined the bank was hopelessly insolvent due to the worthless Avery canal bonds it held and bad loans to men like bank examiner Callender. The chairman had decided the bank would have to be suspended from the Clearing House, freezing its accounts and ending its viability.

Davis also knew his friend Hiland Hulburd had been summoned the night before from Washington. Hulburd was already under pressure; the Ocean would be the largest of the sixteen national banks that had failed under his supervision, his reappointment as comptroller was due to come up in a few months, and a congressional investigation into his widely alleged corruption had already been proposed.

Hulburd arrived shortly after Davis; he had no choice but to close down the bank and appoint a receiver to settle its affairs. After a private ten minutes with Davis, Hulburd signed the papers appointing his friend the receiver. It promised to be a lucrative job; Hulburd agreed to pay Davis 5 percent of the amount he would collect and disburse in closing out the bank, a total of some $200,000 (Hulburd's cut, of course, went unrecorded). Receiverships were frequent subjects of suspicion; Judge Albert Cardozo would resign from the State Supreme Court the following May after it was revealed he had appointed his nephew to be receiver in cases before him and then split the resulting fees. The plan Davis had been mulling for two years was under way; he was beginning his journey to the jackpot.

On January 10, 1907, Davis, Jean, and Nettie returned to the valley and the gold-filled tomb they had entered the day before. The photographer would arrive the following day, but the contents were in such peril that Davis hired Joe Smith to begin some watercolors of the interior and objects immediately. No other work was possible: "[T]he shifting of rubbish so stirred up the dust as to quite obscure all outline, and therefore would be fatal to photography," Ayrton wrote.[19] He failed to mention why the rubbish was being shifted at all.

As carefully as possible, the men again looked at what they had found. The coffin had been broken into two pieces by water flowing from a ceiling crack, a rockfall onto its lid, and the collapse of the bier beneath. It was still an exquisite creation; heavily gilded and inlaid with glass, it was the finest mummy case ever found (until Tutankhamen's).

The irreplaceable golden inscriptions on the shrine were in the greatest danger of deterioration; Smith saw bits of gold leaf float in the air as breezes entered the tomb, and likened the piles of dislodged gold on the floor to snowdrifts. Emma observed ten days later, "I seemed to be walking on gold—and even the Arab working inside had some of it sticking in his wooly hair." When Tyndale visited, his companion noted "bits of gold leaf seemed to be flying through the air in every direction. We felt we must be breathing it in. Tyndale whispered to me he had just sneezed and found seven-and-six in his handkerchief!"[20]

Among the treasures, less glamorous objects were also found: Four "magical bricks," their inscriptions carrying spells for the dead, carried the name of Akhenaten. Other items would emerge inscribed for Amenhotep III and Tiye.

The puzzles of KV 55 were becoming apparent. On the coffin, the owner's name had been cut out and most of the golden face had been yanked off. The shrine had been made for Tiye by her son Akhenaten, but the king's name and images had been removed. The canopic jar heads had lost their royal uraei—cobra or vulture heads—which had been snapped off at the brows and the inscriptions on the jars had been erased.

Why names were removed from some objects but not others has never been determined. That the burial of such an important person as Tiye contained less treasure than that of her parents made little sense. The tomb had clearly been reentered after its initial closure in ancient times, as the two blocking entry walls indicated, but who had come in, and when and why, was a mystery; the amount of gold left behind proved the entrants were not simple robbers. It was equally unclear why the shrine had been disassembled, and why some parts were in the corridor and other parts left in the burial chamber.

The photographer arrived on Friday, January 11, and began taking photographs as Smith painted. The *Beduin*'s passengers amused themselves for the next five days shopping in Luxor and hosting teas and dinners. Davis went back to the valley on January

13 and sent a note to the now-absent Weigall: "I have decided that it is too dangerous for me or for any other man to attempt to move the coffin. Personally I would not think of touching it, and think you will be of the same opinion when you carefully examine it." He explained that the painting and photography would go on for several more days and then "Ayrton will take the measures of everything connected with the tomb and locate by sketch the situ of everything in the tomb."[21]

On Monday, Maspero and his wife arrived in Luxor. Davis visited the *Miriam* and Emma noted, "They are delighted with the finding of Tyi's tomb." A rainsquall the night of January 15 continued into the next day, but Emma loaned Mrs. Maspero her "chair" and the Frenchman visited the tomb for the first time. At their lunch in the valley, Joe Smith records that Davis pressed the director to officially pronounce the find the tomb of Tiye, but Maspero reserved his opinion.

After five days in the tomb the photographer finished his work. In 1910 only seven of his pictures appeared in Davis's book and additional shots, which must have been taken, have disappeared.

Tyndale visited the tomb and noted "it looked more like a wrecked boudoir of Napoleonic times than a mysterious abode of the dead." Yet after he gingerly picked his way across the floor and saw the coffin he was paralyzed by "the most thrilling sight I ever beheld. Arrayed as she might have been when Amenhotep the Magnificent led her to the marriage feast, there she lay, with arms folded and that immovable expression on her face which the contemplation of the vanity of all things might have produced." Then Tyndale realized he was gazing at the coffin lid; to the side he suddenly noticed the mummy's head sticking out of the broken box. "Her dried up face, sunken cheeks, and thin leathery-looking lips exposing a few teeth were in ghastly contrast to the golden diadem which encircled her head." He promised himself to "in future only think of her as she appeared in all her glory."[22]

On January 17 the *Beduin* hosted another member of Parliament who was visiting Egypt, Sir Benjamin Stone. The son of a Birmingham glass manufacturer, Stone was a prolific amateur photographer and had brought his camera to Egypt. He took the most reproduced photo ever made of Davis, standing in front of the entry to the tomb of Rameses IV, just across the path from the new find. Davis is flanked on his right by the Weigalls. Hortense (two months pregnant with the Weigalls' first child) wears a long-

In front of the tomb of Rameses IV, January 17, 1907. From left: Hortense Weigall, Arthur Weigall, Davis, and Edward Ayrton. Across the path from their location is KV 55, discovered the week before, which Ayrton began clearing the same day. Reproduced with the permission of Birmingham Libraries and Archives, Benjamin Stone Collection.

sleeved, floor-length white dress with a high collar; Inspector Wei-gall looks every inch the explorer in a double-breasted suit and pith helmet. On Davis's left Ayrton strikes a dashing pose in a checked jacket and straw skimmer. In the center, wearing knee-high spats, puttees, and a vest and jacket, Davis looks every year of his age and scowls at the camera through his spectacles. Perhaps the sun was in his eyes.

After the photo session, Ayrton began clearing the tomb. The first task was to clear the heap of rubble filling the entry corridor without damaging the shrine sections lying on top. It was decided to prop up the sections in place and dig out the rubble from under-neath, leaving them suspended in air. "The tunneling and propping up was a ticklish performance which Ayrton carried out skillfully,"[23] Smith recalled. With Davis, Maspero, and Weigall hovering about, Emma made it clear in that evening's journal entry who was call-ing the shots in the tomb: "It is all under Mr. Ayrton's charge," she wrote.

Three days later the corridor had been cleared, revealing a twenty-step stairway under the rubble in the first half of the cor-ridor (a few beads and workmen's tools were recovered). Archibald Sayce arrived in his *dahabiyeh* and joined Emma and the group in the valley for lunch and a mummy viewing; Emma "saw the poor queen as she lies now just a bit outside her magnificent coffin, with the vulture crown on her head." She took the time to produce something none of the archaeologists seem to have bothered with and Davis failed to include in his publication: a floor plan of the tomb mapping where the major artifacts had been located. Rough as it is, Emma's plan has been of value to Egyptologists ever since.

Ayrton began removing objects from the tomb on January 20, 1907. His first challenge was to preserve the gold leaf inscriptions on the shrine. "All the panels being treated to paraffin to hold the

gold in place," Emma wrote on January 21. Davis had summoned
Ernest Harold Jones, who had done paintings for the American in
Siptah's tomb, to help record the shrine reliefs. At dinner on the
Beduin on the twenty-third they discussed how to handle the panels. "Decided to take an impression of inscriptions by wax and
plaster of paris," Emma wrote. These were desperate measures;
Davis's agreement with the antiquities service expressly forbade
such techniques because of the potentially destructive result. How
much of the gold was lost to wax or plaster is unknown; the few
wood samples of the shrine displayed in the Egyptian Museum in
Cairo today are devoid of their original covering but bits of wax
are still discernable.

After tea with Ayrton at the Winter Palace the next day, Davis
hosted Harold Jones for dinner. He asked the artist to join him
the following morning when the archaeologists would tackle the
trickiest part of the entire clearance. The damaged coffin and the
mummy would be touched for the first time.

The next morning Davis, Ayrton, Maspero, Weigall, Jones, and
both Smiths crowded into the tomb. The first task was to remove
the broken lid from the coffin trough. The lid had split into pieces
and Ayrton removed it in three sections, placing each on a padded
tray and moving them into the corridor. When the lid was later
restored in the Cairo museum the facial features carved into the
wood, visible in ghostly trace in the tomb photo, were lost.

With the lid removed, the mummy was revealed to be covered
in sheets of gold "so thick that when taken in the hands, they
would stand alone without bending," Davis observed. It was later
determined they had lined the coffin and come loose. Maspero
turned to Joe Smith and said, "You have the delicate hands of an
artist. Please dismember the body."[24] Smith counted twelve gold
sheets that he removed from the coffin. As the archaeologists peered

at them, looking for inscriptions, Smith recalled "Davis's eyes were almost popping out of his head as he stared at the amazing sight of a pile of sheets of pure and heavy gold glittering on the floor."

The mummy beneath the gold sheets was "a smallish person, with delicate head and hands . . . enclosed in mummy-cloth of fine texture," according to Davis. Ayrton noted that the cloth crumbled to the touch. According to Weigall, writing in 1922, the mummy was also bound in gold bands two inches wide. One "had evidently passed down the front of the mummy outside the wrappings, and at right angles to the other bands, which passed around the body." The inspector claimed, most important, that the bands "were inscribed with the titles of Akhenaten, but the cartouche was in each case cut out."[25] Important evidence of the body's identity, the bands were never mentioned by any of the others present. The bands are now missing; if they existed, they may have been stolen later from the Egyptian Museum.

Smith records the body had its left arm bent with the hand on its chest—the standard pose for a royal woman. On the upper left arm were three broad gold bracelets and on the wrist of the right arm were three more. Maspero asked him to feel the bandages at the neck to determine if a necklace was inside, but when Smith touched the surface "it crumbled into ashes and sifted down through the bones." There was a ghastly moment as Smith felt inside the remains looking for necklace pieces, and he found gold pendants, inlaid lotus flower plaques, and some small beads. Maspero concurred the body was in bad shape: "Nothing more than a residue of fibrous bones and disconnected limbs, to which a little dried flesh still adhered in places," he wrote. When Davis attempted to remove a bit of the wrapping, "it came off in a black mass, exposing the ribs."[26]

Smith's version and Davis's agree on the next odd discovery. As he fished underneath the remains, Smith discovered another gold sheet and as he lifted it up he turned to Davis and said, "I have something on my hands which you have never found before." Handing the sheet to Davis, the American "put my hands under it and found them wet with water."[27] The explorers, believing the tomb to be "absolutely airless," concluded the water was 3,000 years old, forgetting the two recent days of rain. Smith claimed the sheet had a cartouche cut out of it.

Attention now turned to the mummy's head, lying a foot away from the body. They removed the "vulture crown," which Maspero described as "the headdress worn by queen mothers . . . The embalmers, in fitting the body into the coffin, had carelessly adjusted it in a reverse position, the beak to the nape and the tail to the face of the mummy."[28] Maspero also records that, at the time, the mummy's face was still visible—"the features had suffered comparatively little"—and he noted a strong resemblance to Tiye's mother, Thuyu: "A visit to the museum at Cairo sufficiently proves the fact."

As Davis described it, "the mouth was partly open, showing a perfect set of upper and lower teeth." He "gently" touched one of the front teeth and, "Alas! It fell into dust, thereby showing that the mummy could not be preserved."[29]

Concerned about the disintegrating corpse, Davis somehow secured the services of two doctors to inspect it. A Dr. Pollack who practiced in Luxor and "a prominent American obstetrician" who happened to be in the valley were dragooned into the burial chamber to offer their opinions. "Both the doctor and surgeon instantly agreed it was the pelvis of a woman," Davis wrote in a letter six months later.[30] Another factor supported their opinion; as noted by American Egyptologist Martha Bell eighty-three years later, "too delicate to mention in 1907, the mummy lacked a male sex organ . . . A mummified penis seems fairly indestructible."[31]

The day's work was finished and the body's identity appeared to have been settled—the sex, the royal arm pose, the crown, and Tiye's name on the shrine seemed to make it certainly hers. It was a surprise to find her there; Akhenaten had dug his own royal tomb at the capitol he had built far from the valley, at modern Tel el-Amarna, and since Tiye had joined him there at the end of her life it had been assumed her son had entombed her there as well. "Davis was almost hysterical at this confirmation of his hopes," Smith reminisced fifty years later, "and insisted he would telegraph the Head of the Expedition at el-Amarna, telling him to stop looking for Tiye because he had found the queen in the Valley of the Kings."[32]

Davis returned to the *Beduin* at the end of the day and shared with Emma one of the most touching moments of their thirty-year love affair. With boyish pride he presented her with the queen's crown; with girlish delight she recorded, "It now lies in the closet at the head of my bed! It is of solid gold, and represents the gold vulture with outspread wings . . . Every feather perfect!" For the next month, until it was turned over to the museum in Cairo, Emma slept beneath the crown of Queen Tiye. Hanging the queen's golden crown over his paramour's bed must have given Davis considerable pleasure. Scholars later determined it was not a crown, and not Tiye's, but nothing diminished the tribute—or Emma's joy—when she received it from her partner.

There was little joy for Davis in closing the Ocean Bank—and taking the Averys' four hundred thousand acres of Michigan—and it took him the better part of a decade to do it. Becoming receiver for the broken bank put him in the public eye for the first time since the burglary; he met with the press the afternoon of

December 12, 1871, and, blaming the collapse on the burglary and
the financial effects of the Chicago fire a few months before, predicted the depositors would receive all their money back and that
an assessment on stockholders—the last resort for a failed bank to
pay its debts—would not be necessary.

The outraged depositors held a meeting two days later demanding their money and calling for Davis's ouster because he was a
friend of the bank officers. President Stevenson was defended by a
lone friend who had served with him in the Army of the Potomac
during the war who did not care, according to *The New York Herald,* "how many bottles of wine the cashier drank or how many -----
the president ----- with. The language of the speaker was of a
character that no journal claiming any respectability can repro-
duce."[33] The following week bank examiner Callender, author of
the rosy report two months earlier, was arrested for bribery.

Davis's job as receiver was to sell the bank's assets at as high a
price as possible and to pay off the depositors and other creditors
with the proceeds. It would prove a complicated task: The Treasury Department had to approve all his actions; ownership of many
bank assets was disputed in court; and the auction of assets he tried
to sell were subject to full public scrutiny. He had more in mind
than getting the bank's customers their money back, however.

His first step was to foreclose on the property of the New York
Printing Company over the debt they had not paid, and in early
1872 the courts approved seizing the company's assets. Davis scheduled an auction at the printing company's plant to sell the presses
and other equipment that had been seized. The auction was conducted rather clumsily, but when Davis closed the bidding his
confederate—his housemate, "Mr. Gilman"—got a million dollars'
worth of equipment for $100,000. When another bidder complained
about the abrupt and sudden close of the sale, Davis fobbed him

off: "It ain't no use bothering about it," Davis said. "Let it go, let it go."[34] Mr. Gilman resold the presses (allegedly back to other Tweed Ring members) for a tidy profit and shared the proceeds with Davis.

The receiver's job kept Davis busy "day and night" for nearly ten years. He never again worked as a lawyer for a client; instead, he employed batteries of lawyers to handle the myriad of Ocean Bank cases that developed (a "lawyers' feast," he later called it). In January, Congress voted to hold an investigation into Hulburd's affairs, and Davis was notified he would be called to Washington to testify.

So Davis had a great deal on his mind the chilly evening of Thursday, January 18, 1872 as he and Annie—who was visiting him in New York—walked down West Twenty-fourth Street to the stately brownstone mansion where his sister Gertrude Galloway was living with her husband. The Davises were on their way to a family reunion. Theodore's half-sister Isabella Titus, now eighteen, was stopping in New York on her way back to school at the Convent of the Sacred Heart in Detroit (she had left school the year before when her father died, to move with her mother to the house Davis had bought for Catherine in Pepperell, Massachusetts). Also visiting was Davis's other half-sister, Kate Lewis, five months pregnant with her first child. It is unlikely Davis spent much time discussing his business affairs with the ladies; he frequently commented on Annie's lack of business capacity and her "inability to understand any business matter."[35] The ruthless businessman left his work at the parlor door and became a charming and affectionate companion among family. The ladies discussed shopping.

The group chatted until around 10:30 P.M., when Isabella bid them good night, adding, "I shall see you no more, as I am going home tomorrow." She climbed the stairs to the fourth floor, sat down on the top step, put the muzzle of a pistol to her temple, and pulled the trigger. A boy in Pepperell had given her the pistol for target shooting.

Gertrude told the reporters who soon swarmed to the scene that the suicide must have been due to temporary insanity caused by ill health: "She never had a love affair in her life," her sister claimed about the girl the press called "the beautiful suicide—she was beautiful beyond description."[36] Kate sent a telegram to a clergyman in Pepperell to break the news to their mother as gently as possible: "I fear the sudden grief will overwhelm her." The sensational news stories identified Davis as the new receiver for the Ocean Bank; it fell to him to appear at the coroner's inquest the next day. On Saturday he traveled on the train with Annie, Kate, the Galloways, and Isabella's coffin to Massachusetts. Davis's mother, who had already buried two children and two husbands, had lost her youngest child.

A week later, Davis was back in New York and made the first partial payment—30 percent of their balances—to Ocean Bank depositors. On February 1, Davis & Edsall formally ended their partnership; Davis devoted himself full-time to the receiver's job and Edsall joined another firm. They remained friends afterward; Davis eventually hired Edsall to help with Ocean Bank matters.

As he proceeded closing the bank, Davis pursued with greater interest the opportunity that would make his fortune. The bank was saddled with $600,000 in Avery canal bonds that Davis, who had read the law regarding the canal, knew were backed by nothing. The Averys, from every indication, were going to blunder away their claim to the Michigan land grant, and Davis saw the reward for building the canal as available to be hooked, like his canoe in 1853.

He held a meeting with the Averys to discuss their bond default and asked why they had not finished the canal; he received no answer. When he proposed a settlement with them to take over their company, offering to pay what he guessed they had already invested, the brothers insisted they would finish the canal, take possession of the land, and pay off their bogus bonds. Davis expressed his certainty they would fail, and the meeting ended angrily.

One afternoon soon after the unproductive meeting, Davis was visited at his Ocean Bank office again by William Avery, who brought along a distinguished-looking man Avery claimed was one of his backers who would provide the money to build the canal. Davis was introduced to Dr. James Ayer, a phenomenally wealthy businessman from Lowell, Massachusetts, who had built the most successful patent medicine empire in the world.

Ayer's Cherry Pectoral was touted as a cure for colds, whooping cough, and consumption; the brew contained half of a grain of heroin in each bottle and was popular for calming children during travel. Ayer's breakthrough was not actually medicinal but one of marketing—for years he had advertised his expanding line of flavored tonics, pills, and potions in every newspaper in the country; his almanac boasted circulation second only to the Bible. Dr. Ayer won endorsements from the emperor of China (who called him "the Great Curing Barbarian of the Outside Country"), the Philadelphia Medical University (which granted him his honorary title of "Doctor") and the press (which dubbed him "the Sarsaparilla King"). He and his brother Frederick invested their profits in Florida lumber, Georgia cotton, woolen mills, railroads, and real estate. In 1870 the Ayers had been persuaded by the Averys to buy a quarter million dollars' worth of bonds in their canal; Ayer had his New York attorney investigate the proposal, and the lawyer confirmed that the Michigan land secured the bonds. The lawyer was given $30,000 in canal stock by the Averys for his lie.

Now Dr. Ayer was in New York to determine the state of his canal investment. The meeting began cordially, although with an edge; Davis told Avery a joke about a man in a story he had read who at the end found himself completely "bandaged and bound" and likened his situation to Avery's. When Davis asked, "Now, what are you going to do about it?" Avery replied with another joke about "dancing to the fiddler's tune." Davis noted, however, that Dr. Ayer was distinctly noncommittal about whether he would provide more money for the canal. Davis arranged a private meeting with the medicine man after Avery had left. The discussion began a long— and profitable—friendship.

Davis revealed to Ayer the lies he had been told and explained the current worthlessness of his bonds. Ayer was stunned; he had thought he was dealing with gentlemen, he told Davis, but now feared he had fallen in with "a band of pirates." (Ayer hired another attorney who confirmed the zero value of the bonds.) Davis was enthusiastic about the value of the land he had walked as a boy, however, and with Ayer he hatched a plot to take the land, redeem Ayer's investment, make the bank's bonds worth something to help cover its debts, and allow Davis to skim the eventual profits. Along with another major canal investor named Isaac II. Knox, they formed what Davis called "the syndicate" to take over the Lake Superior Ship Canal, Iron and Railway Company. Their scheme required the removal of the Averys; the way to do it was to transfer the bank's bonds to themselves and foreclose.

To entice Ayer and Knox into the plot, Davis had to persuade them of the value of the Michigan land they were after. "By kicking and clubbing" he talked them into paying his old boss, George Frost, to examine the land. The survey showed so much pine timber on the land that the deal, if successful, would end up profitable but required the syndicate own all the canal bonds Davis held at the Ocean Bank. Basing their estimates on the standing timber, none of the men involved had any idea how truly valuable the prize would be.

On Saturday, February 10, George Rutter of Memphis reappeared in Davis's new office in the Ocean Bank building. He waved a copy of that morning's *Herald* and raged about its article on the Hulburd investigation, the hearings for which were now scheduled to begin in Washington the following Monday. The article said Rutter had stolen $22,000 from his Memphis bank before it failed, and Rutter began his conversation with Davis by howling for vindication. He was determined to go to the hearings, Rutter said, so he could clear his own name and Hulburd's. All he needed to help Hulburd, Rutter explained, was the money to go to Washington.

The lawyer was skeptical. Davis had seen a copy of a letter Rutter had sent a month before to a congressman on the House Committee on Banking and Currency. "The facts I have are in relation to Mr. Hulburd," Rutter had written, "including Mr. Davis's dirty work as present receiver of the Ocean National Bank."[37] In the letter he accused both men of blackmail.

"Rutter, this is cool," Davis replied. "I hear you made an affidavit down in Tennessee that you paid $5,000 to Mr. Hulburd." Rutter denied it, and then changed his approach; he claimed the anti-Hulburd forces were anxious to have him appear and incriminate the comptroller, and that he had received two telegrams to that effect. Doubting the claim, Davis offered him $100 for each telegram; Rutter sputtered they were "downtown" and unavailable to him. Finally, Rutter got to the point: If Davis gave him $300 he would not go to Washington and his embarrassing past with Hulburd would remain hidden. "I gave him a moral lecture," Davis later testified. "I told him I didn't care a snap, he would get no money from me."

The congressional hearings began on schedule in Washington the following Monday. The first witness was a bank examiner who talked about the extraordinary "private suspension" Davis had handled for the Bank of the Metropolis. Rutter (who had somehow managed to get to the capital) appeared next and claimed he had paid more than $15,000 in bribes to Hulburd and described the $5,000 bribe Davis had paid to the Memphis bank's receiver. He also claimed Davis had offered him $300 not to come to the hearing. None of his allegations could be proven, however, so the committee zeroed in on the carriage Rutter had bribed Hulburd with to keep him from closing the Memphis bank. "The Comptroller gave me to understand that unless I gave him something I would have trouble," Rutter testified.

When the hearings resumed February 22, Davis was in Washington to testify. He denied the allegations against himself, but acknowledged Hulburd had accepted Rutter's "gift." He claimed Hulburd had asked him to pay Rutter back for the carriage only because he felt sorry for Rutter's family. He described Rutter as a man who "made propositions that none but a rascal would make."

The committee also asked Davis what he knew about bank examiner Callender, whose bribery trial would soon begin. Davis swore he had warned the comptroller that Callender was taking loans from the Ocean Bank but said the overly trusting comptroller had not believed him. It was later discovered Hulburd himself had borrowed $10,000 from the bank.

The hearings concluded on March 21. No criminal charges ever resulted. It was a bad time for Hulburd to be convincingly accused of corruption, however; the papers were full of a bribery scandal at the New York Customs House, and just as the hearings ended a report stolen from the comptroller's office was printed in the *New-York Tribune* clearly detailing the carriage episode. The committee voted on March 26 that a change in the Currency department's leadership was required, and Hulburd resigned that afternoon. The story in *The New York Herald* that day carried the headlines "Rueful Rutter's Story—How a Bubble Bank Burst— Gift of a Harness and Carriage to the Currency Comptroller— Hulburd, Davis and Callender."

Davis had little time to mourn the fall of his friend. His efforts to secure the Michigan land for his syndicate had suddenly grown more complicated when syndicate member Isaac Knox (whom the Averys had mistakenly trusted) told Davis the method behind the Averys' apparent madness.

The Averys had sold millions of dollars' worth of bonds, ostensibly to build the canal. The bonds promised a 10 percent return to buyers, and if the payments were not made the bondholders were told they could claim the land to compensate for the default. Knox now explained to Davis why the Averys were not concerned about missing the payments they owed: The 10 percent return they promised violated New York's usury laws and would be legally unenforceable. The brothers had never intended to pay off the bonds; if bondholders sued for satisfaction, the courts would have to find the debts illegal and uncollectable. The Averys would keep whatever cash they had left and, if the canal was ever finished, could take title to the four hundred thousand acres.

Davis and his syndicate realized they would have to declare total war to avoid losing what Ayer and Knox had already invested and what Davis hoped to gain. If they could force the Averys into bankruptcy, finish the canal themselves, and foreclose on the defaulted bonds, they could then take the land. The $600,000 in canal bonds that the Ocean Bank was stuck with had to be acquired by the syndicate; since Davis would be auctioning off the bonds he could guarantee that outcome.

Crucial to Davis, of course, was his cut of the eventual profits. Ayer and Knox would have to pay for building the canal, but they recognized the litigation for the scheme would be long and complicated and Davis offered to manage the entire affair and do the work necessary to realize their plan. In return, when the final profits were divided up the syndicate would pay the lawyer 10 percent.

It was vital that Davis's role be concealed; even in the 1870s, a receiver profiting from his sale of assets was fraud. Ayer later gave full credit for the scheme to Davis, who cajoled him and Knox into it. They agreed the syndicate would eventually pay the bank $480,000 (the amount the bank had loaned the Averys) if Davis managed to get the bonds into the syndicate's hands.

Davis's payoff required him to trust his coconspirators; his trust proved well-founded, and all the men involved committed perjury repeatedly over the coming years to conceal Davis's real interest in the project. The receiver was able to present himself as an uninterested public officer.

The Davis syndicate was an example of the odd sense of honor that existed among the robber barons of the era. Rutter's sin, and the opinion of him as a "rascal," had nothing to do with the bribes he gave Hulburd; it was asking for the bribe back that was seen as dishonest by those involved. Years later, Davis's stockbroker told the story of a secret meeting held in the White House in 1904, where Theodore Roosevelt supposedly won a quarter million dollars for his reelection campaign from steel baron Henry Frick by promising to leave Frick's business alone in his coming term. "We bought the son of a bitch," Frick later complained, "and then he did not stay bought."[38] The tycoons frequently hated each other, but among themselves a deal was a deal—notwithstanding any niceties of law or ethics.

The Averys were not going to go quietly, however. They still imagined they could find a way to get more money to finish the canal, cut the bondholders out of their proper returns through the usury defense, and claim the land for themselves. Davis commenced proceedings to auction off the canal bonds the bank held and to put the Averys in bankruptcy, but the confidence men secured enough lawyers to stymie the bankruptcy proceedings in the courts and bought enough political influence to persuade the secretary of the treasury to delay Davis's sale (although Hulburd's replacement as comptroller of the currency, for reasons that can only be imagined, soon became an ally of the syndicate).

The legal proceedings that followed were of amazing complexity. Court actions in New York, Washington, and Michigan involved the holders of the multiple mortgages the Averys had entered into, the shareholders of the Ocean Bank, the parties to the suits filed after the 1869 robbery, the Averys, and the officials both sides bribed to assist them. Davis later summarized things as they stood in April 1872: "We commenced our legal proceedings in Detroit," he testified. "All this time there was going on between the Avery party and the trustees under these various mortgages a perfectly enormous litigation; suits to foreclose the Sutherland mortgage, to foreclose the Birdseye mortgage, to foreclose the Frost mortgage, to foreclose the Union Trust Company mortgage, met by proceedings in the bankruptcy court, and by answers of all sorts and descriptions."[39] The bank examiner who replaced the indicted Callender called it "one of the most infamous and complicated snarls" he had ever seen. The battle would last for eight years, and grow more complicated and dangerous as it proceeded.

Davis and Knox helped the Averys win another extension from Congress to complete the canal, and then Davis resumed his efforts to put the Averys in bankruptcy. William Avery offered him a half million dollars in canal stock and "all the money he wanted" to back off, but Davis refused—Avery promises did not interest him. He started to try to auction off the bonds the bank held, but the Averys had hired enough congressmen to pressure the secretary of the treasury into stopping the sale. The Averys had won the support of the Ocean Bank's shareholders by promising the bonds the bank held would soon be valuable and the shareholders would profit if Davis was stymied. The bank's depositors, however—still owed the final 30 percent of their balances—pushed for a quick sale that would generate cash to pay off their accounts.

In the summer of 1872 Davis and Knox traveled to Michigan. In Detroit they won their case putting the Averys' Lake Superior Ship Canal, Iron and Railway Company in bankruptcy, a relatively easy part of Davis's plan since the Averys had squandered or hidden the vast amounts they had raised and paid few of their bills. The court appointed Knox the receiver of the bankrupt canal company and granted him permission to issue $500,000 in certificates—which the court stated would be the "supreme lien" on the land—to raise cash to build the canal. The certificates were purchased by Knox and Ayer.

From Detroit, the partners moved on to the Keweenaw to inspect the canal. The trip still had to be made by boat; the railroad would not arrive until the following year, when the trip from Chicago would take twenty-two hours. The scene they found had changed immeasurably since Davis's boyhood; the Upper Peninsula was now providing 70 percent of all the copper mined in the United States, and its timber was rebuilding burned-out Chicago and filling the prairies with farmhouses. As the area boomed, lumberjacks and miners filled the unpaved streets, brothels, and bars of the new settlements, the hogs running as wild as in early Iowa City.

At the canal site Davis and Knox were disappointed, if not surprised, to see the two-and-one-half mile canal was not half finished. What had been dug was not as deep or wide as the specifications called for, and piers, docks, and a harbor had yet to be started. Knox took charge of the project. "We went on from one trouble to another," Davis recalled. "We began the dredging, and pretty soon we struck a cedar swamp buried some fifteen or twenty feet below the surface of the bottom, and everything had to be brought up by rakes."

The Avery construction work, which had originally been scheduled for completion five years before, was a boondoggle, but the canal itself was not. If completed it would allow the constantly increasing lumber, copper, and iron-ore ships on Lake Superior to avoid sailing around the Keweenaw Peninsula, cutting three hundred miles off their voyage and avoiding one of the most dangerous spots on the lake, at the peninsula's tip.

The trip was not all business for Davis. On his way home he stopped in Iowa City to visit the Boal family: Davis's friend George, his five-year-old namesake, Theodore Davis Boal, and his sister-in-law Malvina, who was pregnant. The next Boal son, born in October, would also be named after his uncle, called Montgomery Davis Boal. A stop in Ohio provided Davis time with Emma Andrews and her ailing husband.

Davis finally received permission to sell $200,000 worth of the canal bonds the bank held on November 7. The auction, held in the basement of the Trinity building, at 111 Broadway (demolished in 1903), was "the most extraordinary exhibition I ever saw," according to a witness. Davis gave bidders every impression the bonds were worthless and announced he would recognize only those bidders he wished to recognize. He sold the lot to Isaac Knox for 6 cents on the dollar. On February 10, 1873, Davis sold another $100,000 worth of canal bonds, and this time Knox won them for 5 cents on the dollar. One observer noted that the bonds "would make very good wallpaper, they were so cheap." At a sale in April, Knox bought most of the bonds, again for 5 cents, but a different bidder purchased $105,000 worth. He later testified, "I never paid for those, and never had them. It was a bid by the direction of Mr. Davis," who "asked me to go there and bid, and I did so." Davis "repaid me with interest."[40]

On May 2, Davis lost the first of the cases filed against the Ocean Bank for losses of securities the bank had been holding for other banks at the time of the 1869 burglary. The bank was found guilty of negligence, and the court's award increased the bank's debt. The decision opened the floodgates for similar claims, as well: "If they all go against us," Davis wrote, "there will be nothing left for stockholders."[41] Davis estimated the bank was now $130,000 short of meeting its obligations.

In Washington that year, Davis—as always—dropped in on his friend Nathaniel Wilson at his luxurious, opulent home. Wilson's law firm, with its intimate relations with political power brokers, was now one of the most prominent in the city; clients included the Western Union Telegraph Company and the Catholic Church. At a time when congressmen were routinely and legally hired as amateur lobbyists by interested parties like the Averys, a professional like Wilson was invaluable. The men discussed the syndicate's scheme in Michigan. Although Wilson had not yet surfaced, his involvement was a key part of Davis's plan and he would also emerge wealthy from the plot. Business was interrupted, however, when Davis made a new friend.

"Mr. Davis was dining with my parents," Eleanor "Nellie" Salome Wilson, who was five at the time, recalled years later. "We children came in after dinner. Mr. Davis heard me fussing about a loose front tooth which I would not allow anybody to touch. He took me on his lap and said he would pull it out for me, which he did, and then he gave me a dollar. The whole affair seemed to amuse him very much as I had at once let him do it."[42] As she grew up Nellie would become extremely close to Davis; she and her mother would visit him in New York, and she went on to spend most summers with him when he moved to Newport. In time, he would become her financial protector.

Davis's trip west the summer of 1873 included business in Indiana and Springfield, Illinois, where he foreclosed on bonds the bank held for a railroad "syndicate" he was running on the side. In Iowa City he visited with Buttles and Boals, and also attended the sheriff's sale of tax delinquent property, where the farm of his first legal mentor, G. W. Clark, was up for sale. Clark had never recovered from his Civil War wounds and had lost his home; Davis bought the farm and allowed Clark and his wife to live there rent-free for the rest of their lives. Davis later sold the farm back to Clark's children at a rate they could afford, preserving the family's patrimony. "He saved our bacon," a family member later recalled.

When he arrived at the Keweenaw (by train, for the first time), Davis was pleased with the progress Knox was making on the canal. Although the costs were increasing beyond what the syndicate had planned, the swamp he had seen the year before had been almost completely dredged; the banks were lined with piles of timber and stumps reaching twenty feet high. The canal builders operated five huge steam dredges, had laid track for the two locomotives and dump cars that removed the digging debris, used pile drivers to secure the sides of the canal, and employed more than one hundred horses along with assorted tugboats and scows. Nitroglycerin was used to blast apart the hardpan clay at the bottom. Their deadline for completion was December, and it appeared the requirement would finally be met.

When he returned to New York in the fall of 1873, the world was collapsing into a severe and prolonged economic depression. The "Panic," as such events were called, began on Thursday, September 18, after Jay Cooke & Company (perceived to be the strongest private bank in the country) shut down after a morning meeting where other Wall Street bankers refused Cooke a bailout. "A monstrous yell went up and seemed to literally shake the building" when the Cooke collapse was announced at the New York Stock Exchange, the *New-York Tribune* reported. "Dread seemed to take possession of the multitude." Two days later the exchange suspended trading, and within a week most banks, brokerage firms, and insurance companies had shut down. The panic quickly spread to the rest of the country.

The crash hurt the Ocean Bank; permission was rescinded for another bond sale due to the chaos, and the deflated values of what the bank had left to sell made paying off the depositors— and the possibility of anything remaining for the shareholders— much less likely. Davis recalled six years later, "1873 did for the Ocean Bank's assets what it did for many a private individual's assets."[43]

A flood of letters flowed from New York to Washington that fall from the Averys, their stooges, and bank shareholders decrying Davis's efforts and calling for his firing. The campaign even reached back to Iowa City days when the Averys obtained a letter from Davis's embittered ex-partner, William Penn Clarke, who was now practicing in Washington and called Davis a "dishonorable and dishonest person." A letter Davis sent to his sister-in-law, Malvina Boal in Iowa City, gives an insight into his feelings.

After telling Malvina that Emma Andrews was coming to visit ("I am so glad!!"), Davis wrote, "I am out of sorts today, as near the blues as I ever get . . . [Penn Clarke] has written a letter to one of the stockholders, nominally at his request for information as to me, wherein he expresses himself in no measured terms as to my honesty and integrity." His friends in New York, however, had assured Davis that "my reputation was already too firmly established to be shaken by such a letter. So you see the miserable dog has done his utmost and it amounts to nothing except to expose his own misdeeds . . . I am yet on my feet but between us I wonder that I am, for the influence brought against me was very strong."[44]

On October 15 the syndicate achieved a major triumph. The Michigan state engineer signed a certification that the canal was complete and met the specifications.

The Averys hired another helper in December by employing Massachusetts representative Benjamin Butler. Butler had led the Yankee occupation of New Orleans during the war (he was known in the South as "Beast") and been president of a company formed with Dr. Ayer to sell one of the doctor's inventions, a mining process that was claimed to turn quartz rock into sponge. The company had failed, however, and the two were no longer friends. Butler wrote to the comptroller of the currency demanding Davis be fired, and the barrage of political pressure finally forced the comptroller to submit; he replied, "It would be best that a hearing should be granted to the parties you represent in reference to those matters."

On December 18 the Averys' campaign succeeded. The U.S. House of Representatives voted unanimously to have the Committee on Banking and Currency investigate the receivership of the Ocean National Bank. The charges were that Davis had fraudulently reduced the assets of the bank, and the committee was to determine if he was personally interested in the bond purchases. A congressional investigation into their affairs could derail the syndicate's plot and put Davis in jail; he anticipated the ultimate battle with the Averys (and a public grilling) with cold resolve—and considerable anxiety.

Anticipation of a happier sort consumed Davis and his helpers when the clearance of KV 55 began in earnest on January 17, 1907. Maspero wanted the work done quickly, as in Yuya's tomb, because he feared a robbery. The tomb was a popular stop for tourists crowding the valley, and some of its wealth disappeared before Ayrton could pack it all for transport. By one account, Harold Jones was painting the shrine in the tomb and witnessed Davis allowing favored guests to take small souvenirs away with them; Jones asked if he might take a handful from the floor for himself, and Davis answered, "Certainly, take two!"[45] A box labeled "gold dust from the tomb of Queen Tiye" (containing crumbled pieces of gold foil, a clay seal, a fragment of white glass, pieces of blue glazed ware, and two golden half cowrie shells) was presented to the Swansea Museum in Wales fifty years later by Jones's heirs.

The tomb was quickly emptied, and it was decided the safest way to transport the objects to Cairo would be on board the *Bed-uin*. On January 27, Emma wrote: "About 4 o'clock as we were waiting for tea on deck, we saw coming across the distant sands the procession of the treasures of the tomb on its way to us. Weigall and Ayrton on horses led the way, and a long procession of Arabs following carrying the boxes, the sun striking the rifles of the accompanying sailors. It was really impressive." Jones the Great had a carpenter build a box eight feet by five feet on the back upper deck to hold the larger objects—"safe against everything but a concerted raid," Emma judged—and the smaller and most delicate items, including the canopic jars, joined the "crown" below decks. The large section of the shrine was left in the tomb corridor where Harold Jones continued painting it, and a steel door was installed on the entry.

Davis was in no hurry to leave Luxor, but a constant stream of visitors to share tea and gawk at treasure became a trial for the Americans. By February 14 Emma's patience had reached its end: "We were overwhelmed with people," she wrote, and those who brought guests of their own were "a nuisance and impertinence! 17 people in our little salon is too much!" When Lord and Lady Cromer arrived, however, she felt more hospitable. "They were entranced with the boat and especially my room. She is quite charming and he is interesting because of his achievements and the power he wields."

Among the tea and treasure crowds were Lord and Lady Carnarvon. The earl stepped carefully but steadily across the *Beduin*'s gangplank, turning to offer his hand to his wife to help her onto the deck. Weigall had led the way, bringing the aristocrats to see the sensational crown of Queen Tiye and enjoy afternoon tea with Davis and his mistress.

George Herbert had succeeded his father as the fifth Earl of Carnarvon in 1890, at age twenty-four, an Eton-educated playboy most interested in gambling, golf, horse racing, and automobiles. His wife, despite her official pedigree as the daughter of Sir Frederick Wombley, was actually the child of Baron Alfred de Rothschild, who presented the newlyweds in 1896 with a wedding gift of around $1 million. Soon after, he provided another half million to cover the earl's gambling debts. After a serious auto accident in Germany in 1901, Carnarvon had taken to visiting Egypt every winter for his health and had been in Luxor in 1905 when Davis discovered Yuya's tomb. It had encouraged him to follow Cromer's advice on how to pass the sleepy days in Egypt. "He suffered from ennui," the nobleman's son recalled. "Cromer told him he thought it would be an admirable idea if he were to take up the fascinating subject of Egyptology."[46]

The earl had been provided with a spot to explore (Maspero had made sure the site was easily accessible from the Winter Palace), but in his tent amid the flies, dust, and heat he considered the work "an occupation for the damned,"[47] according to Weigall. He would continue to run his digs, with sometimes disastrous results, until he followed Davis's lead and hired Howard Carter in 1909. The earl and Carter hit it off, partly because the archaeologist suggested expenses "might well be defrayed by buying antiques in the bazaar in Cairo or elsewhere to sell them to collectors at a handsome profit" (again according to the earl's son). "I heard them talk of many good deals brought off in this fashion."[48]

It was the first time the Carnarvons had visited the *Beduin* (perhaps due to social niceties over Emma's presence), and the mood was apparently strained; Davis, now an institution and a legend in Egypt, found a new tomb every year, and Carnarvon's efforts had produced nothing. Davis was far from bashful about his latest triumph and whether due to a tactless comment by Davis or some other reason, the past and future employers of Howard Carter did not get along. Carnarvon later told Maspero "I should not speak to the man again."[49] The earl left the boat planning never to return (Emma discreetly failed to mention the visit at all), a resolution that lasted five years.

Disturbing news arrived on February 17. "Theo was in Luxor this A.M. and Carter told him of various small and precious things which had been shown him by a native which had been stolen from Tyi's tomb," Emma recorded. Carter's notes say pieces of jewelry bearing the Aten cartouche "were in the dealers' shops in Luxor within a few days of the discovery."[50] The pieces were for sale, providing no arrests were made. Ayrton was "deeply distressed about the robbery," Emma noted. "He suspects the trusted *reis,* or rather 2 sons of his." She felt it "humiliating to find that thieves have been among your trusted workmen."

The next day—February 18, 1907—the American rose as usual and dressed in the clothes Jones had laid out for him. Today's outfit was not desert wear; after breakfast with Emma and his guests in the *Beduin*'s dining room Davis took his boat's felucca (a small but graceful short-masted boat with a lateen sail) across the Nile to Luxor.

Whom Davis ransomed the KV 55 items from is as unclear as whom he paid to get back the Ocean Bank's stolen securities in 1869. It is likely, however, that the transaction involved Mohammed Mohassib, the premier antiquities dealer in Luxor and a longtime supplier for Davis as he developed his Egyptian collection. If so, it would have been similar to their other meetings.

Two of the *Beduin*'s crew rowed and steered the felucca to the east bank of the river. Halfway across, the din of the bustling town began to reach them; the contrast of busy Luxor to the quiet mooring where the *Beduin* lay was striking. Davis's escorts tied up their sailboat at the landing used by patrons of the Winter Palace and together they climbed the embankment to the Corniche, Luxor's main drag. Carriages, donkeys, carts, and wagons jostled with pedestrians, the tourists dressed in Western business suits and long-skirted dresses, the Egyptians in galabiyas (the traditional ground-length garments) and turbans, and others wore a sartorial compromise of skirted robes paired with Western jackets, topped by the fez, emblem of the upwardly mobile.

As they proceeded across the Corniche and into town, Davis's companions—in their crew members' uniforms and turbans—kept away most of the street vendors yelling to draw attention to their wares. Everything was out for sale, from water to spices, from clothes to vegetables, and everywhere the omnipresent *antika,* antiquities large and small, some ugly, some lovely, all touted as genuine and all modern fakes. Davis never bought from street vendors.

They soon arrived at Mohassib's shop. The dealer greeted Davis effusively; he had been a valued customer since 1890, when the two had been introduced by Charles Wilbour (president of the old New York Printing Company and a regular visitor to Egypt since 1880). The sailors remained outside while Mohassib escorted Davis into the rear of the store, to a comfortable and expensively furnished sitting room.

Mohassib had sold Davis mummy masks, ancient jewelry, papyri, scarabs, and hundreds of other artifacts, frequently visiting the *Beduin* to display his latest acquisitions; other regular customers were J. P. Morgan and Lord Carnarvon. He had sold Davis the silver statuette of a woman he bought the day after Yuya's tomb had been found, and frequently gave Emma gifts to keep their relationship cordial.

After a lengthy spell of tea drinking and gossip, Davis and Mohassib turned their talk to business. Mohassib normally saved his finest items for his richest customers and held his sales with great discretion. If Mohassib sold Davis the items stolen from Tiye's tomb—he often dealt in illicit antiquities—he would have placed them on a heavy cloth for inspection. Wherever he bought them,

Davis bargained and paid for at least forty necklace pieces and a dozen gold pendants, including one carrying the cartouche of Akhenaten's god, the Aten. The items ended up on display in the Florence villa that Nettie Buttles shared with her sister Mary. True to Davis's word, no one was ever arrested for the theft.

Davis might have believed once a bead or a statue was on the market he had as much right as anyone to buy it, like the hundreds of other antiquities he collected. The fact that these came from a tomb he had discovered—where everything belonged to the government—was not his problem or obligation. If Maspero was aware of the purchase (as he likely was) he may have seen it as simply another way to provide Davis with some small keepsakes.

Davis never saw his collection as a personal treasury but more as an activity. He referred to his systematically collected trove as "the child of my mind," and bought things with an eye to assembling a sampling of all the ages and phases of ancient Egyptian art. Many of the items were displayed in custom-made cases filling the great hall in Newport; Emma mounted his scarab collection for display herself. There were occasional mistakes; a visitor told the story of "the mummy of a monkey which Mr. Davis brought home in great triumph from the Nile—almost a unique treasure." The mummy was placed in the chief cabinet in his hall until the drains of the mansion seemed to go out of order; plumbers investigated twice, but the bad smell persisted. "At last an enterprising person opened the cabinet and disturbed the slumbers of the Monkey supposed to have been undisturbed since 7000 B.C. Unwrapping him a dead cat was found in an indescribable state! Mr. Davis's theory is that American sea air is bad for mummies."[51]

Davis intended all his items—including a few fakes, such as the monkey mummy—to remain together forever in a museum (eventually decided to be the Metropolitan). Such largesse was ahead of its time. Just as his willingness to fund his digs without any guaranteed return was more generous than other sponsors' agreements, his intention to give everything away was unusual for his period. After Heinrich Schliemann found "Priam's Treasure" in Turkey, he smuggled it out of the country illegally and at one point tried to trade some of it to the United States in return for an appointment as U.S. consul in Athens. The Egypt Exploration Fund was able to raise money for excavations because donors were promised artifacts in return; the policy was greatly helpful for museums but also resulted in "minor" items going directly into individual contributors' parlors and attics. J. P. Morgan, Lord Carnarvon, Charles Wilbour, and most of the other collectors left their treasures to their heirs, who in most cases sold them to the highest bidder (in Carnarvon's case to the Metropolitan, in a sale brokered by Howard Carter that may have been as rigged as any of Davis's bond sales).

The idea that all the things found by archaeologists should go to science and museums instead of rich men's mansions was not yet accepted. Davis's posthumous gifts might have been partially a desire to create a legacy—his friends said it was because he had no children—but his impulse might also have been a genuine belief such things should be "seen and appreciated by the greatest number," as he had claimed when he declined any of the Yuya treasures. It was a concept that distinguishes Davis from his peers and set a precedent. It was another example of his contributions to archaeology that became the standard. By sending the finest things to the Metropolitan only when he died, Davis made the point that immortal masterpieces should be shared with the entire world—just as soon as he was done with them.

• • •

Philanthropy was the furthest thing from his mind as Davis and Nathaniel Wilson traveled together from Wilson's Washington home in one of his company's horsecars to the Capitol building on the chilly morning of St. Valentine's Day, 1874. The cast-iron dome of the Capitol had been completed for seven years, and no matter how often he had seen it, the dignity of the surroundings moved Davis with respect. He had no such feelings about the men he would be meeting inside.

The two conspiring lawyers climbed the steps to the entry and proceeded through the building, where its first elevator was being installed, to the House of Representatives wing. The Capitol housed the Library of Congress and the Supreme Court as well as the legislature's offices, and Frederick Law Olmsted (who had finished New York's Central Park in 1873 and in a few years would design Davis's gardens in Newport) had just been placed in charge of planning the Capitol grounds. The committee room where the congressional hearings into Davis and the Ocean Bank bankruptcy would be conducted was a dignified, wood-paneled room lit by gas fixtures and heated by steam. Seating for the committee stretched along one wall and the opposing parties and their lawyers sat at tables facing the congressmen.

Davis and Wilson took their seats and were joined by Davis's personal New York attorney, his close friend John E. Parsons. Parsons was a New York aristocrat and a partner in one of the city's biggest firms; years before he had lost most of his paternal inheritance by investing in the Averys' canal scheme in South America. At the other table William Avery and his lawyers were ready to begin; William's brother Perez had been laid low by ill health and did not attend.

Like most such meetings, most of the participants did not really want to be there. Davis had the most to lose; if his participation in the syndicate was established he faced disbarment and jail for fraud and perjury. Avery had the most to gain; even if Davis was not proven to be a crook, the committee might dictate his discharge as receiver. A more agreeable receiver would stop selling the syndicate the rest of the canal bonds and stop resisting the Averys' usury defense. The lawyers, of course, were all being paid to attend, although Avery's attorney later revealed the brothers already owed him $50,000 and he saw little chance of payment if Davis prevailed.

The high-stakes investigation would entail eight full days of testimony over the next five months. The full Committee on Banking and Currency would vote their recommendations at the end of the process. It was encouraging that the committee, like Congress, was filled with Republican friends of Davis and Wilson. The only Democrat on the committee was a businessman who had worked for the Averys. Despite the presence of the attorneys and the three subcommittee members who ran the hearings, the primary battles during the inquiry were between Davis and William Avery.

The first witness called to testify was Avery, who stated the heart of his case: "Mr. Davis, on receiving these collateral securities as receiver of the Ocean National Bank, soon formed a syndicate, the object of which was to purchase in these securities that the bank held and, by legal sale on the foreclosure of the mortgages of the canal company, to possess themselves of the property."[52] He named Dr. Ayer and Isaac Knox as Davis's coconspirators. Avery was followed by a Michigan businessman who claimed Davis had offered him a place in the syndicate. The final witness, after a long day of testimony, was the former secretary of the treasury George

S. Boutwell who testified he was never sure if Davis was "acting in good faith to the Government and the parties."

At the next session, in New York on March 4, ex–bank examiner Callender (still awaiting his bribery trial) testified that Davis had been plotting to take over the canal since 1869 and had sold the bonds "most injudiciously." A man swore he had purchased canal bonds at one sale as Davis directed and delivered them to Knox: "I did not ask who it was; I did not want to know so long as I got the money."

When Dr. Ayer testified, he condemned the lawyers who had misled him for Avery bribes and called Caleb Cushing—who had just been nominated to become chief justice of the Supreme Court—a "prostitute of the bar." He swore Davis stood to make nothing out of the deal, denied the syndicate existed, and told Avery, "I do not know anything about any syndicate . . . I have heard you tell about a syndicate, but nobody else. You have committed frauds enough for you to be sent to Sing-Sing."

Another witness was Charles L. Frost (no relation to the Michigan real estate man), who was a self-described "railroad wrecker"; by lies, bribes to reporters, and rumormongering, he would depress the value of railroad stocks, buy them, and then sell at a profit. Frost was involved with Davis's other syndicate to take railroad bonds held by the Ocean Bank, and had been involved with the Averys until a disagreement led to a fistfight with William in the middle of Wall Street. Frost called the canal company "a great fraud" and told the congressmen, "It is your duty to have these men arrested." He denied any railroad syndicate existed; when Davis asked if they had any transactions together, Frost replied, "No, you are too sharp for me." He said he owned none of the canal bonds (although he had cosigned for one series). "I would rather buy a rotten egg."

• • •

While the committee hearings were suspended, Callender's bribery
trial finally was held in New York in March. The ex-president of the
Ocean Bank testified he made loans to Callender that he would not
have made to "anyone except a bank examiner." Nine bankers testified they had made loans to their examiner that were never repaid.[53]
The clearest charge was that the examiner had only written his
positive report about the collapsing Ocean Bank after the president
had allowed him to cash $76,000 in checks drawn on banks where
Callender had no account—"a mere cloak to cover the bribe," as
Davis described it. Callender's only defense was that the entire prosecution was a "conspiracy set on foot by Theodore M. Davis." *The
New York Times* published a document showing Callender had received $400,000 in unpaid loans from banks he examined.

After two days of deliberations, however, the jury was dismissed,
hung by a vote of ten to two for conviction. The newspapers spoke
of "unpleasant rumors" that Callender had bribed his way out. The
former examiner was retried in May, and again the jury found itself
hung ten to two for conviction; one of the two not-guilty votes was
cast by a former police commissioner. Callender was never tried
again and was free to walk away with his $400,000 in unpaid loans.
He died in 1910, a respected citizen of Philadelphia.

When the hearings into the Davis receivership resumed in
New York in June, the lone Democrat on the committee was con-
veniently absent. The committee granted Davis a private session to
explain how he would produce payment for the bank from the
bonds he was selling; he apparently explained the agreement that
Ayer and Knox would pay the bank when they owned the rest of the
bonds. The committee decided Davis's secret testimony "need not
be disclosed to the creditors of the bank or their representative,"[54]

ruling the testimony would not be published. Davis then took the stand for a protracted battle with Avery.

Davis unequivocally denied forming a syndicate, denied any personal interest in the bond sales, and denied masterminding the legal proceedings. It was certainly not the first time Davis had committed perjury, but it was likely the most dramatic. The Averys had thrown everything they had at him, and he finished the hearings offering an absolute denial of any sins whatever. The audacity and energy of the lie, even today, is almost inspiring. He attacked Avery: "I swear positively that what you swore to is false," he said at one point, and referred to "a thousand schemes you laid before me that had nothing in them."

Davis was followed by Isaac Knox, who with equal vehemence denied Davis had any interest in the bonds or syndicate; he claimed he had "no partners and no understanding, directly or indirectly, with anybody." On the final day of the hearings Davis called the Averys' company "a fraud, a deceit and a swindle," and contrasted himself to the Averys: "*I* am not in the business of selling property which I do not own."

When the hearings ended, the subcommittee blamed their stenographer for not preparing the testimony in time for the full committee's review. Congress adjourned with no decision on the investigation; Davis would have to wait until the following March to learn the verdict. Whether he was worried about what the committee's findings would be is unrecorded, but he proceeded to act with a confidence about the future that implies small concern; the majority of the committee members were Republicans, after all.

Davis's personal life in New York was one of extravagance and high living. Friends recalled his "bachelor's existence" in his apartments at the upscale Barmore Hotel at Fifth Avenue and Thirty-sixth Street (a block from where J. P. Morgan would build his library in 1902). The Barmore had a restaurant, a confectionary, and an ice-cream parlor and was one of the city's most fashionable caterers. His broker, Thomas Manson, was one of a group that convened at Davis's elegant rooms every other Saturday night for poker games; players included Ocean Bank officers, his lawyer friends, ex-Comptroller Hiland Hulburd (who now lived in New York), and the mysterious Mr. Gilman. Manson recalled that Davis always adjourned the games promptly at midnight.

What other entertainments Davis enjoyed are less well documented, but some years later he likely joined Manson at the notorious midnight salons hosted by another wealthy broker named James L. Breese. At the male-only dinner parties the lascivious proceedings included waitresses in dresses made of paper, which were set on fire and then extinguished with champagne. The most infamous of these gatherings, attended by Davis's lawyer Parsons, was the "Pie Girl Dinner," where a naked sixteen-year-old girl emerged from a giant pie. The newspapers learned of the scandalous affair and described the girl as "covered only by the ceiling."

Davis's domestic life took a more restrained turn after his trip west in the summer of 1874. Stopping in Iowa City, he visited George Boal's family and made an offer the parents felt was too good to refuse; he had grown very fond of his namesake, seven-year-old Theodore Davis Boal, and he proposed the boy return with him to live in New York. His parents saw the chance as a good one for "Terry" and they agreed. Annie returned to New York as well, and Terry later described his life in Davis's household: "I was put in Charlier's Institute on 58ᵗʰ St. opposite Central Park. It was considered a very desirable school and everything was done for me that was possible. Uncle had our riding horses at the stables which later became the riding club, the stables being on 58th St. We used to ride daily in Central Park which was then the extreme northern end of New York City and quite in the country."[55]

In a letter to his aunt Sarah, Terry described "my most exceeding particular corner" in his room at the Barmore: "Aunt Annie has gotten me a bookcase and I have a beautiful nook, a deerskin hung on the wall and antlers above . . . I am going to have drawing lessons and jumping lessons at the riding school."[56] Having the boy in the house was clearly a pleasure for Davis, who wrote to Terry while away on business, "I want to see you very much, but must content myself—like many a little boy—in 'taking it out in wanting.' I shall however see you early in July when, if there is any water in the sea, I shall have the pleasure of *ducking you!* . . . Now, my dear little boy, consider yourself kissed. Keep your hands clean, and don't pick what you are pleased to call your nose!"

The separation was hard for Terry's parents; his father wrote, "I miss you greatly and continually. Do not forget me," and his mother wrote, "Oh! If only I could have you with me this one day—it is almost more than I can bear at times to have you so far away."

The Iowa relations later suspected Davis had spoiled the boy. Judge Buttles wrote to Terry, "I am afraid that your Uncle and Aunt will pet and indulge you too much for your own good. It is well for a boy to know by experience what it is to earn a dollar by the sweat of his brow," while his mother, Malvina, wrote that Davis "thinks you appreciate your advantages. Do you know what that means?"

For Christmas, Terry wrote to his aunt Julia, he received a play theater, a fishing reel, ice skates, marbles, and a knife. One of Davis's cronies gave the boy "soldiers on horseback—very nice ones." The family attended a performance of "Rip Van Winkle" and had a

box in the theater. On Christmas day they went to Grace Church—
"it was a simple sermon I could understand," he wrote. The day
after Christmas Annie took him to the park to skate, and that night
they attended the opera. Davis formed a strong attachment to
Terry; in his first will, Davis identified him as "my adopted son."

Congress was scheduled to adjourn on March 4, 1875. That morning the Davis investigation committee's majority report (signed by
five members) and the minority report (signed by three) were released. It was the closest Davis ever came to losing his battle, being disbarred, or going to prison, and marked the turning point in
the fight between the ruthless schemers on both sides to claim the
Michigan kingdom.

The majority found that Davis had acted "faithfully and hon-
estly." They absolved his bond sales of any rigging and found that
if he had a personal interest in the plot "the only persons that can
know are James C. Ayer, Isaac Knox and himself. Each swears
positively that he has no personal interest in it in any way."[57] In
other words, nobody could prove anything. The majority went on
to say they believed Davis had acted in good faith "and not for his
private interest, and would therefore recommend that he be continued as receiver." The whitewash meant Davis would stay on the
job to finish the syndicate's business. The Averys had failed in the
courts and in Congress to get the receiver fired; lies and bribes
had been defeated by the same tactics.

The minority report, irrelevant at the time, saw things differently. The bond sales had been manipulated and were a sham, "the
real sale being the secret, verbal, tripartite agreement between
the receiver, Knox and Ayer." The syndicate was "grossly illegal,"

they found, and was "a scheme to absorb and become possessed of the land grant and property of the canal company." Time would prove the accuracy of the minority's opinion, but long after any action could be taken.

Whether the verdict came as a surprise to Davis is unknown, but the lengthy period between the end of the hearings and the release of the reports suggests some conversations and transactions took place. Perez Avery had already been convicted of bribing U.S. senators; Davis had confessed to paying blackmail to cover Hulburd's bribes. In an era of rampant corruption, if the committee members were solely concerned with truth and justice they were congressional anomalies.

It took until September 1875, for the Averys to surrender. "That is the time that peace was declared," William Avery said later, "and the weapons of rebellion all laid down."[58] Hoping he could find investors in England to salvage the deal, Avery offered to pay off the syndicate. Assuming he could raise $2.25 million, Avery, Ayer, Knox, and Davis agreed how the money would be divided up. The agreement marked Nathaniel Wilson's first formal involvement in the scheme; he would take $689,000 to administer the legal loose ends and settle the costs the long battle had created and keep any money left after he had delivered a clear title to the English investors.

The deal called for the Averys to raise the money by July 1, 1877. William headed to England on borrowed money. Davis loaned him some, saying, "If the ship goes down, remember when you are going down that I got this money for you."[59] The trip ended in failure; when William Avery returned in 1876 he explained that the investors would not agree to the proposal until the title to the land was clear of the dozens of lawsuits that were still under way. While he was gone, Davis submitted a bill to the comptroller for his services to date as receiver and was approved to collect $58,520—equivalent of well over $1 million today.

Davis had yet to collect anything on the canal bonds, and with Avery's English failure it was now impossible to come up with the cash to pay off the depositors. On January 25, 1877, Davis resorted to the final alternative for meeting the bank's debts: He sent the bank's shareholders official notice they were being assessed 40 percent of the face value of stock they held and included a copy of the order of arrest that would be served on any shareholders who failed to pay within sixty days. The share owners, who had been continuously assured by Davis that they would receive some money when the closure was finished, reacted predictably and began efforts to derail the assessment.

Meanwhile, developments in the Michigan courts regarding the land were coming to a conclusion. Recognizing the concerns of Avery's English investors, in February all the contending parties consolidated their lawsuits and the court decreed the lands—now that the canal was done—would be placed for public sale (ostensibly with the proceeds to go to the bondholders). The court also ruled that the certificates Knox and Ayer had bought to provide the money to finish the canal would be accepted at the sale as cash. Title to the land, following the sale, would finally be clear.

Davis then concocted a plan the conspirators signed that called for all their bonds to be deposited with Nathaniel Wilson as trustee, and for Wilson to attend the sale and bid on the land using the syndicate's certificates. A new company would be formed, Wilson would convey title to the four hundred thousand acres to it, and stock in the new company would be issued. Avery would return to England, and if he came back with the money by July 1 it would be divided according to their earlier agreement and the stock would be turned over to the new investors; if he failed, the stock would be divided up among the conspirators in the same proportions that the cash agreement called for.

Avery headed back to England, with four months to close his deal there. While he was gone, Davis sold the bank's remaining canal bonds, fully realizing they would soon be worthless. "While this English negotiation was going on there were parties who believed that the first mortgage bonds of the canal company were going to be valuable, and they came and offered me 10, 15 or 20 cents for them and I sold all I could."[60]

The land sale took place in Houghton, Michigan, on May 11, 1877 (four days after Davis's thirty-ninth birthday). Davis and Wilson made the long trip to the sale together. Houghton, named after the explorer Jonas Titus had canoed across Lake Superior with in 1838, was a copper mining town and the largest settlement on the Keweenaw, with a population of 1,500. The sale drew a good crowd. "There were parties there prepared to bid," a Davis accomplice explained, "but it went double beyond what they expected to pay." Wilson used the syndicate's certificates to offer a bid of $792,000, and the entire four hundred thousand acres went to him. The sale can be seen as another of Davis's rigged ones; the terms the court had approved completely cut out any bondholders not in the syndicate and made it impossible for anyone else to match their bid. The losers sued in Detroit, charging the syndicate with conspiracy and the judge with collusion, but a year later the suit was thrown out.

Davis and Wilson hurried back by rail to New York, and four days later the next step in the plan was accomplished when the syndicate formed the Lake Superior Ship Canal, Railway and Iron Company (changing the name only slightly from the Averys'). Davis's role was revealed when he was voted president: "I have been a sort of father of the company," he testified later, when it was safe to do so. "I carried through actively all this litigation. I was at least the New York brains of it, and knew all about it from the beginning to the end, and in my early days I had very considerable experience in the pine woods of Michigan."[61] The board members next bought the land from trustee Wilson for $100 and issued forty thousand shares of stock.

Dr. Ayer had gone insane and been committed to Bellevue Hospital in Manhattan shortly after the congressional investigation had been completed, and his interests were now handled by his brother Frederick. Not all the participants were happy after the new company was formed. "The stockholders were extremely pessimistic as to the future of the company and whether they would ever recover their money," a company history written in 1981 records; Davis and Frederick Ayer were the "spark plugs."[62] It was estimated that the battle to win the land had cost the syndicate $2 million; if they had simply bought the land from the government at the going rate in 1866 it would have cost around $500,000.

Having little confidence in Avery's ability to close his sale in England, Davis set off to help him. The highlight of this trip to Britain for Davis was attending a private dinner at the Grosvenor Hotel in London on June 29 with former President Ulysses S. Grant, who was taking a world tour after leaving office. Davis had met Grant at least once before; as acting secretary of war in 1867 Grant had refused to honor a voucher issued by the army and held by Davis's Bank of the Metropolis. The party was also attended by the elite of London's journalists, the American ambassador, and Republican power broker Roscoe Conkling.

When Davis met Avery, it was the final time he would be disappointed by him. The deal had gone bust; Avery blamed it on the outbreak of the Turko-Russian War. Davis wired Wilson the negotiations had failed, and Wilson distributed the stock in the new Lake Superior Company when Davis got home in July.

The parceling out of the stock was clouded by the participants' need to mask what they were doing: Knox received 9,287 shares, the Ayer interests 12,608, the Averys' lawyer got 4,000 shares, and the Ocean Bank received 5,315. Wilson, in his crucial role, held 8,387 shares to settle the final details of the transaction, but no incriminating description of his disbursements was ever made. By the time of his 1895 will, however, Davis was safe to list 3,262 shares as his own (he had already given away 600 shares to Wilson's daughter, Nellie). When Wilson handed over the stock to his friend is unrecorded, but 1877 would have been far too soon in light of the charges that were still being made against the receiver. The ultimate dispersal of the stock was well concealed; only Davis, Ayer, and bagman Wilson were in a position to know, and the partners held to their secret agreement.

For the thirty-nine-year-old Davis, it marked the culmination of years of plotting, conspiring, and scheming. He was president of a company that owned four hundred thousand acres of the land he had tramped across as a youth, and a huge payday was looming. Although lawsuits and political attacks would continue for another five years over the land and the still-unfinished Ocean Bank settlement, he knew he had finally made his fortune. He would never be a financial power on the order of a Morgan or Carnegie in America, but he had reached the point that would allow him to become a true tycoon in Egypt.

News of the tycoon's discovery of the tomb of Queen Tiye hit front pages in New York and London on February 8, 1907. "American

Finds Crown of Queens of Egypt," the *New York Times* headline blared; the tomb was "Literally Full of Gold." The paper called it "another sensational discovery," and described the find as more important than even Yuya's tomb. *The Times* of London reported the mummy's head was "still encircled by an object priceless and unique—the Imperial crown of the queens of ancient Egypt." While it was still sitting above Emma's headboard, the paper described the crown "of solid gold . . . It was difficult to avoid a feeling of awe when handling this symbol of ancient sovereignty which has thus risen up, as it were, from the depths of a vanished world." Five days later a short item by Ayrton was published titled "The Tomb of Queen Thyi," and announced his work with Davis "has again been crowned with success."[63]

Maspero brought four guests to the *Beduin* for another tea and treasure session on February 11, and Emma records he "delighted Theo by saying they wanted him to have one of the canopic heads and he hoped he would choose the best one. Theo replied he would not do that but would choose the one having a stain across the head caused by dripping water." Davis was answering disingenuously; the one he picked, after the stain had been cleaned off, was clearly the finest of the four and nearly undamaged. Maspero also gave the patron six of the gold sheets from the coffin and a few other small pieces. When Lythgoe joined the flood of visitors to the boat, Davis told him as soon as he got home the jar itself would be presented to him at the Metropolitan; the exquisite head, however, remained on Davis's desk until his death.

Exhausted by the stream of distinguished gawkers who had been flooding the *Beduin* for a month, Davis finally set sail for Cairo on February 26. With the most fragile items stored below and the rest in the huge box on deck, they arrived without mishap. The treasures were cataloged and restored at the museum, where they joined Yuya's equipment in the Salle Theodore M. Davis.

Just before leaving England for home in June, Davis was interviewed and asked about the canopic head of Queen Tiye. He said he would keep it as "a memento of a very beautiful and attractive lady whom I am sorry I did not have the opportunity of meeting."[64]

During the ocean voyage home he played whist every day with author William Dana Orcutt; director of the Bank of England Gaspard Farrar; and a future U.S. ambassador to Italy, Thomas Nelson Page. Orcutt recalled that Davis was "full of enthusiastic detail concerning his great find of the tomb of Queen Tiye."[65] When they landed in New York, *The New York Times* reported that "an arriving passenger yesterday on the Cunard *Carmania* was Theodore M. Davis, the archaeologist, who brings to this country one of the oldest relics in the world. This is the alabaster statue of Queen Teie, a famous Egyptian, whose tomb Mr. Davis recently discovered."[66]

Davis had been basking in glory for a month when the first discouraging words about the find arrived from Egypt. Weigall had sent the bones from the coffin to Dr. Grafton Elliot Smith for examination. "It may be imagined my surprise was considerable," Weigall later wrote, when Smith sent him a note asking, "Are you sure the bones you sent me are those which were found in the tomb? Instead of the bones of an old woman, you have sent me those of a young man." Weigall found the physician's conclusion "somewhat disconcerting";[67] he had already sold an article to *The Century Magazine* titled "The Recent Uncovering of the Tomb of Queen Thyi" in which he had described the mummy as "the beautiful heroine of an almost fairy-like story."[68]

Davis did not accept the conclusion as quickly as Weigall (who immediately shifted his guess to the body being Akhenaten's) and resisted the sexing for some time. He fired off an angry letter to

Dr. Smith disputing his finding on August 5, and Weigall wrote to his wife, "I hear Davis is furious about Queen Thiy . . . It seems he is viciously fighting the idea of it being anybody but Thiy."[69] The argument soon became public; both Dr. Smith and Professor Sayce had letters on the topic published in *The Times* of London, and Sayce wrote to Weigall "I'm afraid you might as well try to stop an avalanche as try to stop Mr. Davis when he is bent upon doing a particular thing."[70]

Weigall wrote, rather condescendingly, in 1922 that "owing to some curious idiosyncrasy of old age, Mr. Davis entertained a most violent and obstinate objection to the suggestion that he had discovered the body of Akhenaten. He had hoped that he had found Queen Taia."[71] By 1910, when he published his volume about the tomb, Davis had surrendered and wrote, "Alas! Dr. Smith declared the sex to be male." He excused the error by the doctors in the valley, who had been "deceived by the abnormal pelvis,"[72] but he never agreed that the bones were those of the heretic pharaoh. Weigall could not resist a jibe at the American when he dedicated his 1910 biography of the pharaoh to "the discoverer of the bones of Akhenaten." Although Davis never concurred, *The New York Times* put a positive spin on the story when they published it on August 18, stating the body "is that of an even more important personage, the 'Heretic King' . . . the most curious and fascinating figure in all Egyptian history."

Like much of KV 55's legacy, the argument continues to this day. The body has over the years been identified as Tiye, Akhenaten, another king named Smenkhare and—until 1922—Tutankhamen. Although DNA testing reportedly proved the bones were male in 2010, there is no definitive test for the age of the person and many opinions, Dr. Smith's included, make the mummy a man in his mid-twenties. Sayce felt the age made it impossible for the man to be

Akhenaten; as *The New York Times* noted in 1907, it was doubtful that "even in an Oriental country is a King of only twenty-five years likely to have been succeeded by his son-in-law!"

The identity of the mummy is only one of the unsolved mysteries of KV 55. The alabaster canopic jars were found to be from different sets (the lids do not match the jars), it is by no means certain they depict the same person, and with their inscriptions erased they cannot even be proven to depict a man or a woman. They have been theorized to belong to all the proposed occupants of the coffin and also to Kiya, a minor wife of Akhenaten, and to his daughter Meritaten; the Metropolitan has variously displayed the jar Davis donated as Tiye, Akhenaten, Smenkhare, and Kiya. Perhaps the most exciting item of all—the crown of Queen Tiye—has, on reflection, been recognized not to be a crown at all but a pectoral ornament, which only landed on the mummy's head when the coffin collapsed.

The coffin trough had a journey of its own; the wood disintegrated, probably in the tomb, but the gold foil trimmings were sent to Cairo (perhaps along with Weigall's "gold bands") until they were stolen sometime between 1915 and 1931. After decades of concealment, they were secretly presented to the State Collection of Egyptian Art in Munich, Germany, by an antiquities dealer's daughter in 1980. Remounted on a Plexiglas base, their existence was revealed by the American journal *Kmt: A Modern Journal of Ancient Egypt* in 1999, and in 2003 the reconstituted trough was returned to the Egyptian Museum in Cairo, where it is today displayed next to the lid.

A few conclusions have been generally agreed to by Egyptologists: The find was the reburial of at least two different Amarnaera interments, the objects were probably moved to the valley from tombs at Akhetaten, and the tomb was reentered more than once after it had been originally sealed. Scholars universally agree, however, that the excavation was seriously botched; KV 55 will always be an archaeological "one that got away," that could have helped fill in a number of historical blanks if the clearance had been better handled. "One of the worst pieces of excavation on record in the Valley,"[73] is a typical judgment.

The greatest loss from the tomb was the irreplaceable information that was inscribed on the shrine, lost in flakes of gold that landed in peoples' hair, handkerchiefs, and pockets. Today only two charred-looking planks are displayed in the Cairo museum. Why was no map of the find (other than Emma's) ever produced? Why was no complete inventory of the objects (which included faience foundation deposits, cups, vases, statuettes, the coffin's false beard, and other items) ever compiled? Why was no measurement ever even taken of the shrine parts? And why was security at the site so lax, with the archaeologists themselves taking home souvenirs and Davis apparently handing out trinkets like party favors? The answer cannot possibly be simple indifference or incompetence by the discoverers.

The mummy crumbling like cigar ash and the other failures in the clearance cannot have been any less horrifying to the diggers, who through profession or passion had dedicated themselves to reaching just such a moment, than they seem today. Archaeology was an infant science in 1907, however, and had not developed solutions to the problems that confronted the explorers—or, if solutions did exist, they were unknown to the most skilled and experienced professionals in Egypt. "If objects in such a condition had been found in the tomb of Tutankhamen," Weigall wrote years later, "they too would have perished before means of preserving them could have been procured."[74] Davis postponed any work in the tomb until the photographs had been taken, trying to preserve it; perhaps he believed the photos would eliminate the need for a drawn chart of the chamber. He hired two painters, Joe Smith and Harold Jones, to record the treasures. Their efforts to use wax to preserve the shrine, known to be potentially disastrous, illustrate their desperation.

In the light of such an acknowledged loss, criticism of the excavators has dominated study of the tomb ever since. Davis has come in for more than his share, depicted as a bully who forced the weakling archaeologists into hasty mistakes—an odd opinion, since of all the men involved the American was the least likely to have been giving instructions (and the least likely to have been listened to by Weigall or Maspero). Davis's agreement called for any work to be managed by the antiquities service as soon as a discovery was made, and in light of his respect and liking for Maspero it is highly unlikely he would have risked their friendship by challenging the Frenchman's authority or expertise. Maspero was the supreme authority on the scene in 1907, and any faults in the work are ultimately his responsibility.

Maspero was a busy man, however, and for just that reason Weigall had been hired to serve as the site's inspector, and he relished his important role. "I supervised it on behalf of the government and officially took charge," he wrote in 1923—but with his next breath, astonishingly records, "Mr. Ayrton was in charge . . . I kept in the background, and to a great extent left the clearing of the tomb in his efficient hands."[75]

Command, therefore, devolved to twenty-four-year-old Ayrton (as Emma also stated), living on Davis's payroll, and none of the participants had anything but praise for his efforts. He unquestionably approached the task with competence and dedication. It seems the most likely explanation for any failures, therefore, is simply the technical limitations of the age and the fact that none of those present saw themselves as fully responsible for the work. All of them did what they thought they should, and when the *Beduin* left for Cairo they all felt satisfied with the job they had done. The centrality of the Amarna-era mysteries to Egyptology (and popular culture) has dictated that the excavation of KV 55 be dissected and second-guessed for more than a century, the debate now buttressed by DNA tests and CT scans. While far from perfect, the work might not have been much inferior to other clearances of the time. The continuing controversy is not necessarily an indicator of the quality of the archaeologists' work, but of the still painful lack of knowledge about ancient Egypt's most romantic episode.

For Davis, rescuing the glamorous Queen Tiye from obscurity was clearly more exhilarating than even finding the more orderly and better-stocked tomb of her parents. To have the prize snatched from him was a biting disappointment, although he had already learned how to accept disappointment (notably, in art collecting). If his enthusiasm waned as he approached his seventieth year, his determination did not. After a summer of emotional deflation (perhaps a bit mitigated by receiving the title of chevalier in the Legion of Honor from the president of France), he would return to Egypt; the valley was not yet exhausted.

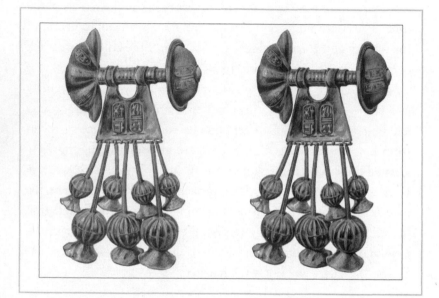

"Ceremonial Wig Ornaments" (actually, earrings), painted by E. Harold Jones on the Beduin *in 1908. From Davis,* The Tomb of Siphtah: The Monkey Tomb and the Gold Tomb.

Five

TAWOSRET'S
GOLDEN EARRINGS

Masterpieces of the ancient goldsmith's art, the identical earrings[1] are composed of two narrow tubes that fit inside each other and were passed through pierced earlobes, a hemispherical cap on one end and a convex rosette with eight petals on the other. Suspended from the tubes by two rings is a trapezoidal plaque inscribed with the cartouches of King Seti II of the Nineteenth Dynasty, and hanging from each plaque are seven pendants, four small and three large, possibly depicting pomegranates or poppy heads. The mummies of kings and queens have revealed ear piercings even larger than the pure gold tubes on these earrings, which together weigh 5.5 ounces. They likely were worn by Seti's wife, Tawosret, who served as regent for King Siptah after her husband's death; after Siptah's own mysterious death in 1190 B.C., for two years Tawosret herself was pharaoh of Egypt.

. . .

In May 1907, Davis was interviewed by *The Washington Post* regarding his plans. "I calculate that it will take two more years to complete my excavations of the tombs of the kings in Thebes," he predicted. "If the reward in the next two years is as great as in the last, I shall have no complaint."[2] In November, two days before he and Emma left for Egypt, he spoke at the National Geographic Society in Washington; despite the continuing controversy, he titled his lecture "The Discovery of the Tomb of Queen Tiye."

In Luxor they met with Edward Russell Ayrton, serving one more year beyond his contract heading Davis's excavations. Ayrton had accepted a job for the following year with the Egypt Exploration Fund, and working on his team during his last season would be a new Davis employee.

Ernest Harold Jones (always known as Harold) paused before stepping onto the gangplank to join Davis and Emma on the *Beduin*'s deck in late December, seized again by a fit of the racking cough that had bedeviled him since he was diagnosed with tuberculosis five years before. The son of the master of an art academy in Wales, Harold had inherited his father's talent and attended the Royal College of Art in London. When his doctors prescribed a warmer climate for him in 1903, Percy Newberry had found him a job painting and taking photographs for archaeologist John Garstang in the tombs at Beni Hassan. The Egyptian sun improved his health, and soon Jones was Garstang's number two man. He also painted watercolors to sell to tourists on the side. He had moved with Garstang to Esna in 1905, supervising a crew of one hundred men unearthing the ancient necropolis.

When Davis had needed another painter to copy in Siptah's

tomb he had hired Jones at Newberry's recommendation; Jones also drew "Davis's dog" in one of the animal tombs. He had become part of Davis's circle, visiting the American at Shepheard's and on the *Beduin*. He had been working with Garstang at Abydos the season before when Davis had summoned him to help record the contents of KV 55—and had spent three uncomfortable weeks in the tomb, trying to copy the sections of the shrine as they disintegrated. He spent another week living on the *Beduin* painting the canopic jars. Before he returned to Abydos, Davis had offered him a job for the next season in Luxor. Jones had been pleased to accept the higher pay and better living conditions.

His coughing fit over, Jones proceeded onto the boat and joined his hosts. He would be the prime candidate to take over the Davis digs after Ayrton departed, and it was not certain the situation for the next few months would be altogether pleasant; relations among Davis, Weigall, and Ayrton had become strained, and everyone on the site would be working behind gritted teeth. Davis told Jones his job for the coming season: Hundreds of minor items were beginning to crowd the storage space at the dig house, and Davis wanted Jones to draw them. Jones suggested an improvement Davis agreed to—a studio with large, northern-lighted windows was added to the house for Jones to work in.

By December 1907 Davis had finished exploring most of the hillsides and gullies in the valley, and the remaining area was in the central part where KV 55 had been found the season before. Ayrton had started work in November (first clearing the floor of the "lunch tomb" enough to add a third table), and began clearing the slope above the entry to the tomb of Seti I. Their first find came on December 21; as Davis described it, "I found a small pit tomb about three-hundred feet from Tiyi's tomb. It was covered with rock and sand about three feet deep. It proved to be about seven feet square and six feet deep. It was filled with white jars sealed with covers."[3]

Two years later Davis expanded his narrative a bit, adding that they had found "dried wreaths of leaves and flowers, and small bags containing a powdered substance. The cover of one of these jars had been broken, and wrapped about it was a cloth on which was inscribed the name of Touatankhamanou."[4] The cloth, translated by Maspero, recorded year six of Tutankhamen's reign and provided the first clue for Egyptologists in gauging the length of Tut's life. Apparently one of the jars—which were about three feet high with mouths eighteen inches across—was opened and revealed an interesting object, a small yellow mask of a human face similar to those found with packets of mummified organs in canopic jars. The otherwise boring jars were of no interest to the diggers and were sent to the dig house and stored.

Davis came up with a theory—now discredited—that when the time had come to move Tiye's burial from Akhetaten to the valley, a "poor man's tomb" (KV 55) had been emptied for the purpose and the jars in it had been moved out to the new discovery (later designated KV 54). The new tomb had been covered with chippings from later tomb construction that had kept it hidden. "We know that insignificance spares many people from various troubles," Davis noted.

As Ayrton continued working down the hillside, Davis's social life proceeded as usual. In addition to hosting visitors on the boat, he and Emma had dinner with Arthur Weigall in his Luxor house, meeting the inspector's new baby. The Americans dropped by Carrie Buchanan's school, and Professor Archibald Sayce arrived in Luxor, moored his *dahabiyeh* next to Davis's and came to tea.

Having found nothing noteworthy, Ayrton finished the hillside and moved the crew to the path where the animal tombs had been discovered. "We had already explored the south side of the Valley," Davis wrote, "and beginning now at the western extremity we dug along the north side of the mound of rock,"[5] near the tomb of Rameses VI. The sides of the hill extended deeper into the earth than had been expected, and voicing a now-familiar refrain, Davis wrote, "I frankly admit it seemed a waste of time and expense, but I determined to follow the rock as long as it remained perpendicular."

The uneventful digging was interrupted by a rather strange note that arrived at the *Beduin* from Sir Eldon Gorst, Britain's newly named consul general following Cromer's resignation. (Davis had met Gorst several years before; Inspector Weigall grumbled that Gorst's manners were "never gracious or engaging").[6] Gorst "had heard that [Davis's] men found a royal tomb every winter," and his note requested "as he intended to be in the Valley of the Kings in a few days, that all discoveries be postponed until his arrival."[7] What Davis thought of Gorst's request is unrecorded, but the chance to impress the new ruler of Egypt was one the American wanted to take advantage of.

In the meantime, Ayrton literally struck gold. On January 5, 1908, Davis sent a snippy note to Weigall—they were still at odds over the KV 55 bones—saying he had found a new tomb. It would be saved for Gorst's arrival. Davis asked Weigall to "exercise your rights and duties under your Inspectorship in the matter of guarding the site."

The note angered the inspector, who sent a note to Gaston Maspero complaining that Davis's amateur status hurt the antiquities service's image and asking the Frenchman to intervene. Maspero replied with a stirring defense of the American patron: "Do not call him an amateur," the director wrote. "[H]e has Ayrton with him . . . All the people who do not find a royal tomb are a little angry with Davis for finding them, but I have not seen that any of those who are hard on him have ever given us the whole of their finds, and published the account of it in such a splendid and complete way." Any critics of the service's operations will receive "my candid opinion of their sayings. It will be done with all the courtesy of which I am capable in such a case,"[8] the Frenchman concluded.

The new shaft Ayrton had discovered was near the entry to the tomb of Rameses VI, some twenty feet beneath the level of the modern path. When the diggers reached the bottom of the twenty-foot shaft they discovered the door to a tomb that, dug under the watercourse through the valley, had been flooded and filled with debris. "Doubtless the unknown man who excavated it paid no attention to the fact that it would be flooded by the subsequent rainstorms," Davis wrote. "As a matter of course we undertook to clear it, using carving knives to break up the mud" that filled the tomb; "the use of heavy implements would destroy any possible deposits." Davis and Ayrton had learned their lesson from the pilfering of KV 55. "As none of our workmen were allowed in the tomb, Mr. Ayrton did this most disagreeable work with his own hands—a task requiring skill, endurance and patience."[9] The undecorated, single chamber tomb filled nearly to the ceiling with mud did not promise a dramatic experience for Gorst.

On the morning of January 12, however, as Ayrton chipped down through the fill with his knife, he came upon a small piece of glittering gold. Davis arrived shortly after and the two had a leisurely lunch. Ayrton feared further work with the carving knife would damage whatever he had found, and after lunch he resorted to flooding the spot with water to dissolve the mud—and found two magnificent golden earrings. Suddenly excited, Davis and Ayrton flooded an area about four feet square and before sundown retrieved a cache of jewelry that gave the chamber its name—"the Gold Tomb." In the course of the afternoon, according to Davis, "among the objects was a pair of silver gloves, evidently intended for a woman with small hands. I dissolved the mud with which they were filled by soaking the gloves in water, and when I poured out the contents there came eight unique gold finger rings." The rings displayed the cartouches of King Seti II, his queen Tawosret, and Rameses II. Unwittingly, in dissolving the mud Davis might have also dissolved the hands inside the gloves.

Emma was enthusiastic when Davis came home to the boat that night. "A deposit of silver and gold objects of most unique importance and value," she wrote in her journal, "all of which Theo brought home with him." Despite the animosity brewing between them, Ayrton and the Weigalls joined Davis and Emma for dinner that night.

Clearing the tomb took the rest of the month, as Ayrton continued with knife and water to clear the mud as more jewelry emerged. The find proved to be the richest collection of golden objects ever found in the valley (until Tutankhamen) and totaled 78 ear pendants, earrings, amulets, bracelets, a head circlet, a silver sandal, rings of gold, silver and electrum (a combination of gold and silver), and 151 filigree gold beads forming a necklace, the earliest example of filigree work found in Egypt. In terms of bullion, the spectacular trove was the high point of Davis's career. In a letter to a friend, Davis described his latest triumph. "Some of the objects are the most beautiful ever found!" he crowed. "It would seem that I have more success than any other explorer, but I brave the danger of conceit by saying I find because I exhaust every spot in the valley regardless of time, expense and promise."[10]

The Gold Tomb (now KV 56) is still a mystery. Maspero guessed it was a cache moved when Tawosret's tomb was usurped in ancient times, and Ayrton suspected a robbers' collection that was never reclaimed. Opinion today holds it was probably an intact tomb destroyed by the floodwaters where a child—perhaps of Seti II and Tawosret—had been interred. Between 1998 and 2002 the tomb was reexcavated by archaeologists Nicholas Reeves and Geoffrey Martin, who found a few items Ayrton had missed. British novelist Paul Sussman was assisting them and he found a plaque of sheet gold from a necklace with Seti's cartouche on it, as well as a dog carcass and an empty pack of Ayrton's cigarettes. Reeves has theorized the tomb might have belonged to Nefertiti or Kiya.[11]

Meanwhile, Davis was preparing for Consul General Gorst. Emptied of its treasure, the Gold Tomb was distinctly dull, but Davis decided it might be exciting if the jars from KV 54—which had so far provided the small yellow face—were opened in the important visitor's presence. A new acquaintance—archaeologist Herbert Winlock, who had studied under Albert Lythgoe at Harvard and been hired by his former teacher when Lythgoe joined the Metropolitan Museum of Art—was visiting Ayrton at the time and described the scene at the dig house on January 17: "The front lawn had about a dozen gigantic white pots lying on it where the men had placed them when they brought them from the work."[12] Davis and Emma joined Gorst at the house when he arrived with his wife, his secretary, and Hortense Weigall. "It was a very pleasant lunch," Emma recorded. "I liked Sir Eldon very much—Lady G. exceedingly pretty and chic." Emma was discreet, however, in not mentioning what else happened.

Winlock had been banished from the event and had lunch

with Howard Carter at Medinet Habu, where Maspero was letting the still-unemployed Englishman live and paint in a government-owned house. "That evening I walked back over the hills to the Davis house in the Valley," Winlock recalled, "and I have still got a picture in the back of my head of what things looked like. What in the morning had been fairly neat rows of pots had been tumbled in every direction, with little bundles of natron and broken pottery all over the ground. The little mask which had been taken as a harbinger of something better to come had brought forth nothing, and poor Ayrton was a very sick and tired person after the undeserved tongue-lashing he had had all that afternoon. Sir Eldon complimented Mr. Davis on his cook."[13]

While Davis's verbal abuse of Ayrton over the ancient Egyptians' failure to fill the jars with gold is bad enough (which only Winlock records, hearsay from Ayrton), that afternoon Davis may have indulged in an even more damnable action. Among the pots had been found a half dozen floral collars made from papyrus and decorated with strings of blue faience beads. According to Winlock, who talked to Ayrton, "some were torn by Mr. Davis to show how strong they still were." The image of a frustrated Davis ripping ancient wreaths to shreds to entertain his self-invited guest has done much to damage the American's reputation ever since; the caption for a photo of one of the wreaths published in 1981 called it "one of three that escaped the attentions of Davis's after-dinner tricks."[14] The Gorsts returned to the *Beduin* for tea and viewed the Gold Tomb's bounty.

The disappointing jars from KV 54 turned out to be important. With Maspero's approval Davis gave them to Lythgoe for the Metropolitan the following year. Davis has been criticized for not appreciating the cache's importance ("they were of no intrinsic value to the treasure-hunting amateur digger"),[15] but neither did

Maspero, or the museum. They were left to languish—unexamined and unpublished—in storage in New York until 1941, when the retired Winlock inspected them and concluded they were leftovers from the embalming and burial of Tutankhamen. In the 1950s, the Metropolitan passed some of the objects on to the Oriental Institute in Chicago, the American Museum of Natural History in New York, and the Textile Museum in Washington. In 2010, however, the cache items had become interesting enough to be mounted in a special exhibition at the Metropolitan, titled "Tutankhamun's Funeral." Carter later mentioned that the embalming cache—and the blue cup Davis had found—were clues that encouraged him to look for the unfound tomb of King Tut.

The small yellow mask, which had led Davis to think the jars would provide thrilling revelations for Gorst, has its own complicated history. In 1915 Winlock told Carter the mask from the jar was covered in gold leaf and in the Cairo museum. Writing in 1941, however, Winlock stated the jar had held a painted plaster head that went to the Metropolitan when Davis died. When Carter discovered two mummified fetuses in Tutankhamen's tomb, one with a gold mask, he concluded the other gold mask had been made for the second fetus but not used because it was too small and left in the cache. In 1983 Nicholas Reeves argued persuasively that this was the case, and that the plaster face in the Metropolitan had come from one of the animal tombs in 1906. In light of the confusion at the dig house, such a slip ("cross contamination" of the two finds, in archaeological terms) can be understood.

With the Gold Tomb's riches on board, the tea and treasure sessions of the season before resumed on the *Beduin*. Despite whatever bad feelings he held, Weigall could not afford to alienate Davis since he needed to bring guests like the Duke and Duchess of Devonshire to see the gold. The duchess made it clear she wanted an invitation from Davis to have lunch at the dig house. "I don't think he will be able to escape it," Emma correctly predicted. A week later they were joined there by the duchess, who was "painted and enameled, with reddish wig, an old black hat, with painted lips," according to Emma's journal.

Davis and Weigall continued to feud; the American wanted access to KV 55 so Harold Jones could paint more of the shrine pieces left inside, and he resorted to sending Maspero a note asking him to order the inspector to loan them the keys. Nonetheless, two days later Weigall invited himself to the *Beduin* and brought along an Italian princess and Sir Ernest Cassel, financier of the Aswan dam. At the end of January Davis formalized his plans for the next season; Harold Jones wrote home happily that "Davis has asked me to take it on for 250 pounds for 3 months work."[16] There was still the specter of Jones's tuberculosis, however. A month later he wrote, "I cannot get rid of that horrid morning cough . . . I am feeling fit were it not for being short-winded."[17]

Having finished the Gold Tomb, Ayrton resumed digging down the valley. Davis left the bickering archaeologists behind (in a later note Ayrton wrote petulantly to Davis "you did not receive my theories at all kindly,")[18] and set out on a leisurely sail to Aswan. While they were there, Davis received one of the few honors ever granted to him in America; the board of the Metropolitan Museum, doubtless in recognition of Davis's signed bequest, voted him an honorary fellow. The Gold Tomb was already making headlines; *The New York Times* titled its story "Mrs. Pharaoh's Gems," and E. A. Wallis Budge of the British Museum called it "of the greatest importance, and it is a further triumph for Theodore M. Davis, the American millionaire who is backing the excavation."[19]

Starting north back to Luxor, on February 22 the *Beduin* was tied to the river bank north of Aswan due to a hard gale. They were passed by the Duke of Connaught's boat, the duke again in Egypt to inspect the army. As usual Davis's boat had been fully decked out in U.S. flags and bunting to celebrate Washington's birthday and the duke and duchess "thought it was in their honor, and did everything except fire a salute to express their appreciation of the attention."[20]

That same day in the valley, Ayrton sent a note to Weigall. "We have just found another tomb . . . Keep this information private until Davis' arrival."[21] The inspector arrived immediately and later wrote, "We were able to look down from the surrounding mounds of rubbish upon the commencement of a rectangular cutting in the rock . . . The excavators were confident that the tomb of either Tutankhamon or Horemheb lay before them."[22] The opening into the hill was similar to other Eighteenth-Dynasty tombs in the valley, and since only three of those kings' tombs had not been found, Weigall made a safe guess.

By the time Davis arrived back in Luxor on February 24 Ayrton had found a twelve-step stairway descending into the hillside, and on the twenty-sixth the group returned to the valley. "The first door of the tomb is cleared—the corridor filled with rubbish," Emma wrote. "Ayrton crawled through with great difficulty and said he could see another door quite filled up." Davis went to greater length in describing what he saw: "It was impossible to advance except by digging our way with our hands—and, as we were most anxious to find out whose tomb it was, my assistant Mr. Ayrton, in spite of the heat, undertook the difficult task of crawling over the sharp rocks and sand on his hands and feet for a distance, when to the astonishment of all of us he found on the sides of the wall a hieratic inscription containing the name of Harmhabi [Horemheb]. This was a surprise."[23]

King Horemheb, who reigned late in the fourteenth century

B.C., was of nonroyal birth and the last king of the Eighteenth Dynasty. He followed the brief reign of Ay, who had succeeded Tutankhamen on the throne. Horemheb is generally credited with returning Egypt to religious orthodoxy after the Akhenaten period and, as a former general, with restoring Egypt's military might. The discovery of his tomb did not add significantly to the historical record, but ultimately provided tremendous insight into the artistic and technical details of royal tomb construction. He had an earlier tomb in Saqqara that was well known; his presence in the valley was unexpected.

After two days of clearing rubble, on Saturday the twenty-ninth the tomb was ready to enter. According to Emma, when Davis and Harold Jones arrived and met the others, "in spite of their protestations Theo insisted on entering the tomb, and going first." He recalled, "I made my way down into the tomb with Mr. Ayrton and three others" (Weigall, Harold Jones, and a visiting official of the Egypt Exploration Fund named Max Dalison). "It was necessary to drag ourselves over the stones and sand which blocked the way, with our heads unpleasantly near the rough roof. There was little air, except that which came from the mouth of the tomb, 130 feet above, and the heat was stifling . . . We came to an open well or pit, cut vertically in the rock."[24]

The explorers crossed the well using a ladder as a bridge. In a lecture fifteen years later, Weigall recalled he was about to climb the ladder when Davis tapped him on the arm and said, "Oh, please let me go in first. I have paid $1,000 for this sensation, and I do want to have it!"[25] Davis recorded they found "the walls on three sides were covered with paintings, but the one opposite to the entrance to this pit had been partially destroyed, showing that the robbers had not been deceived by the painted wall but had broken through the concealed entrance and found their way to the funeral

chambers, ruthlessly destroying their beautiful and valuable contents."[26]

As usual, Weigall's account is more dramatic. "Wriggling and
crawling, we pushed and pulled ourselves down the sloping rubbish until, with a rattling avalanche of small stones, we arrived at
the bottom of the passage . . . The surrounding walls were seen to
be covered with wonderfully preserved paintings . . . The colours
were extremely rich, and though there was much to be seen ahead,
we stood there for some minutes, looking at them with a feeling
much akin to awe." As he had felt in other tombs with Davis, "it
was almost desecration to climb into those halls which had stood
silent for thousands of years."[27] (In fact, the tomb might not have
been so silent for so long; when reexcavating the tomb in 2010,
British archaeologist Geoffrey Martin discovered two lamp-black
graffiti on the ceiling of a side chamber dated 1887 and 1896; he
believes they are evidence of earlier, undocumented entries.)[28]

After gaping at the paintings at the well, Davis records, "we
made our way for 180 feet to the bottom of the tomb. The walls of
this corridor were adorned with paintings of the king and the
gods—many of them unfinished. At the lowest point of the tomb,
in a room about ten feet square, is a remarkable painting of Osiris
on stone—somewhat larger than life—and quite unique. The last
and largest room contained the sarcophagus of Harmhabi, made
of red granite—8 feet 11 inches in length, 3 feet 9 ½ inches wide,
and 4 feet in height—in perfect condition, and one of the most
beautiful ever found."[29] Emma summarized the condition of the
find that evening: "Walls beautifully ornamented with paintings,
wonderfully fresh, of Gods, a magnificent Sarcophagus, and figures in wood and marble—a few bones—no mummy."

Davis rested from the tomb's exertions the next day by visiting
Karnak temple and ran into the Duke of Connaught; he invited

him to tea the following afternoon. Emma found the Duke's entourage "quite an imposing array—several mounted guards arrived before them." With the duke and his wife were their daughter, a lady-in-waiting, four army officers, and Weigall. They looked at the gold and went on deck for tea.

On March 7, Davis was back at Horemheb's tomb with Harold Jones, Ayrton, and a photographer from Cairo who was to take photos before any more clearing was done. The photographic record for Horemheb is far more extensive than for previous Davis tombs; nearly one hundred shots, including pictures of the valley and other tomb sites, appeared in Davis's 1912 publication. The book fails to credit the photographer, but Egyptologists believe most of them were taken later by Harry Burton,[30] whom Emma had first met in Florence in 1903 and who came to Egypt with Davis the next season.

Horemheb's tomb (designated KV 57) was Davis's last great discovery in the valley and is significant for demonstrating the differences in tomb design between the Eighteenth and Nineteenth dynasties; it is the first in the valley to proceed into the hillside in a straight line, a pattern followed by later tombs. Conditions in the hundred-yard-long tomb were chaotic; although there had been no flooding beyond the well, movement of the hill had shattered some columns and ceilings had collapsed. The original builders had left the tomb half filled with chippings, and the objects remaining in it (including around twenty wooden statues of gods and animals) had been scattered everywhere by ancient robbers. The lid of the sarcophagus had been shattered when the robbers dumped it on the floor. Weigall noted that "vivid and well-preserved wall paintings looked down on a jumbled collection of smashed fragments of wood and bones, [and] one felt how hardly the Powers deal with the dead."[31]

The most striking aspect of Horemheb's tomb proved to be its unfinished state. It was the earliest tomb in the valley to have its artwork carved into the walls in relief, and the workmen left an almost perfect display of the stages they followed in creating the beautiful images that are KV 57's glory. In some places the walls are still unsmoothed, in others only preliminary sketches have been made on the walls, in others corrections to the sketches have been drawn in, in others preliminary carving has been started, and in others the painting is unfinished.

The next day the entire Davis group visited the tomb one last time, the American having decided to leave Luxor the following morning. Ayrton came to dinner on the *Beduin* that evening and spent the night on board, sleeping on a deck divan. Emma noted it was a "very jolly evening," but the friction between the archaeologists was putting everyone on edge.

Davis and Emma set sail for Cairo on March 9, carrying the treasures of the Gold Tomb and leaving the clearance of Horemheb to Ayrton; Jones began painting its scenes along with another painter Davis hired named Lancelot Crane. Ayrton, finishing his time with Davis, decided not to remove the tomb's rubble up the steep shaft but instead dumped much of it in the well and in unfinished rooms beyond the burial chamber. There was again theft by the workers; some of the wooden statuettes were purchased on the antiquities market by the British Museum, and one found its way to a collector in Kent, England.[32]

Davis's departure did not bring peace to the valley; in a letter accompanying his official report on the season, Weigall wrote that "Ayrton behaves as badly as he could while there . . . resenting my appearances on what he considered his own field."[33] In a letter home, the inspector wrote that Ayrton "had quite a row with me, and was awfully babyish and rude . . . I am rather glad he is leaving. He is always so frightfully on his dignity." Artist Joe Smith received a tour of the tomb from Weigall with Lady Carnarvon (one of Weigall's complaints about Davis was that he ran the excavations as a "social affair") and Smith was even blunter in a letter to his mother. "Ayrton has suddenly gone mad. I can hardly explain his babyish action otherwise—he has gone out of his way to insult Arthur . . . We think he has gone off his head really."[34]

When the *Beduin*'s treasure was deposited in the Cairo museum's Salle Theodore M. Davis some days later (Emma called it "a good riddance"), the patron noted that one of the display cases had been left half empty "against the chance that Theodore Davis may find new material in his excavations," as the new *Guide to the Cairo Museum* (1910) optimistically noted. The guide devoted thirteen pages to the *salle*. When Davis met with Maspero, the Frenchman presented Davis with another keepsake: the twenty-four-inch gold filigree necklace with twenty-six gold pendants of cornflowers from the Gold Tomb, now in the Metropolitan.[35] Before leaving for Europe the Americans were feted at a luncheon hosted by Gorst at the British Embassy, and on the twenty-first Maspero held a dinner in Davis's honor attended by the British and French officials of the antiquities service. Joe Smith also attended and noted that Davis "made an excellent speech without his usual wisecracks and tactless sayings."[36]

A memoirist in 1938 recorded a rather confused account of Davis's passage home. "One night, during a violent storm on the Mediterranean, the walking stick of an Egyptian dead these five-thousand years saved the life of an American." The story claimed Davis "would have slipped overboard but for the stout cane he carried, and which I knew he had found leaning against the wall of the tomb chamber in one of the mastabas or pyramids he had excavated. The foreman of the workers had forgotten it there. 'It was old,' remarked Mr. Davis, 'when Pharaoh's daughter found Moses in the bulrushes.' "[37]

As he traveled home through Europe, publicity continued worldwide about the Davis discoveries. A lengthy, syndicated profile of the millionaire appeared in U.S. papers, quoting Davis as saying, "The only way to find a tomb is to dig for it. Like the miner, one must take his chance of finding anything. Thus far I have been fortunate in uncovering a tomb each year; still, one might dig an entire season and find nothing to reward him for his work . . . These tombs are cut in solid rock, on hillsides, and the sands of ages have drifted firmly over them."[38]

On May 21 *The New York Times* discussed Horemheb and christened the finder "Professor Davis," who "by close observation proved himself a greater detective than even Sherlock Holmes, for he discovered indisputable evidence of the robbery of the tomb some 3,500 years ago." A month later, *Punch* made the same joke: "[T]he matter, we understand, has been placed in the hands of the local police."

Davis was back in Cairo on November 19, 1908. That morning at Shepheard's, Jones laid out a frock coat and top hat for his boss to wear (Emma was amused, knowing he disliked such formal clothes). After breakfast Davis met American Consul General Lewis M. Iddings (who, like Judge Buttles, had been born in Warren, Ohio, and been a newspaperman in New York for twenty-five years). The consul general had known Davis since his appointment in 1905— Iddings's signature was required on customs forms for antiquities exports. The two Americans took a carriage to the five-hundred-room Abdeen Palace of Khedive Abbas Hilmi Pasha (where a month before two servants diagnosed with plague had been quarantined). The lavish palace, designed by Europe's most extravagant architects and decorators, had served as the monarch's seat of authority since 1874 and included magnificent gardens on its twenty-five-acre site.

The Americans passed through the two-story surrounding walls and entered the compound. They were greeted at the palace door by elaborately costumed servants, and walked through the vast halls and marble-floored salons decorated with elaborate chandeliers, sculpted ceiling decorations, and fine paintings. They finally arrived at the audience chamber, where Davis was formally presented to the khedive for a private meeting.

Like the pretense that Egypt was still part of the Ottoman Empire, the khedive was—in theory—the hereditary monarch in a dynasty more than a century old; in reality, he was a prop mounted by the British. Their conversation was fluent (the khedive had been educated by British tutors and taught English by his governess), but predictably inconsequential. The audience with the khedive was an honor for Davis, but Iddings had been hoping to arrange such a meeting for three years. The khedive's antipathy to the British occupiers (military man Herbert Kitchener called him "that wicked little Khedive") had been greatly reduced by Gorst's appointment, and Iddings hoped to increase American influence with the throne as well. Davis attended alone; protocol did not allow the company of a mistress. Emma did join Theodore later that day for a garden party at the British embassy hosted by Gorst.

The *Beduin* set sail from Cairo for Luxor on November 22. There were still "unpromising" areas left in the valley to explore, and Davis was especially pleased to have along Nellie Wilson Knagenhjelm, the widowed daughter of his friend Nathaniel Wilson. He hoped that with Ayrton gone and Harold Jones in charge, the mood of the diggers would be less stressful. "The disturbing element has passed away," Davis wrote to Inspector Weigall. "Doubtless the sky will be brighter!"[39] Optimism was Davis's usual attitude; he had a long history of responding to changes successfully.

In the summer of 1877, the president of the Lake Superior Ship Canal, Railway and Iron Company had important tasks ahead. The company owned four hundred thousand acres of Michigan, but there was no organization in place to do anything with it. Davis traveled west that summer and while in the Upper Peninsula sold $30,000 worth of fallen timber the company now owned. He also hired a geologist to prepare a report on potential iron deposits on the land. The owners hoped to sell the property quickly and pocket their profits, but economic conditions stalled their plans—and complicated Davis's trip.

The still-depressed economy had caused the Baltimore and Ohio Railroad to cut its workers' wages twice in 1877, and on July 16 a skirmish broke out between B&O strikers and police in West Virginia. The "Great Strike" quickly spread throughout the country; militiamen shot at rail workers in Pittsburgh, the protestors set fire to engines and cars, and the resulting urban warfare claimed more than one hundred lives. The disturbances resulted in general strikes that paralyzed Chicago and St. Louis, the governor of New York declared martial law and ringed Albany with troops, and rail traffic was stopped across the country. After a crowd of twenty thousand in New York City's Tompkins Square Park (a mile from Davis's office) heard an orator claim that all the government had offered the victims of the depression was "the hangman's rope and the soldier's bullet," the police attacked the crowd and clubbed the protestors indiscriminately. The harsh response brought the

Great Strike to an end by August, but the most violent labor confrontation the country had ever experienced revealed a widespread hatred of the railroads and big business.

When the trains started running again and Davis returned to New York, he still had the Ocean Bank settlement to complete. He spent the fall preparing twenty-two lawsuits against shareholders who had not paid the assessment ordered in January; a later newspaper account recorded, "[T]he assessments were paid with much the same feelings that the belated traveler on the lonely moor surrenders his purse at the muzzle of the pistol."[40] The most publicized of the cases was against a widow named Henrietta Redfield, whose lawyer argued she should not have to pay the assessment because of fraud by receiver Davis who "was appointed in the first place by a corrupt agreement with Hiland R. Hulburd," and had conducted things "to improperly make a large sum of money for himself which really belongs to the bank . . . [He] had now become rich by his manipulation of the property in his hands."[41]

All the stockowners shared her suspicions, but Davis's battery of lawyers succeeded in making them pay; by the end of March 1878, Davis had collected $332,000 of the $400,000 in assessments and sold $1.2 million in bank assets. He was still $100,000 short of what he needed to finish paying the depositors.

Back in the Keweenaw that summer, Davis arranged for the harvest of some of the company's pine timber; as was the common practice the land was clear-cut, the endless vistas of forest discouraging any thoughts of conservation. Since a quick sale of the land appeared impossible, Davis had realized it was going to be necessary for the company to hire a local manager and had conferred with Frederick Ayer, the majority partner now that his brother had died. Davis proposed to hire George Frost, his boss of a quarter century before in the Soo canal days, but Ayer had another idea. A young landlooker named John Munro Longyear was the son of a judge who had helpfully presided over some of the company's legal battles in the past, and Ayer thought the young man might be capable.

Davis and Longyear met in Escanaba in late May 1878, and traveled to Marquette, where they discussed the company's prospects for several days. Davis assumed the twenty-eight-year-old Longyear's inexperience would eliminate him from consideration and asked the landlooker to design a system for managing the land. "I asked him what features he wanted incorporated in this system," Longyear recalled, "and he said, 'None of us know anything about it. Go ahead and see what you can do.' "[42]

When Davis returned five months later, "I had my system sufficiently perfected to show him," Longyear wrote. "He spent nearly an hour examining the books, blanks, forms, etc., saying nothing except to ask a few questions. When his examination was finished he turned around, looked at me, and exclaimed, 'Most admirable!' From that time on he became my friend." Davis hired the landlooker and signed a contract with him that Longyear put in his pocket and "immediately set off for Mrs. Frazier's boarding house to find a certain little schoolteacher and propose to her." The landlooker and the teacher married the following year and eventually had seven children together.

Longyear was soon earning his pay. The survey Davis had ordered had revealed extraordinarily promising iron deposits, but the nature of the steel industry complicated the pleasures of owning iron lands. Andrew Carnegie and John D. Rockefeller (at the time the other big steel magnate) refused to buy iron ore from outside sources, desiring to control the entire steel-making process from start to finish. Carnegie was unwilling to pay to buy the land, so the solution that fit the times was to lease the lands to Carnegie subsidiaries and negotiate a royalty fee with the mine operators, paid per ton of ore mined. Davis was approached by James J. Hagerman, president of the Milwaukee Iron Company, to lease what became the Chapin mine. Soon another lease was signed for the Norway mine.

The mining companies hired workers, began tunneling into the earth, and built railroad lines, shipping docks, and tramways. The Norway was soon shipping an unprecedented five hundred tons of ore per day, and the first full year of mining operations won Davis and his partners more than $100,000 in royalties. Within two years the New Vulcan, the Cyclops, the Curry, and the Ludington mines were operating on company property; over the life of the company's mining activities the royalties amounted to more than $50 million, equivalent to well over $1 billion today. Riches had started flowing into Davis's hands, and the spigot would never be shut off.

Meanwhile, however, the Ocean Bank still owed depositors some $64,000, and Davis suspected another assessment on the shareholders might be necessary. The shareholders were bombarding the comptroller of the currency with letters criticizing Davis for stealing their assets. The bank still held stock in the Lake Superior Ship Canal company that Nathaniel Wilson had distributed to it, per the conspirators' agreement, but there was no discernable market for the shares.

The bank shareholders joined forces with Charles Frost, the "railroad wrecker," who had now decided Davis had cheated him on the railroad and the canal syndicates and sworn vengeance. "When I take a man to my bosom and he stings me," Frost warned, "I hurl him away as a serpent, and denounce him." On February 14, 1879, the bank shareholders filed suit against Davis and Wilson alleging "divers [sic] dishonest, corrupt and fraudulent practices" that had reduced the bank's assets, kept the depositors from being paid in full, eliminated any payout for the shareholders, and forced the assessment. The suit claimed the stock Wilson had received was "for the personal use and benefit of the said Theodore M. Davis," and charged there was an agreement between them for Wilson to deliver stock to Davis "at some future time."[43] The shareholders demanded that the canal stock the bank held be transferred to them and a new receiver appointed.

No matter how accurate the charges were, however, they rested on one fatal flaw: The only evidence they could produce was a sworn statement signed by railroad wrecker Frost. In his sworn response to the suit, Davis denied being "interested in the stock which Mr. Wilson holds. To all such allegations, suggestions and insinuations I give an unqualified denial." When the case went before a judge, it was tossed out because Frost and his affidavit were deemed "not entitled to credit." The loss, and the affront to his reputation, made Frost even more enraged at Davis.

The conflicting pressures of the depositors and shareholders had now squeezed the receiver to the limit. The depositors knew the bank still held the canal company stock and, as Davis recalled, "they became indignant about it, and said the stock must be sold . . . They petitioned the Comptroller and sent delegations to Washington; they did everything they could; they made my life miserable by constant applications . . . There was nothing to do but sell the stock." By the end of March Davis had received the necessary court permission to sell the 5,315 shares in his company that the Ocean Bank owned.

The sale took place on April 30 and was another confusing and rigged Davis auction. With the comptroller of the currency watching and conferring with him, Davis offered the stock in hundred-share lots and then withdrew the offer when the wrong bidder came in high. He provided literally no information about the company; he answered one question by confirming there was a canal on the land but denied it was generating any profit, and to another he admitted there were mines on the property but denied they were leased to anyone. After more false starts and more lies, the entire lot of stock was suddenly put up for sale and was awarded to Ayer's lawyer for 20 cents on the dollar. One of the shareholders was present and later testified, "If I wanted to make property bring as little as possible I should conduct the sale as Mr. Davis did." It was too late, however; the sale had generated $120,000 for the Ocean Bank and Davis's syndicate had hung on to all the Michigan land.

On May 23 Davis paid out the money to the depositors; most had agreed to settle for their remaining balances and 30 percent of the interest they were legally due, and the total amount distributed was $117,000—another $6,000 went to Davis for running the auction. The shareholders and Charles Frost were not finished, however; on May 29 a petition was delivered to the House of Representatives Committee on Banking and Currency accusing Davis of having stolen $1 million from the shareholders, and on June 4 the House voted to hold another investigation. Once again, Davis would be subjected to a public grilling—and perhaps prison.

Davis did not allow the upcoming investigation to spoil his trip west that summer. He visited the family in Iowa City and Emma Andrews in Columbus, and spent three weeks with Longyear in the Keweenaw. Another survey had just been completed and it identified an enormous iron-bearing formation on the company's land, beginning at the western border with Wisconsin and known later as the Gogebic Range. Work was under way dredging the canal to remove sand that was beginning to block it; since the state set the canal tolls, Davis had been truthful when he said that it was operating at a loss. Two towns were being platted on company land; one was named Frederick, after Ayer, and the other Theodore. Theodore, Michigan, is located in a county named after one of the Averys' lawyers (and later postmaster general), Donald Dickinson.

Davis arrived back at the Barmore Hotel in New York on June 26, 1879. As he and Annie and Terry Boal rode home in a cab from the train station, they might have discussed the news that the khedive of Egypt had just announced he would present the city with an ancient obelisk lying on the seashore at Alexandria. It would take $100,000 donated by William Vanderbilt and two years to get the monument to New York, but as *The New York Herald* had warned, Europeans would "point the finger of scorn at us and intimate that we could never rise to any real moral grandeur until we had our obelisk." As they walked up the street to the hotel they noticed that telephone wires were beginning to join the forest of telegraph lines that almost blocked out the sun; the stock exchange had just installed its first phone. They raised their eyes to see the towering St. Patrick's Cathedral, fifteen blocks away, finally dedicated after twenty years of construction.

Davis was in no position to reflect on the progress of the city, however. The entire front page of that morning's *Sun* was filled with an article titled "The Ocean National Bank: Robbed By Its Officers, By Thieves, and By Its Receiver." The sensational piece, obviously placed with the paper by Frost and the shareholders, charged that bribed police had let the 1869 robbers escape, that the officers had stolen more than the burglars, and that "the able Receiver has finished the work begun by the bank officers." Letters from Davis to Frost were quoted to demonstrate how deeply Davis "was interested in the success of the syndicate which had been organized at his suggestion to swindle the stockholders and depositors."

Preparing for the upcoming congressional investigation, Davis did not face the same risks as he had in 1874. His company now owned the Michigan land, the depositors had been paid off, and there was little doubt the assessment had been legal. He still faced possible prosecution, however: If it were proved he had profited from the wranglings of the past eight years, then he would be indicted. The president of the Second National Bank would soon flee to Canada after being charged with criminal acts and spend nineteen years hiding in Quebec; when the president of the Marine National Bank was convicted of mishandling funds he received ten years in the penitentiary. Frost had made it clear he intended to send Davis to jail, and the biggest worry for the receiver was that, unlike 1874, the committee holding the hearings was predominantly composed of Democrats.

On Thursday, October 30, 1879, Davis and his lawyer John Parsons took a carriage downtown from their dwellings in the now fashionable northern end of New York City. As the horse's hooves clattered against the brick pavement and traveled through the crowds of pedestrians, carts, wagons, and horsecars, they passed Delmonico's—the finest restaurant in the city—at Fifth Avenue and Twenty-sixth Street; the establishment had moved steadily north over time and had been in its fourth home for three years. At the intersection at Fifth Avenue and Broadway at Twenty-third Street (where in two decades the Flatiron Building would rise) the buildings on the site advertised competing mustard plasters; the Erie Railroad building supported a huge banner advertising the FINEST TURKISH RUSSIAN HEATED BATHS in the city.

They passed under the delicate Victorian tracery of the Metropolitan Elevated Railroad station at Fourteenth Street and Sixth

Avenue, the architecture suggesting a Swiss chalet; the whimsical station belied the screeching noise, darkness, and falling cinders the elevated provided at street level. The modest R. H. Macy store on the corner would move farther north in a few years. They passed the elegant neo-Venetian building between Ninth and Tenth streets on Broadway housing E. J. Denning's store, with its cast-iron façade; it would later become Wanamaker's. They went by dry goods stores, photographic studios, auction halls, theaters, churches, and sheet-music shops. Elegant Greek Revival row houses, most still there today, surrounded Washington Square.

Their destination was the imposing Grand Central Hotel at Broadway and Bleecker Street. The hotel had opened in 1870 as the largest in America, standing eight stories high and topped by a mansard roof and a central dome. The hotel boasted 640 rooms and featured a dining room that could seat six hundred. It was one of the most elegant and expensive hotels in the city, charging $25 per day for a suite. Seven years before, Tweed Ring member Jim Fisk, who had almost cornered the gold market in 1869, had been shot to death by his mistress's jealous lover on one of its marble staircases.

Davis and Parsons passed the stores and shops on the hotel's first floor and proceeded upstairs to one of the meeting rooms, where the Committee on Banking and Currency had scheduled the first session of hearings in the Davis investigation. The lawyers were joined by the two Democrats and one Republican on the subcommittee that would conduct the hearings, and as the ten o'clock starting time arrived and then passed, the tone of farce that would mark the inquiry began. No one showed up to represent the opponents, and after waiting awhile the congressmen decided to adjourn until the following Monday. Davis, fuming, went back to his office and sent the committee chairman a letter calling the failure of his persecutors to show up "quite incomprehensible" and providing the committee members with the addresses of the shareholders so notice could be sent to them.

The enemy also failed to appear on Monday, and Davis was galled by the congressmen's decision to try again Wednesday. When the hearings finally got under way, the first witness was the chairman of the shareholders' committee, who admitted he had paid no attention to the bank's affairs until the assessment was levied but expressed certainty the problems were due to Davis's chicanery. He admitted everything he knew had come from Charles Frost, now Davis's passionate enemy, and suggested that "when rogues fall out they say that honest men get their dues, and we got some information from him." Parsons expertly skewered the witness over contradictions between Frost's 1874 testimony, when he had described Davis as honest and fair, and the affidavit the shareholders had filed.

Another shareholder was called and displayed an ill-informed understanding of what had happened, although he was certain things had been "mismanaged" by Davis. One of Ayer's lawyers next testified Davis had no financial interest in the scheme. A depositor accused Davis of dishonesty but admitted "you are apt to think bad of a man if he doesn't pay you." A shareholder accused Davis and the comptroller of collusion.

William Avery appeared the next day and gave his opinion of Davis's accuser, Frost: "He is a noisy talking, bloviating, swearing, rearing, tearing sort of a fellow ... The last time I saw him for several years I took him by the collar in the street and shook him and told him I had a good mind to lick him." It was the last time Davis and Avery saw each other; Avery moved on to Mount Clemens, Michigan, and found partners who funded construction of "Avery House," a hotel covering two square blocks that catered to patients using the natural salt baths there, reputed to cure arthritis. He also bottled and sold the water as a cure for catarrh. Dr. Ayer's old enemy ended his career as a patent medicine peddler himself.

On November 7 Frost appeared at the hearings, his testimony providing a masterpiece of unintended comedy. "Although I dealt with Davis, and although it turned out to be a robbery of the Ocean National Bank, I did not do it as a thief. I did not make that trade with Davis with the view to rob the bank, as he did," the railroad wrecker swore. He demanded the leading bankers, merchants, and real estate owners in New York be called to testify to his character. The *New York Times* account of his testimony was headlined "Mr. Frost Boils Over—Amusing the Congressmen with an Exhibition of Rage." By the end of the session, "Mr. Frost had become thoroughly warmed up, his eye glasses had dropped from his nose, and everybody was roaring with laughter." When Frost complained his papers had been stolen and he was unprepared to testify further, lawyer Parsons suggested "the gentleman don't dare to take the stand and swear to the truth of what he has said against Mr. Davis." Frost replied, "Dare? Don't dare? You dare to say I don't dare? I dare to show you I do dare! . . . I'm here to denounce that man Davis, and I do dare it, I dare!" The paper reported, "The committee and everybody else in the room were convulsed with laughter."[44]

The congressmen retreated to Washington, consulted with the rest of their committee, and decided to continue the hearings in the capitol on January 26, 1880. Davis and Parsons attended and the first witness was Nathaniel Wilson, who did a masterful job of confusing the committee. (The Supreme Court later found his answers "indefinite and unsatisfactory.")[45] He categorically denied Davis had any interest in the Michigan land, and when questioned about his division of the new company's stock revealed that 223 shares had gone to "executors of Almerin Hubbell"—without mentioning that Hubbell had been Davis's grandfather and had died in 1822. He went so far as to say rather disingenuously that if Davis "had followed my advice he would have quit the bank long ago . . . Talked about and misrepresented and abused as he was, I thought it was time for him to quit."[46]

Frost was then recalled, and denounced Davis as corrupt. After being questioned about the railroad syndicate and his belief that Davis had cheated him, he said "I am willing to go to prison if they will send Davis there." When Parsons pointed out how different Frost's 1874 testimony had been, Frost replied that the transcripts had been copied incorrectly. "Davis deceived me in every way," he raged, "and I gave that testimony with a misconception about this man Davis . . . If you want me to go to prison, I'll go with him . . . I would never have peached on Davis if he hadn't swindled me."

On January 28, Davis was called as the last witness (although the comptroller had also been accused, he was never asked to testify). Davis did a masterful job, in every case arguing in convincing detail that he had worked only to benefit the Ocean Bank and denying he had any personal interest in the canal company or the Frost railroad syndicate. At the conclusion of his testimony he asked to make a voluntary statement: "I have never bought an asset or any property of the Ocean Bank of any kind or description, and never have been interested in a deposit or an asset of any kind in any way, shape or manner from the date of my appointment." Having seen nothing could be proven against him, his denial was doubtless delivered with passionate sincerity.

As Davis traveled back to New York, he should not have had to worry. The hearings had produced no evidence against him, and the shareholders' ignorance and the absurd posturing of Frost should have made it clear there was no case to be made. After reviewing the testimony, however, the decision from the full committee—which included six Democrats, two Republicans, and one Greenback Party member—could not be guaranteed.

Otherwise, the future appeared rosy. The money was beginning to roll in from Michigan and Davis knew his fortune had been made. He began planning for his future life; on February 18 he resigned from the New York State Bar, knowing he would never need to practice law again. The work pace he had followed since 1871, "working day and night, for years," was behind him. Davis was now a capitalist businessman, and ready to enjoy the fruits of his labors.

When the congressmen came in with their report on May 19, 1880, Davis was not even in town to note it; after three months of private discussions, he was so sure of a safe outcome that he had already left for his annual trip west. As Davis and Longyear paddled a canoe down seventy miles of rivers inspecting their property, camping every night, and hauling their boat and gear across land three times, the committee report was released with the signatures of all its members—except the two Republicans. The Democrats found Davis "motivated by corrupt and improper motives and guilty of intentional wrongdoing." Davis's plan, the committee said, was to "ultimately obtain the control and ownership of the property and franchise of the canal company for himself," and cited a "gross perversion of the facts in attempting to justify his illegal action." Even the minority report by the two Republicans stated his actions had been "unwise and in violation of law."

None of it mattered. Both reports, amazingly, concluded their damning indictments by recommending that Davis be left in place to finish closing the Ocean Bank. "The estate in his hands has been nearly administered," the majority explained, "and his accounts are in a condition soon to be closed." Davis had failed to keep the issue from coming to Washington, but once it got there he had won—or likely purchased with bribes—permission to continue the corruption the congressmen had found him guilty of. The committee did helpfully suggest the shareholders file another suit.

The answer to the question the committee was supposed to illuminate in 1880—whether Davis was a crook who had robbed the Ocean Bank—is clearer after the passage of time. The receiver had succeeded in a number of tasks; he had paid off the depositors, turned the worthless Avery bonds into money, completed the canal, and carried things through the Panic of 1873. His objective, however, had not been to pay off the depositors promptly—it took eight years—or to save shippers' money and sailors' lives by building the canal. He had been entrusted, at a lucrative rate of pay, to resolve the wreck of the bank and preserve as much money as possible for the depositors and shareholders. Instead, he manipulated the situation to end up owning a company that generated more for him each year for the rest of his life than the entire pay he received for eight years' labor as receiver.

The casualties Davis left in his wake included the buyers of Avery bonds not lucky enough to be in his syndicate, who saw their investment wiped out. He gleefully sold Avery paper to the unwary up until the day he made it all worthless. The other losers were the bank shareholders. Perhaps they deserved no better; for years they had allowed criminals like Tweed, Callender, and Wilbour to plunder the bank without complaint, but they suffered a 140 percent loss on their investment after Davis's assessment. The shares in Davis's new canal company, had they been sold at an honest auction or held until their value became obvious, could have cut that loss. Certainly the shares Wilson and Davis skimmed for themselves would have made a significant difference.

Conventional wisdom in the Keweenaw forever after was that Davis and his cronies had stolen the canal, with some justification; the ruthless deceit they practiced was completely unethical and, even under the relatively lax laws of the day, fraudulent and illegal. There was no proof in 1880 of Davis's "steal" (as Frederick Ayer called it), however, due to the conspirators' steadfast and bald-faced lies about Davis's involvement. The perjuries kept him out of jail.

What will never be known is the amount Davis had to pay in bribes to ensure the syndicate's triumph. The receiver had become renowned for what were euphemistically called his "peculiar methods," and otherwise inexplicable decisions by courts and government officials from Michigan to New York to Washington permeate Davis's rise to fortune—as do accusations of payoffs, though he always escaped the charges in court. Absence of evidence, as Davis's archaeologist friends would later point out in a different context, is not evidence of absence.

Tweed had died in prison two years before, "his influence more pernicious than that of any other public man of his generation,"[47] according to *The New York Times.* Many of Tweed's partners were in exile, hiding from arrest. Former bank president Columbus Stevenson was working as a station inspector for the Third Avenue Elevated railroad. A month after the report on Davis was issued, disgraced former comptroller Hiland Hulburd died along with forty others when the boiler on the commuter steamer *Seawanhaka* exploded and sank the ship as he was headed home to Long Island. Dr. Ayer had died in an insane asylum. But although Davis's reputation had been damaged, he was rich and in the clear. With Nathaniel Wilson he had entered the wreck of the Ocean Bank and emerged with pockets overflowing.

. . .

One summer afternoon in 1881, Davis took a carriage ride with Emma to inspect the place where he had decided he would spend the rest of his life. Brenton Point, on Ocean Drive (now Ocean Avenue) in Newport, Rhode Island, is at the extreme southwestern end of Aquidneck Island, the farthest tip of Newport, and was named after the original owner who had cleared it for farming in 1639. Surrounded by water on three sides, the point overlooks the meeting of Narragansett Bay and the Atlantic Ocean, one of the most commanding and spectacular views on the East Coast. During storms, violent ocean waves crash into the seawall and shoot high into the air, cascading down onto Ocean Drive in a deluge of water and seaweed. The rocky coast provides a dramatic view and a feeling of immense privacy.

After walking up the broad incline to the top of the rise from the shore, Theo and Emma viewed the site and discussed where a house might be built and where the gardens could be located; Emma was a passionate gardener. They gazed out to sea where the waters concealed Brenton's Reef, a hazard to ships that had claimed many seafarers' lives beginning with a Spanish brig that hit the reef in 1810 and drowned its crew of ten.

After inspecting the property, Davis drove the carriage on to Castle Hill, the neighboring mansion of his friend Alexander Agassiz, president of the Calumet and Hecla copper mining company in the Upper Peninsula. (The Agassiz house is a hotel today.) Their friendship had resulted in Davis owning a good number of shares in the C&H.

Agassiz, the son of a famous Harvard professor of natural history who had debated evolution with Darwin but never saved any money, nonetheless benefited from family connections. His sister had married a wealthy Boston investor who enlisted Alexander to turn his Michigan land speculation into money, and Agassiz had established C&H as the most profitable metal mine in history after living in the wilds for two extraordinary years (his rivals blew up a dam that Agassiz had built and his wife had worn a pistol on her hip at times of labor unrest when she took their baby to the outhouse). He controlled a company that operated its company town in a relatively generous if thoroughly paternalistic way, and generated profits that were huge even for the Gilded Age.

He had built his mansion in 1874. His interests were more in oceanography than in copper mines; his first two books, *North American Acalephae* and *Embryology of the Starfish,* had been published in 1865. He had built a laboratory on his property where students from Harvard gathered every summer to learn fieldwork, research, and specimen gathering. Agassiz was now a widower who enjoyed putting on fancy dinners for his friends, his table graced by two Benvenuto Cellini candelabras.

Theo and Emma also visited another friend who had moved to Newport and just completed his mansion on Gibbs Avenue. Raphael Pumpelly was one of the fathers of American geology and, as a distinguished Harvard scientist, had received high pay from the Averys and others to explore the Upper Peninsula. He had kept his eyes open and purchased for himself a two-mile tract in the Gogebic Range (which he is credited with discovering) that ultimately produced twelve million tons of iron ore. He had also written a bestselling memoir about his youthful travels through Japan, China, and Mongolia. He had first met Davis in New York in 1867, when the Averys trotted him out to verify the value of the Michigan land; he had advised them against trying to dig their canal through the cedar swamp but been ignored. After being hired to conduct the census of mineral resources for the U.S. Geological Survey, he had headquartered the census in Newport and operated a laboratory on his grounds for classifying ores and metals from around the world.

The Newport to which Davis was moving was not yet the emblem of extravagant excess that it would become. Newport had been the fifth largest city in the pre-Revolutionary colonies but been burned by the British in 1779. In the 1840s it had reemerged as a summer resort, rivaled only by Saratoga Springs, but much of the clientele was from the South and the Civil War had caused the business to collapse. In 1860, however, August Belmont had built the first of the New York robber barons' mansions there and the town soon became the summer playground for much of the New York elite. Although Davis was never interested in the social climbing that characterized Newport's classic Gilded Age period, he was attracted, like Agassiz and Pumpelly, to the distinctly intellectual society that had developed there.

William and Henry James had grown up in Newport, as had Edith Wharton. In 1871 Julia Ward Howe (author of "The Battle Hymn of the Republic") had formed the Town and Country Club, which became a focus of Newport's intelligentsia. Visitors to the club, which met in her home, included Henry Wadsworth Longfellow, Mark Twain, Oscar Wilde, Bret Harte, Oliver Wendell Holmes, Edgar Allan Poe, and most other literary lights of the time.

In 1879 James Gordon Bennett, owner and publisher of *The New York Herald*, had built the Newport Casino, a 100,000-square-foot multipurpose pleasure palace with theaters for concerts and plays, a restaurant for fine dining, a bowling alley, a billiard room, and outdoor courts for the newly introduced game of lawn tennis. In 1881, as Davis was shopping for real estate, the first national tennis championship (now the U.S. Open) was held at the casino, where it would stay for thirty years. Matches were accompanied by an orchestra playing classical music; when pleased by a point, the ladies in the audience waved their parasols.

Davis bought the 18-acre site at Brenton Point for $20,000, with the title in his name only. To build his "cottage" (as the mansions were always called) he hired the prominent Boston architects Sturgis & Brigham, who had designed the Museum of Fine Arts building. He worked with the architects on the design for six months; not coincidentally, Emma was in New York visiting the entire time the house was being planned. The home they designed exemplified the custom of the day of wealthy Americans to ape the style of English aristocrats. The 25,000-square-foot, thirty-room mansion was a Queen Anne style, built of stone with a shingle roof. The property was surrounded by a stone wall; entry from Ocean Drive was through a stately gateway. The ground rose from the ocean front across a huge lawn to level ground where the house was constructed. Surrounded on three sides with a wide veranda, the house featured four tall chimneys, a distinctive three-story tower on the north end with a steep conical roof, and wide windows overlooking the sea.

The interior of the house was as opulent as the exterior seems whimsical. The main hall, lined with oak paneling, featured a high open beamed ceiling and a huge fireplace with an intricately carved mantel; a majestic double-wing stairway led to the second floor. Light entered the hall from every direction, either through the windows or entry doors to other parts of the house. The dining room paneling was mahogany; the room featured a vast ocean view. The drawing room was oak paneled with elaborately carved window cornices and ceiling moldings, as was the library. The library had capacity for around one thousand volumes on its shelves; when Davis died, another five hundred books were found stored in the attic.

The grounds included an L-shaped stable with room for a dozen horses and carriages and upstairs rooms for ten servants with a kitchen and dining area. Another building, known as the Bungalow, offered quarters for other servants, the laundry, and the heating plant for the house. Behind the land side of the house a regulation grass tennis court was included. The gardens became Emma's pride ("I never saw a being who could enjoy a garden as she does," Davis wrote) and were renowned as among the most extensive and beautiful in Newport—in 1897 the Society of American Florists, meeting in Providence, made a day trip to Newport to view them. Planned by Frederick Law Olmsted (designer of Central Park), they included an "open air playroom" with marble statues of fauns and satyrs from an old Venetian garden among the flowerbeds. A sunken garden and a

Architects Sturgis & Brigham's drawing of Davis's Newport mansion, the Reef, *showing the tennis court where Davis played every day. (Author's collection.)*

courtyard fronting a small Japanese tea room completed the idyllic scene.

In later years Davis bought more adjoining land and added
greenhouses, a thirty-foot-tall round tower with a four-faced clock
and chimes, and a windmill. He had fishing stands built into the
sea (across Ocean Drive) where he frequently caught prize-
winning bass and other fish. As was the custom, the estate was
given a name; in honor of the deadly hazard outside, Davis named
his home the Reef. It would be the only house Davis ever owned.

Construction began in June 1882. Still living in New York,
Davis busied himself managing the company lands in Michigan
but limited his other business activities to occasional projects that
interested him or promised a rich payoff; he declined an offer
from Collis P. Huntington, president of the Southern Pacific Railroad, to be his personal attorney. He appears to have had no special plans for the rest of his life, but the fact he could walk so
cleanly away from business sets him apart from many of his peers
and argues an acute degree of common sense.

His semiretirement allowed Davis to spend more time on developing his family life. Annie's sister Mary, who had lived with
the couple since their marriage, had died in 1880 and Davis had
added another young person to his household that year. His trips
to Columbus had usually involved visits to Emma's cousin Levi
Buttles, a professor at Kenyon College in Gambier, Ohio, who had
six children. Davis was most charmed by Levi's daughter Ellen
Mary, known in the family as Mamie. In 1879 Mamie was fifteen;
Davis, seeing that Levi's resources were limited, asked if he could
adopt the girl.

Her parents refused the offer, although Mamie recalled she
"went to her room and cried her eyes out because she thought she
would be stuck in Gambier forever and would never see the world."[48]

By the following year, however, Mamie (and likely Emma, who was also especially fond of her) had convinced her parents to agree, and the sixteen-year-old girl joined Theodore, Annie, and Terry Boal in New York. Moving to the city and the lavish lifestyle Davis offered, with new gowns, the theater, and expensive restaurants was a considerable change from small-town Ohio for Mamie. She later recalled living with Davis sharpened her wits. "Uncle" Theodore, she recalled, "trained me to answer questions directly."

Davis took Annie, Mamie, and Terry with him on a lengthy trip to Europe as the Reef neared completion in late 1882; in Venice he bought two crates of glassware, including fingerbowls, cups, and vases for the Reef. They returned in April 1883 and were in New York to see the opening the next month of the finally completed Brooklyn Bridge. The same week, work began on building the pedestal in New York Harbor that would support the Statue of Liberty.

In June Davis left New York and moved his family into the Reef; the cost for the "large, handsome cottage," according to the *Newport Mercury,* had been $50,000. Maintaining the estate required a household staff of around two dozen; in addition to the servants he had employed in New York, gardeners and stablemen were added to the maids, cooks, and menservants. Davis's butler supervised the house servants, his coachman the stables, and the head gardener the outdoor staff. He became a stockholder in the Newport Casino and was invited by Mrs. Howe to join the Town and Country Club. On August 30 the participants in the annual conference of the American Institute of Architects, meeting in Newport, were driven in carriages down Ocean Drive to inspect the Reef. Another member was added to the household soon after, when Judge Buttles died in Iowa City and Annie's sister Sarah joined them.

Based on Davis's merciless business approach and the cold reserve of the few remaining pictures of him, it would be easy to conclude he was a grim and crusty character. In fact he was an extroverted, wisecracking joker whose self-confidence invigorated his wide circle of friends. A rustic tinge added an air of eccentricity to a quintessentially American disregard for social pretense or intellectual mystification. He had a competitive nature; the Reverend Arthur Powell, who married into Emma's family and became a close friend, recalled Davis as "an aggressive, very active man in mind and body, and fond of all out of door sports . . . remarkably successful when playing at cards and other games, which was due very largely to the power of concentrating all his faculties of his mind upon the subject in hand, whether it be work or play."[49] Powell called him "kind, very determined and generous." His broker, Thomas Manson, remembered Davis as a man "who always knew exactly what he wanted . . . He saw the gist of everything; he had one of those minds that never bothered with the circumference of anything, but he went to the kernel of the nut."[50]

Reverend Powell, the doctor of divinity, called him "distinctly intellectual," and while that may be an overstatement, Davis was a man of intellect who read voraciously and remembered much of what he read; in personal letters he quoted Shakespeare and French phrases as well as popular songs. His formal education had been brief, but he had approached his self-education with the same energy he brought to making money or playing cards. He appears to have bought books to read rather than simply to collect; his personal library did include rare items like Belzoni's narrative of his Egyptian discoveries and the full twenty-one-volume *Description de l'Egypte,* produced by Napoleon's savants in 1798, but also included works on art, literary classics, poetry, and history. He owned the complete works of Charles Dickens (they had had dinner together at Delmonico's in 1868), Samuel Taylor Coleridge, George Eliot, Edward Gibbon, Washington Irving, Sir Walter Scott, Alfred Lord Tennyson, William Makepeace Thackeray, and Montaigne. Along with 191 law books, he owned one Bible.

When Davis moved from New York to Newport, his life assumed a tone of almost benign satisfaction with the pleasures it offered. He was as indulgent of others as he was of himself, curious if not especially contemplative, enthusiastic though not obsessed. He found many good things in the world, which he shared with genuine ease.

His life in semiretirement took the pattern he would follow until his death. Winters were spent abroad traveling to Europe and, later, Egypt. Summers were home at the Reef, although business and pleasure usually spurred a trip west for part of the season. His trips were always done in the highest style: private train cars, the finest first-class quarters on ships, and the best suites in the most luxurious hotels around the world. He always traveled with an entourage of family and friends, and Jones the Great handled the inconveniences of luggage and other details.

The mansion was always full of visiting friends, relatives, and business partners. William James (often called the "father of American psychology") visited in 1898 and found Davis a "sort of eccentric grand Seigneur."[51] William's novelist brother, Henry, visited with his reported lover, sculptor Hendrik Andersen (who spent several summers at the Reef) and spoke of "that far kind Mr. Davis . . . the opulent collector and charming host."[52] The American Egyptologist James Henry Breasted spent a week at the Reef at the height of its grandeur in 1903, and his description of his time there (in a letter to his mother)[53] sounds like a stay at a five-star resort hotel.

Every morning one of the "brass buttoned individuals" would

silently glide into the room, lay out the guest's shaving gear and clothes, and take away any shoes needing polish. Downstairs a huge breakfast buffet was offered on a sideboard in the dining room. The morning papers from throughout the country were available in the library, where the men read and smoked.

Then, according to Breasted, "a big red automobile full of girls comes chuff-chuffing into the garden" and everyone played tennis until an hour before lunch (Breasted neglects to mention where the girls came from). Davis himself was an avid tennis player; he wrote a friend that "I play tennis with all comers every morning . . . Every summer I have two trials or tests of my condition to undergo, first I must jump over my wall on the way to the house from the fishing stands and second, I must play my first game of tennis. If I succeed at both I am assured that old time has left me undisturbed."[54]

After the tennis players had bathed and dressed lunch was served, "of course, an elaborate affair," Breasted continued. "After an hour's smoke in the library, everybody goes for a drive, and the flunkies in top boots and white buck-skin breeches draw up the carriages at the door." Breasted counted thirteen carriages in the stables. "Mr. Davis is fond of driving himself and has a special team of beautiful bays for his own driving." After the drive it was back to the mansion to dress for dinner, always a formal event.

Davis liked horses and rode every day; he wrote a friend in 1900, "my dear saddle mare is dead lame for life; I am about sending her to a stock farm where I hope she will spend her days in motherhood and pleasure." Theodore and Emma were both animal lovers; they took their dog Toby to Egypt in 1898, and when Toby was ill in 1900 Emma summoned her own doctor to care for him. By 1901, Davis wrote to a friend that "dear old Toby" was slightly blind and deaf: "What a dreadful pity that such a dear soul should ever lose his faculties . . . He is dearer than ever, and his present attachment to me is even greater than ever, so great that it breaks my heart."[55] In Egypt in 1893 Emma adopted a stray cat she named Mish-mash; Jones the Great was assigned to bathe the new pet.

There were other amusements available in Newport; Davis always rented a box for the annual horse show, and his gardener entered the Reef's best specimens in the yearly horticultural exhibits. He was a regular at the Newport Polo Tournament (Breasted was taken to a polo game one afternoon during his stay) where players vied for the Brenton's Reef Cup. Davis took Mamie (and sometimes Annie) to the annual gala Subscription Ball at the Newport Casino, and they attended many society weddings. In 1890 Davis's neighbor T. A. Havemeyer, kingpin of the "sugar trust," brought the sport of golf to Newport when he rented forty acres at Brenton Point and built a nine-hole course; it may have been the first course in the United States, but Davis never took up the game.

After leaving New York, Davis continued to keep a close eye on operations in Michigan; it gradually became obvious that more money was to be made from the iron-mining leases than from selling the property, and eventually sixteen mines were dug into the Davis lands. By the mid-1880s another battle against the company was under way; claims to land the company had taken began to clog the courts. As railroads began connecting the wilderness areas—with rewards in acres of government land—it became their object to invalidate the claims Davis had made so his land would be available to the latecomers. The Marquette, Houghton and Ontonagon Railroad Company hired a local newspaperman and Democratic politician named Alfred P. Swineford to conduct their attack.

The railroad men decided the most productive way to get at the Davis land was to attack both the legality of the company's claims—many of which had been originally filed by the Averys with their usual scrupulous attention to detail—and to establish that the canal had not been built according to the specifications, invalidating the company's titles completely. The fight, like that of the Averys to keep the land and the Ocean Bank shareholders to get some of their money back, ended up in Washington. The House Committee on Public Lands was persuaded to investigate the situation, and the third congressional investigation of Davis's doings began on March 28, 1884. As in 1880, the committee was weighted with Democrats, but the investigation seemed doomed from the start; Davis was able to pay for a multitude of witnesses to support his case and scores of ship captains, land agents, and engineers were brought to Washington for the proceedings.

The charge the canal was inadequate was effectively refuted by the fact that nearly five hundred ships had traveled through it in 1883. The claiming process, however, was more troublesome for Davis; the Averys' acts now had to be defended, and the testimony revealed awkward incidents like the night in 1868 when, after a number of Avery claims had been voided, the land office mysteriously burned down, forcing the cancellation of the resale scheduled for the next morning. Allegations of bribery, extortion, and forgery were lodged against elected officials, land agents, and officers of the court.

Swineford committed a major error when his paper in Michigan printed an article charging the hearings had been rigged by Davis; the committee chairman, who was singled out for attack, quickly received a copy and questioned Swineford about it. Alluding to Davis's renown for paying off officials, he pointed out that in the article, "I am the 'dear friend' of Mr. Davis. Of course it would be inferred from that that I am a costly friend, and as to the peculiar methods which Mr. Davis has the reputation of adopting, I do not know what that can mean except that he is a wealthy man."[56] Swineford apologized profusely and blamed the story on his partner in Michigan. Davis, George Frost, Raphael Pumpelly, and John Longyear all testified.

The hearings dragged on until the end of April, and were a debacle for the railroad men. Longyear recalled there was a furious quarrel between Swineford and the chairman of the full committee when the hearings ended. "When he realized he had spent twenty-five thousand dollars of government money in the investigation and that none of Swineford's statements had been substantiated, he found himself in an embarrassing position."[57] When the full four-hundred-page transcript was published, considering that the company had spent at least as much as the government, Longyear noted "it was perhaps one of the most expensive documents of its size ever published."

When the committee's report was released, along with thousands of others on the last day of the congressional session on March 4, 1885, the results were predictable. The eight Democrats on the committee found that the canal had been so poorly built that it was a "fraud," and that 280,000 of Davis's acres had been illegally selected; they recommended suits be filed to recover the land. The report of the seven Republicans found the canal to have been splendidly constructed, and suggested the recommended lawsuits would be useless.

Nothing ever resulted from the investigation; the railroad men might have realized their case was weak, or that they could not match the enticements Davis was willing to offer. Swineford's prominence in Washington was enhanced, however; on May 7 he was appointed the first governor of the newly designated District of Alaska by President Grover Cleveland. By most accounts, he did a creditable job.

In 1890 Davis concluded he needed to reorganize his company legally. Michigan law placed a ten-year limit on corporate ownership of lands not actively developed by a company, and it was not clear if Davis's leasing activities satisfied the requirement. With his partners, Davis organized the Keweenaw Association, Limited, and then transferred the assets of the Lake Superior Ship Canal, Railway and Iron Company to the association, sidestepping the Michigan law's limitations. Davis continued as president, and stayed intimately involved with the company almost until his death; in 1894, while fighting another attempt to invalidate the company's land claims, a friend noted "the poor man has been having so many committee meetings of stockholders that he looked about a thousand years old."[58]

In January 1886 Davis began his last major business undertaking when James J. Hagerman, the first iron man to lease a mine from Davis, arrived in New York in a private railroad car (leased from the Pullman Company for $35 per day) from his new home in Colorado. He had just been elected president of the Colorado Midland Railway, which was intended to connect the silver mines in Aspen to the main line in Colorado Springs, and his task was to raise the money to build the line. Davis bought 2,400 shares and became heavily involved in the road and in Aspen. He became a major partner in the Aspen Mining and Smelting Company, which benefited his friends as well: In 1886 his old New York law partner, Thomas Edsall, joined the board of the company; the next year George Boal left Iowa City for Colorado to accept a five-year, $10,000-per-year contract to run the mining company's business affairs; and in 1888 the son of a friend of Davis's, a young mining engineer named Wolcott Newberry, was named the company's general manager. Davis also became a partner in the Compromise Mine, which produced $11 million worth of silver in five years.

Building the Colorado Midland was a massive undertaking; the work employed more than one thousand men to lay more than 250 miles of track and trestles in some of the most forbidding country in America and required a tunnel cut through 2,100 feet of granite in the Continental Divide using steam-powered compressed air drills and dynamite. The line reached Aspen in February 1888. That May the railway's board met in New York and, Hagerman's health having deteriorated, elected Davis president, neatly coinciding with his fiftieth birthday.

The road operated profitably, hauling silver, coal, and passengers, but the new president recognized more money was to be made by selling out to one of the rival lines in Colorado. He spent much of 1890 playing two rival bidders—the Denver & Rio Grande and the Atchison, Topeka & Santa Fe railroads—against each other. At the last minute, Davis proposed to his Midland partners a deal that required Hagerman to take his pay in stock from the Santa Fe, while Davis would be paid in cash. Davis said Hagerman could afford to make a sacrifice, and knew Hagerman would pay almost any price to thwart his hated rivals at the Denver & Rio Grande. "To be called on at the last to take any risks not shared by the others was a great wrong," Hagerman later complained. "I do not wish to be considered such a dolt as to have done it willingly,"[59] but he agreed. Davis cleared over $120,000 (well over $2 million today) on the deal. Four months later, in September 1890, Davis sold the Keweenaw canal to the federal government—after years of trying to unload the unprofitable waterway—for $350,000.

That fall he traveled west to inspect another railroad tunnel he was building in Colorado and with him were Agassiz and lawyer Frederick J. Stimson. "First we went to Wisconsin and Minnesota," Stimson recalled, "where some of the party also owned a railroad, but really, I found, to enable Davis to inspect his iron mines." The tycoons traveled in a private train, but the nature of the territory made it difficult nonetheless. "We got snowed up in the forests of northern Wisconsin," Stimson noted. "The heating apparatus went out of commission, and all we had to survive on was a barrel of canvas-back duck Fred Rhinelander had shot." Rhinelander, a partner with Davis in the Milwaukee, Lake Shore and Western Railroad, had been treasurer of the Metropolitan Museum of Art since 1871 and in 1902 would become its president.

"A great railroad war was going on in Colorado," Stimson recalled, referring to the battle over the Colorado Midland, "and another object of our trip was to try and settle that." In Colorado Springs Davis linked his train to that of David Moffat, president of the unsuccessful bidder for the Midland, the Denver & Rio Grande, and they traveled together. Past wounds were healed by the trip. "Moffat's habit was to start drinking champagne at ten in the morning, always insisting on a companion," Stimson writes. "As I was the youngest in the party, I was deputed to go on at ten. Davis spelled me at lunch, and Jo Busk went on at tea time."

An English financier and yachtsman who was Davis's partner in building the new tunnel, Joseph Busk was considerably larger than Davis. "I well remember Davis (he was a thin, nervous man)," Stimson recalled, "coming back to our car one day at five, wiping the perspiration from a wearied brow, having entertained Moffat for four mortal hours. 'Ah, Jo, it's all very well for you not to get tired,'" Davis complained. "'You chaff from fat. I chaff from brains—and there's a lot of difference!'"[60]

In addition to drinking champagne (and visiting the finest

brothel in Leadville), Davis inspected another Colorado investment. The previous year he had bought 8,232 shares in the Mollie Gibson silver mine from his partner Hagerman for 90 cents per share; now the stock had soared to $10, and when Davis sold it generated more profit than the entire cost of buying, building, and furnishing the Reef.

The Colorado ventures were Davis's last significant business undertakings; finally having as much money as he wanted, he devoted more of his time to personal affairs. The Reef was filled with people he cared for, beginning with the two young relatives he had brought with him from New York.

Terry Boal, who Davis referred to in his 1885 will as "my adopted son," had been living with Davis for seven years when they moved to Newport, and Davis enrolled the fifteen-year-old at the elite St. Paul's School in Concord, New Hampshire. John Jacob Astor IV, Cornelius Vanderbilt III, J. P. Morgan Jr., and William Randolph Hearst had all attended. Davis was disappointed with Terry, however, when the boy was asked to leave the school after his second year. Whether it was for misconduct or academic failure is unclear (Hearst had studied for nine hours every day with a tutor, but such rigor was never Terry's style). Davis then enrolled Terry for his last year before college at Phillips Exeter Academy (where Ulysses S. Grant's son had attended). It was not a success; Terry had little interest in his studies and big trouble hanging on to money. Davis wrote Terry's mother complaining about his "character," saying the boy needed to apply himself and work harder.

Things came to a breaking point in 1886 when Terry went to Boston with some friends to take the entrance examinations at

Harvard. The boys got into a fight with a cabdriver one evening (they wanted to drive) and in the ensuing scuffle a window of the cab was broken and the young men were arrested. To pay their fine, Terry pawned a gold watch Davis had recently given him. When he returned to the Reef and Davis found out, an angry argument followed that ended with Davis cutting off his relationship with the boy. He sent Terry home to Iowa City, retrieved his will, and crossed out the "adopted son" mention and reduced his bequest from $50,000 to $10,000. For the finale, Davis retrieved the watch from the pawn shop and sent it with $100 to Iowa.

The fight might have been due to simple hurt feelings about the watch, or perhaps because by bailing out the other boys Terry appeared to Davis to have been a patsy, but it marked the final step in their estrangement. Davis did not see Terry again for years, and they were never fully reconciled although Annie and Emma were both fond of the young man. For the rest of his life Terry was a disappointment to his uncle. Eventually he graduated from Iowa State University in architecture and commenced a life spending money his family gave him. He followed his parents to Colorado and formed a partnership with another architect in Denver, where he used his social connections to win jobs for the firm. Thanks to his father's prominent role in the Episcopal Church, the firm designed the St. Barnabas and St. Peter's churches there.

The financial panic of 1893 ruined Terry's firm. After seven years of estrangement, Annie and Emma prevailed and Davis invited Terry back to the Reef. With the ladies' encouragement, Davis agreed to pay for Terry to go to Paris and enroll in the École des Beaux-Arts to further his education. His time in France, however, was spent with society. In 1894 he sent a cable to the Reef announcing he had met a twenty-three-year-old French aristocrat named Mathilde Denis de Lagarde, asking for Davis's permission to marry—and for money. Such apparent irresponsibility made Davis extremely angry, but Emma argued his case and Davis sent $4,000 for the wedding.

By the time Davis met Terry's family in Paris in 1897, a baby named Pierre had been added. Davis was charmed by Mathilde, and even more by her sister Cecile (Davis always called her "Baby") but Terry's unproductive life did nothing to endear him to his uncle. "I detest being so largely dependant as I find myself for the moment," Terry complained in a letter to his mother. "This leading a six-thousand dollar a year life on my limited income will drive me not mad, but home, and at no very distant date."[61] Even Emma sniffed, "Their plans seem very vague and uncertain."

After his father died in 1898, Terry used his inheritance to buy the family home in Boalsburg, Pennsylvania, from his aunt and turned it into a mansion, adding a ballroom and servants' quarters. He opened another architectural firm in Denver and won the commission for a 24,000-square-foot mansion in Redstone for coal-mining millionaire John C. Osgood, now known as Redstone Castle. It appears unlikely he did any of the actual design; he and Mathilde spent their time at her family's plantation in Cuba, in Boalsburg, the Reef, and in Europe. In 1902 he bought a house in Washington and at an auction of White House furnishings bought a piano that had belonged to Dolley Madison and later found its way to Boalsburg. In 1904 Davis recommended Terry to Alexander Agassiz to design a clubhouse for the workers at the Calumet & Hecla mines in Michigan, but Agassiz decided the place might be used for meetings of "labor unions or things of that sort"[62] and canceled the project.

Terry's high-flying lifestyle caused his money problems to continue. He wrote to his mother in 1905 blaming his strongest advocate, Annie, for a lack of help from Theodore: "I fear my affairs with the Reef too are in bad shape just because Aunt Annie wished to do things her own way . . . There is nothing more fatal than to think you know business when you do not at all. I don't pretend to."[63] Nonetheless, he and Mathilde traveled that summer to Spain where Mathilde's aunt Victoria, widow of a direct descendant of Christopher Columbus, offered the family titles—which included High Admiral of the Ocean Seas and Governor General of Panama—to nine-year-old Pierre if he would remain in Spain. His parents declined the offer.

While in Spain, Mathilde contracted "undulant fever" (brucellosis, at the time believed to cause depression and neurosis) from drinking unpasteurized milk; her condition worsened with time. After what must have been prodigious requests from Annie, Davis loaned Terry $39,000 that year to help him shore up another undertaking called the Arapahoe Realty Company in Colorado; the firm failed.

Davis had grown very fond of eleven-year-old Pierre by 1906 and planned to send him to St. Paul's School, hoping for better luck than his father had had there, but then decided Pierre's teeth needed fixing more urgently: "The projecting tooth will disfigure him for his whole life," Davis wrote to Terry's mother. Davis had explored the case with several dentists and identified a new type of specialist, called an orthodontist, who could fix the boy's mouth in a year in Washington. "I will furnish the money to pay for his dentist work and such clothing, food, etc. as may be necessary."[64] When Pierre did enroll at St. Paul's, Davis picked up the tab.

A violent storm hit Newport in September 1906 and Davis wrote Terry "the lightening [*sic*] burned up my stable last night and came near burning my house, but did not. Horses, carriages and harness all escaped."[65] (The four sleeping stablemen also survived, saving only their nightshirts.) Since he was about to leave for Egypt, Davis asked Terry to take on the rebuilding. He wrote to another friend, "I am building a very large cement stable . . . Terry is my architect and can devote his time to the construction, consequently we have agreed on all the plans. I deposit to his credit a sum which shall cover all his expenses and shall sail away for my Egypt with a mind discharged of anxiety in respect to the work."[66]

Once again, Davis was disappointed. Terry wrote to him a few months later that the cost would be double his estimate and that the work was far behind schedule. Perhaps Davis was also irritated by Terry's closing; after asking for more money, he mentioned Tiye's tomb and cheerfully wrote, "Dear Uncle, please accept my most sincere and affectionate congratulations!"[67]

Davis's relations were more harmonious with the other young relative he brought to New York, Mamie Buttles. Mamie's common-sense sensibility, developed by her first sixteen years in small-town Ohio, was enhanced by a degree of sophistication and poise that life as a millionaire's ward inevitably added. After the household moved to the Reef, for four years she was "Cousin Theodore's" favorite—the two formed a genuine and lasting bond. She also became almost a sister to Terry, but there was no question where her loyalties lay—it was Mamie who told Davis about Terry's pawning the gold watch.

Mamie's affection for Davis was in part due to her closeness to "Cousin Emma"; the two traveled together to Europe in 1885. By 1887, Mamie was ready to begin her own life and married mining engineer Wolcott E. Newberry (no relation to the English Egyptologist), the son of another Davis friend. The wedding took place in Gambier, Ohio, and Theodore, Annie, and Emma all attended.

Uncle Theodore used his position to place Wolcott as general manager of the Aspen Mining Company. The newlyweds moved to Colorado, where they lived in "the prettiest and best arranged little house in Aspen,"[68] and were visited by George Boal and Terry and his family. In 1889 Mamie had their first child, a daughter named Doris, and in 1891 son Roger was born. The Newberrys were frequent visitors to the Reef; a dinner Davis held in Wolcott's honor in 1896 was covered by the *New-York Tribune*.

In 1897 they visited the Reef to say good-bye before Wolcott moved on to a new job developing a silver mine in Ecuador. The children stayed in Colorado Springs while Mamie traveled with her husband through the Ecuadorian interior for several months. Mamie and the children came to the Reef again in June 1898, to meet Wolcott on his return. It was immediately obvious he was extremely ill (he might have contracted malaria in Ecuador), and he died at the mansion. Mamie, now a thirty-four-year-old widow with children ages seven and nine, was confronted by a difficult situation; her family had never been as wealthy as the other Buttles, and Wolcott's father had left only a small estate. She moved to New Haven, Connecticut, where Wolcott's family had lived, and rented a suite in a boardinghouse.

Mamie never remarried, although she considered at least one proposal. She visited the Reef frequently, but apparently did not confess her money problems to Davis for several years. One afternoon, however, Davis told her he wished she would wear some new dresses because he was tired of seeing her in the clothes she was wearing, and Mamie burst into tears and explained her financial straits. Davis immediately began providing for her, although she remained in the boardinghouse. Eventually, Davis paid for Roger to graduate from Yale.

Mamie's departure from the Reef when she married in 1887

marked the moment when Theodore and Emma Andrews publicly acknowledged their relationship; Emma had been an almost
constant visitor in New York and at the Reef for years, but in 1887
she moved permanently into Davis's home. While her invalid husband, Abner, remained hospitalized in Columbus until his death a
decade later, Emma was Davis's constant companion from the
time she moved to the Reef. Theodore's estrangement from Annie
had reached the point that they were apart more often than together; Annie traveled with her sister Sarah much of the time, and
even in summers the two sisters spent vacations away from the
Reef, frequently staying with Terry in Boalsburg or Denver. Emma,
shortly after moving in with Davis, was elected vice president of
the Newport Industrial School for Girls.

For appearances' sake, as Annie wrote after Davis's death, "I
tried for all these years to cover up this situation to avoid a scandal, hoping to win back my husband, who was a very kind man,
but this woman is much deeper than I am." She called Emma "his
mistress who has lived in our house."[69] Davis, for his part, remained cordial and solicitous to the wife who bored him, always
providing her with every comfort money could buy, but the distance between them was obvious. Compared to her husband's
friends, "she was intellectually inferior," one recalled. Overawed
and restrained by the company at the Reef, she seldom partici-
pated in conversations at dinner. "[S]he did not do anything or say
anything in particular."[70]

Whether Theodore and Emma were physically intimate is, of
course, unrecorded (Emma, Theodore, and Annie all had their
own bedrooms at the Reef), but they were both healthy and physically active into their seventies. Adultery was common among
Davis's social peers—J. P. Morgan had a host of mistresses, Sen.
Roscoe Conkling had an affair with the married daughter of a

member of Lincoln's cabinet, Cmdr. Cornelius Vanderbilt had had simultaneous affairs with women's rights advocates Victoria Woodhull and her sister—and Newport's mood of vacation probably increased people's mood to stray, but Davis's circle of friends did not include notable philanderers. Agassiz lived as a lonely widower, Pumpelly's family was conventional and happy, and Frederick Ayer, Nathaniel Wilson, and John Longyear all had long, stable marriages.

Divorce was probably not even considered by Davis (although in 1881 his half-sister Kate had divorced Samuel Lewis, twenty-five years her senior, and six months later married another lawyer, Warren Atwood, who was three years younger). While extramarital sex was generally recognized as a prerogative of Davis's peers, marriage among the upper classes was still seen as a permanent commitment and divorce as a scandal. A divorced woman was an object of pity and contempt; after he visited the Marquesas Islands on an oceanographic expedition in 1899, Agassiz wrote of the queen who, "not liking her first husband, she ate him and married the great chief. Would it not be a good recipe for Newport divorcees? It would lessen the later scandal so greatly and simplify matters."[71]

Society contrived to keep the matter quiet; Emma was variously described as Davis's sister, his cousin, Annie's sister, and Annie's "companion." The blatancy of the attachment, however, could not be concealed and kept the couple from being received in some circles; painter Mary Cassatt, who came to tea on the *Beduin* in 1911, wrote that "I hear no one at Newport visits them, that woman pirate has made the wife walk the plank and brazen facedly takes her place . . . She is the *mistress* in every sense of the word."[72]

In publically acknowledging his wife's cousin as his honored partner and moving her into his house, in any case, Davis violated the mores of his time. It may have been to his advantage; while a Newport scandal in 1906 revealed J. P. Morgan had paid a black-mailer $2,500 to avoid publication of his liaisons ("Willie K." Vanderbilt had paid $25,000), Davis's blatant installation of Emma at the Reef apparently saved him from such threats. Emma's deci-sion had nothing to do with money; through her inheritances she was one of the richest women in Ohio. Emma and Theo simply decided it was better to be together than any other alternative, and it is evidence of their devotion that they chose to alienate much of society. Having agreed to pay the price of social disap-proval, the reward they bought was a luxurious and stimulating life together.

Eventually the climate in the Reef between Annie and Emma became toxic; the strain was evident even to children in 1898. Frederick Ayer's twelve-year-old daughter Beatrice, who was en-tranced by Egypt (she had stolen a mummy's toe from a tomb when her family visited) was anxious to visit the Reef that year, both to see Davis's collection of antiquities and to experience the fabled life in Newport. The Ayer children saw Davis as a bit in-timidating and eccentric; he was the only one of their father's friends who brusquely called him "Ayer." Her father finally agreed to let Beatrice and her sister go, but the morning they left he warned them at breakfast, "You should know that Mr. and Mrs. Davis have not spoken directly to one another for thirty years."

"A distant cousin named Mrs. Andrews lived with the Da-vises," Beatrice's daughter recalled being told. "When Mrs. Davis said something to the effect of 'Theodore, I would like to take the Ayer girls for a drive this afternoon, may I have the carriage?' Mrs. Andrews would answer, 'Mr. Davis, Mrs. Davis would like to have the use of the carriage this afternoon to take the young ladies for a drive.' Mr. Davis would reply, without looking up from what he was reading, 'Mrs. Andrews, please tell Mrs. Davis she is most welcome to use the carriage for the pleasure of our young guests.' And so it went."[73] Beatrice herself formed an appreciation for strong, if eccentric, personalities; in 1910 she married George S. Patton, the now-legendary general of World War II.

On the evening of July 16, 1895, Davis took his place at the head of the twenty-foot mahogany table in the Reef's mahogany-paneled dining room. The dramatic view of the ocean through the huge picture windows did not distract the diners from the fine table-ware in front of them; Davis owned three different sets of silver, and the after-dinner coffee set was engraved TMD, a gift from Emma. In the corner over the sideboard hung Giovanni Bellini's four-hundred-year-old painting, *Madonna Adoring the Sleeping Child,*[74] one of a half dozen pictures Davis had bought three months before in Europe ("a pure masterpiece" according to the Metropolitan). The dinner guests were not there to admire the painting, however; as they waited for their soup, Davis rose to make an announcement.

There were ten for dinner that night. Terry Boal had returned to America from France for his father's funeral, leaving pregnant Mathilde at home. Emma, Annie, and Sarah Buttles took their usual seats and were joined by a guest named John Proctor Jr., son of a friend of Davis's and a student at Harvard. Also in attendance were Nathaniel Wilson and his wife; the guests of honor were Wilson's daughter Nellie and Nils Knagenhjelm, the Norwegian charge d'affairs in Washington. As the servants withdrew from the room, Davis proudly took a father's role and informed the group that Nellie and Nils would be married in two months. It was not necessary for him to mention that an hour earlier he had agreed to make the wedding possible.

Davis had been especially fond of Eleanor Salome Wilson since she had let him pull out her loose front tooth the first time they met, when she was five. Although Nathaniel had turned down Davis's offer to adopt her, Nellie had been a regular visitor to the Davis home in New York and she spent most of every summer at the Reef—she and Emma had come along when Davis enrolled Terry at St. Paul's School, and she had witnessed their argument when Davis sent Terry back to Iowa. After Mamie left the Reef, Nellie "occupied all his attention," according to Annie's disapproving sister Sarah.

Nellie and her brother Charles had traveled for seven months in 1887 with "Uncle Theodore" and "Aunt Emma" to England, France, Spain, Morocco, Egypt, Constantinople, Greece, and Italy. In letters he called her "my own dear child" and his "sweetly eyed girl," and showered her with gifts including pearl earrings and a matching necklace, antique jewelry, money, gowns, and one hundred shares in the Keweenaw Association.

Nellie Wilson was an attractive woman; in 1890 *The New York Times* had printed a story about "the Washington Girl," and called her "a stylish belle . . . In looks, manner and costume she has the stylish *chic* that is supposed to belong exclusively to the French, and which therefore renders her very popular in diplomatic circles."[75] She was certainly popular with the young diplomat Knagenhjelm, who had been courting her for three years. She had brought "Knogs" (as Davis called him) to the Reef for visits and shown Davis his letters to her, and Davis had formed a strong liking for him. "He was extremely anxious for me to marry 'that nice Norwegian,'" she recalled. There had been a problem when Nils proposed, however; the diplomatic service forbade its members to marry unless they had a significant income of their own, and Nils did not.

Before dinner Davis and Nils had met privately in his office, and when they emerged Davis had told Nellie he would provide the couple with an allowance of $5,000 every year and signed over 497 shares in the Keweenaw Association to her as a wedding present. Davis's willingness to take on responsibility for her was perhaps not necessary, since her father was a wealthy man, but Nellie's reliance on Davis gave her a degree of independence from her family. In light of their close relationship, becoming financially dependant on him might not have seemed so big a step. He would fulfill the role for the rest of both their lives. "I find more satisfaction in knowing your happiness," he wrote to her, "than in anything I ever did."

The wedding took place at the Wilsons' summer house in Rockport, Massachusetts, and was performed by Rev. Arthur Powell, the husband of Emma's niece Helen. Terry and Emma joined Davis at the wedding. Annie did not; in the growing tensions at the Reef, Nellie and her family were squarely on Emma's side. Twenty years later the wedding was recalled as "an interesting event in the social history of the time, uniting the charming and accomplished young daughter of a prominent Washington family [Nellie was twenty-seven], with a young diplomat whose prospects promised a brilliant life."[76]

The following year Knagenhjelm was made secretary of the Norwegian/Swedish embassy (the two countries did not become formally independent of each other until 1905), and when their first child was born in 1897 the boy was named Nils Theodore. The next year Knagenhjelm was assigned to the embassy in Copenhagen, and it became a regular part of Davis's European agenda to visit Nellie, usually in Florence or Paris. In 1901 she and her three sons traveled with Theodore and Emma back to America for a visit, and while at the Reef Davis took Nellie to the horse show. In 1902 Nils was moved to the embassy in St. Petersburg, Russia, and Davis provided Nellie an extra $1,500 for clothes.

Tragedy was brewing, however. Nils became afflicted with "inflammation of the brain," and when his mental condition made it impossible for him to carry out his duties Davis decided the family should move to Dresden, the "German Florence," and paid to install Nils in a hospital there. Davis found Dresden "a place full of pictures and art, music and learning," and provided Nellie and her boys with a home there. "I want you to go out to see people, theatres, concerts etc.," he wrote. "You have been for years, and are now, and will be until I depart from this world the dearest human being on earth."[77] Every year, after leaving Egypt, Davis would visit her there.

Nellie came to love Dresden, and after Nils died in the asylum in 1907 she continued living there. Her three boys, ages eight, nine, and eleven, were being schooled with the German aristocracy. She spent much more time with Davis from then on, regularly traveling with him from Dresden through Europe. Davis's correspondence with her was extensive, and the largest surviving collection of his letters.

Davis's series of wills provides an overview of his personal attachments. According to his private secretary, Davis "often stated that he had made his money himself by hard work and saving, and that it gave him a great deal of pleasure to think that those he cared for would enjoy the money he had made."[78] His first, written in 1885, left the bulk of his estate to Annie but provided bequests of $100,000 to Emma and $50,000 each to Mamie and Terry (Terry's was reduced to $10,000 after their split). If Annie died first, her share went to Terry's mother, Malvina.

In 1902 Davis drastically changed the disposition of his estate, naming as executors his broker Thomas Manson and his new lawyer, John Parsons' son Herbert. He provided $100,000 in cash for both Emma and Annie, gave another five hundred shares in the Keweenaw Association to Nellie, and distributed $175,000 in other bequests. The income from his remaining estate was to be divided each year between Annie and Emma; the Reef was left to Annie for her lifetime (but the gardens and Egyptian collection went to Emma); if Annie died first, the Reef went to Emma. When both women had died, his estate was to be liquidated and divided into thirty-eight equal parts that were to be distributed to twenty-two people. He intended for Nellie to receive $100,000 for each of her three sons.

In 1906 Davis revised his plan; in the new document, Annie and Emma were granted a joint life tenancy in the Reef (although Mamie predicted Emma would never live there if Annie was present). The other major change was the result of Albert Lythgoe's move to the Metropolitan Museum; Davis decreed his entire art collection should go to the Metropolitan, although Emma could retain the Egyptian collection until her death if she wished to. His secretary recalled Davis saying "he had put all of his estate in trust, and Mrs. Davis and Mrs. Andrews were to have, each of them, half of the income for life. And that they were both old ladies and wouldn't know what to do with it afterwards . . . He said he would rather leave it to women than to men because men were better able to look after themselves."[79]

The year 1908 brought more changes to his will. Davis called for his estate, after Annie's and Emma's deaths, to be divided into forty-two parts and distributed to twenty-eight people. He added the proviso, however, that each part had to equal $50,000; if there was insufficient cash to meet that level, enough of his collection— now destined for the Metropolitan—was to be sold to make up the balance. He estimated his fortune, therefore, at between $2 and $3 million—not including the art and Egyptian collections. It is equivalent to more than $75 million today.

Travel took up half of each year after Davis moved to the Reef, and in November 1897 he and Emma set off as usual for Europe, on board the *Kaiser Wilhelm II* (known to passengers as the "Rolling Billy"). With them was Terry's younger brother, Montgomery Davis Boal, and sculptor Hendrik Andersen (who had spent the summer at the Reef). Also on board was Julia Ward Howe, who played whist with Theodore and Emma every morning ("and a very good game the delightful old lady played," Emma noted). In Naples they picked up Emma's niece Nettie Buttles (now living with her mother and sister in a villa in Florence) and proceeded on to Egypt.

Davis's archaeological work had not yet begun; their time in Egypt was spent, as Maspero described tourist life there, visiting with the foreign "scholars, idle folk and invalids. They chatter, intrigue, exchange cards, invite each other from hotel to hotel, or from boat to boat; they play tennis and bridge, plan picnics in the Valley of the Kings."[80] One topic of the chatter that season was the discovery by then-director of the antiquities service Victor Loret of the tombs of Thutmose III and Amenhotep III in the Valley of the Kings.

By April 9, 1898, the group had moved on to Rome. They dined with Mrs. Howe, who wrote in her diary, "Davis showed us his treasures gathered on the Nile shore and gave me a scarab."[81] Davis bought antiquities regularly in Egypt, but it was not yet his great passion. In 1898 he was gripped by a different desire that had been his focus for a decade—buying fine art. "Theodore is trying to get a precious picture," Emma noted cryptically on April 19, when they dined with art dealer J. P. Richter.

The compulsion of robber barons like Davis to collect art was partially a desire for standing and display; after conquering the world of business and building their mansions, owning old masters was another way to show their superiority, obtain a bit of immortality, and satisfy their natural acquisitive urges. Lewis Mumford wrote, "It had not a little of the cruder excitement of gambling in the stock market . . . They wanted an outlet for their money; collection furnished it. They wanted beauty; they could appreciate it in the past, or what was remote in space, the Orient or the Near East."[82]

It appears, beyond the more crass motives, that Davis developed a genuine appreciation for art, but the excitement of the chase to find an available masterpiece was also an outlet for his competitive nature. He strayed from the old master canon on occasion, especially enjoying works by Monet (he owned three, although his neighbor Agassiz grumbled "the only way to have them is about a mile off—then they are superb.")[83] When the Metropolitan received his collection after his death it obtained forty-nine exquisite works; the Metropolitan's memorial publication stated—notwithstanding his Egyptian treasures—that the most important part of his bequest were the paintings.

His first major purchases had been at an auction at Madison Square Garden in 1891; Davis left with paintings by Daubigny and Corot. His obsession took off, however, in 1893. In Rome that year he was talking to a Mr. Bliss—"the agent or envoy or something of the English government at the Vatican," according to Emma—who suggested getting advice from an expert before buying some paintings Davis was considering. When Davis asked where to find one, Emma wrote, "Mr. Bliss advised writing to Mr. Berenson who was then in Florence and asking him to come down to look at them, saying he probably knew as much if not more about Italian art than any man living . . . So we wrote him, and he came, and we have been going about with him and seeing for the first time with discerning eyes."

Bernhard Berenson (he would change his name to Bernard during World War I) was a Lithuanian-American art student from Boston. He had come to Italy with money from friends after graduating from Harvard in 1887. Never willing to subject himself to the banalities of earning a living, Berenson was eking out an existence guiding tourists through Florence art galleries for one lira apiece, between frenzies of study and writing. Destined to be recognized as one of the greatest art scholars of the twentieth century, when Berenson reported to Rome in 1893 he was impoverished and found himself meeting "a party of American billionaires. I saved them from spending $60,000 on four daubs not worth a hundred dollars."[84] He quickly charmed and impressed Davis and Emma, taking them through the Vatican, the Colonna Gallery, and the Villa Burghese. They met again in Florence, and at Berenson's recommendation Davis bought an early sixteenth-century Madonna by Boccaccio and another painting by Moroni.

Connecting with Davis marked a significant turn in Berenson's fortunes and career; he took commissions from the sellers and buyers of the art he recommended, played customers off against each other, and wrote his sister he hoped Davis "will trumpet my name far and wide as the only original patent back-action, double running art critic." Meeting again in London Davis bought a painting by Rembrandt's student Ferdinand Bol and Berenson wrote, "I made a lot of money out of them . . . They are likely to prove a pretty constant source of income."[85]

They did. Davis entrusted Berenson to shop for him, and the following summer he bought, through the mail, another painting that Davis wrote he was awaiting "with anxiety and pleasure . . . The blind confidence I have in your judgment and taste gives me great hope . . . If you see any very fine picture which can be bought very cheap, please advise me."[86] Unlike his hard-nosed approach to business, Davis gave way to enthusiasm in his art purchases and his trust for Berenson. When the connoisseur visited the Reef in 1894, Davis took him to the Newport Casino and the Town and Country Club and then to New York, where he installed the aesthete at the Union League Club and introduced him to his rich art-collecting friends. Perhaps most valuable for Berenson was an introduction to Henry Duveen, partner in the premier art dealership in the country; the union proved extremely profitable for both.

Every trip Davis made to Europe from then on involved Berenson, with visits to each others' homes as well as to galleries, museums, and churches. At the Reef in 1903, Davis taught Berenson a limerick (requiring an affected English accent) he frequently quoted to friends:

There once was a monk from Liberia;
Whose existence grew dreary and drearier;
So he broke from his cell,
With a hell of a yell,
And eloped with the Mother Superior.[87]

Over time the connoisseur's opinion of the millionaire changed from appreciation to condescension. At one point he called Davis "half-cultured," expecting to "ravish art at a blow," and another time, "half red Indian, half genius." Berenson's wife, Mary, had equally conflicting opinions of the American. "It is strange how much ingenuity the Creator has put into the making of bores!" she wrote to her sister. "Mr. Davis is one of the most fancy varieties I have ever met." The Berensons' income rose as the relationship continued, however; Berenson sold paintings to Davis by Bellini, Tintoretto, and many others, and the money made a difference. "It is astonishing how interesting and unboring society becomes when you have something to get out of it," Mary wrote. "I am surprised to find how interesting Mr. Davis is in his own house, when you have the patience to let him take his own rope. He is a man of power and character, who observed a great deal."[88]

It was Berenson's opinion, although not his direct participation, that triggered Davis's most thrilling acquisition in 1898. Donna Laura Minghetti was the widow of an Italian statesman who had inherited a profile portrait of a lady from an art critic friend, and in 1886 Berenson had seen it in her home and declared it a "not quite finished" work of Leonardo da Vinci. The dealer Richter had learned it was for sale ("the rumor is that she wanted to save her son from some bad business," according to Berenson), and on April 20 Emma recorded "a very exciting afternoon. Mr. Richter and Theodore went off at 3 o'clock in a closed carriage to Donna Laura Minghetti's to actually bring home in great secrecy, into our own possession, the incomparable Leonardo, to which we thought it such a privilege only a few days since, to be allowed to see. It is hard to realize that we have actually acquired it, it seems almost as if we had bought the Vatican or St. Peters! If only we can get it out of Italy without arousing suspicion!"

Owning a da Vinci was the pinnacle of Davis's collecting career, a coup that made him the envy of the art world. When Berenson learned of it, he wrote, "Davis buys in the first place for the pleasure of getting a thing cheap, and then for glory. He got this Leonardo for 3,000 pounds [$15,000 at the time, equivalent to $300,000 today and since then he has been swaggering it about."[89]

After successfully smuggling the picture out of Italy, Davis took it to Paris. "Theodore has had a great success with his Leonardo," Emma wrote on May 4. "[S]he [the picture] was invited to the Louvre." Experts compared the picture to other Leonardos approvingly. It was shown at the Burlington Fine Arts Club in London, and Berenson listed it in a journal titled *The Golden Urn* as "Leonardo. Portrait of a Girl." Davis spent his sixtieth birthday in a mood of triumph.

Back at the Reef, according to a friend of Berenson's, "Davis seems to be quite mad with joy about the Leonardo . . . He is bursting with pride." A few other connoisseurs had voiced skepticism about the picture, however, and Berenson replied that "Davis has gone stark mad . . . He is but half a civilized man. As for his Leonardo, I fear I am the only person entitled to have an opinion who sincerely believes in its genuineness."[90]

Within a year it became clear, even to Berenson, that the painting was a forgery. Berenson had to reverse his opinion (his wife had been skeptical from the beginning, believing if it had been genuine it should have cost thirty times what Davis paid for it). In December 1899 Berenson admitted his mistake to his customer. "He has taken it like a brick," Berenson wrote, "simply, sensibly and gracefully. I really do not know what can make one happier than when a friend behaves rather better than one expected. If he only knew how he has risen in my esteem. I simply love to be able to approve of people."[91] The episode seriously damaged the critic's reputation; at his request Davis wrote a letter published in *The Nation* absolving the connoisseur of any involvement.

His disappointment over the fake Leonardo was keen. Among

all his paintings it was the only one he did not leave to the Metropolitan; he gave it to Nettie and Mary Buttles. Although he continued to buy art (notably, a Goya in 1902 and a Rembrandt in 1905), the Leonardo failure was a very public embarrassment; eventually, fictionalized versions of the story using transparent names for the participants were published. The revelation of having been fooled took much of the joy out of the art hunt for Davis. Having grasped an ultimate prize and then lost it, he never again took such pleasure in a purchase—nor did he ever again trust Berenson so blindly. He began to hunger for a new channel for his energy and his money.

In the early 1890s, after a bout with pneumonia, Davis was advised by his doctors to spend future winters in a warm climate, and the advice was in line with his whims. He had first visited Egypt in 1887, after Agassiz had visited and suggested it; Charles Wilbour (the ex-president of the New York Printing Company and now a summer resident in nearby Little Compton, Rhode Island) had spent every winter there since 1880 and also recommended it. Davis's first trip, with Emma and Nellie, took him no farther than Cairo, but it made a lasting impression. The romantic charm of the exotic country was attractive to growing numbers of Westerners. "The land of the Mysterious River, the magic country of one's longing dreams," a typical visitor wrote; "of Pharaoh and pyramid and sphinx, of desert and of camel . . . perplexing tokens from when the world was young."[92]

Davis returned in December 1889, with Emma—who began her journal of their visits that year—and Mary Buttles. They rented a *dahabiyeh* from one of the khedive's family (Emma got the largest bedroom), raised the Stars and Stripes from the flagpole and set sail south. They stopped in Dendera, Luxor, and Aswan, where Emma was struck by the beauty of Philae temple's paintings: "such lovely greenish blue, such delicate red pinks and tender greens . . . worn by time to such soft brilliancy." Their future plans were not yet set. "The thought rose again and again," Emma wrote in Aswan, "will I ever see this again?"

On the way north they tied up in Luxor on January 29, 1890, and met Wilbour, who introduced Davis to the antiquities dealer Mohammad Mohassib. Davis bought two mummy masks[93] and papyrus pieces from a *Book of the Dead* (stolen from their tomb days before) when the dealer visited the boat, but when Davis dropped in at Mohassib's shop and was offered a mummy cloth supposedly from the mummy of Queen Tiye his dragoman advised against it. "He keeps an eagle eye on us to see that we are not cheated," Emma wrote, "and when he says quietly 'You don't want that, Governor,' Theodore will not buy."

On February 2, Davis visited the Valley of the Kings for the first time. The Americans were overwhelmed by the timeless atmosphere of the valley's silent, unearthly gullies and hillsides, and intrigued by the occasional gaping holes in the landscape where the ancient kings had dug their tombs. They were also appalled by the condition of the tombs and the widespread looting taking place. "It is against all law," Emma wrote. "The government allows no digging or excavations—but they seem powerless to prevent it . . . They have not the money to undertake thorough and intelligent excavations themselves. I feel in a rage about it when I think of it . . . Valuable things are destroyed and injured by hasty and forbidden search." They decried the crime, but Davis had not yet decided to do anything about it.

According to Agassiz's son, Davis's "first interest in the land of the Pharaohs was excited by a little book by Mr. Martin Brimmer, lent him by Agassiz."[94] Brimmer was a Boston Brahmin and the first president of the Museum of Fine Arts, from 1876 until his death twenty years later. His book, *Egypt: Three Essays on the History, Religion and Art of Ancient Egypt* (published in 1892), presents an informed digest of Western thought on the subject as Davis began his own studies. "The essential elements of Egyptian life and thought have been laid open," Brimmer believed. "The manly virtues were wanting in the early Egyptians, just as they are wanting in the Egyptians of today"; the lack of invasions ("substitution of a superior to an inferior race") had stunted the society's development. Present-day Egyptians were similarly crippled by "the Mahometan religion, which has at least this resemblance with the ancient religion, that it is crystallized and fixed in forms and dogmas immovable, incapable of progress, and admitting no independent thought within its domain." Brimmer seems to have preferred the ancient Greeks.

Having concluded the ancient Egyptian was a mindless drone ("his mind was not, like ours, informed by the traditions and discussions of all the centuries"), Brimmer and others of the period focused their attention on the kings and priests "holding all the resources of knowledge, commanding all the resources of religion, constituting an aristocracy which rested on birth." Readers—and scholars—of the period paid attention only to the "best" of Egyptian art. Brimmer was as fascinated by the romance of the period as most tourists. "It comes down to us from the earliest ages with perfected grandeur, expressive of a great idea which we vainly seek to grasp in its completeness," he concluded, "without known origin, without filiation, strong, grave, solitary and inscrutable."[95]

Whatever effect Brimmer's book had on his thinking, Davis set off for Egypt again in late 1892. Annie made what would be her only trip to Egypt, joining Theo and Emma as well as Nettie Buttles, Jones the Great, and a dozen trunks and suitcases. As they sailed south in another rented *dahabiyeh,* Davis read Matthew Petrie's *Ten Years Digging in Egypt* and other books by the Egyptologists E. A. Wallis Budge and Auguste Mariette, a significant step up from Brimmer. In Aswan in January 1893 they tied up next to Wilbour's boat and were introduced to Professor Sayce for the first time. Sayce may have planted more seeds in Davis's mind; in his preface to Schliemann's book on Troy in 1882, Sayce had wondered why other rich men did not "spare for science a little of the wealth that is now lavished upon the breeding of racers or the maintenance of a dog kennel?"[96]

Nettie found a Hathor-headed sistrum (a musical instrument used in temple ceremonies) and a Greco-Roman oil lamp on the ground on Elephantine Island. Emma was disappointed ("at least Theodore and I were") when an accident damaged the boat and forced them to cancel travel farther south; she sniffed that Annie was relieved for she had "cherished, I am sure, many secret dreads and fears of dangers and dervishes." They took a train to visit Kalabsha temple and the Temple of Dendur (now rebuilt in the Metropolitan Museum) and then boarded a steamer for their first visit to Abu Simbel. Back in Aswan, "Mr. Wilbour came over and made us a long visit this evening," Emma noted. "The talk was all of Egypt and Egyptian things." Apparently there was no mention of William Tweed or the New York Printing Company.

Theodore, Emma, and Nettie returned in late 1894. In a letter to Nellie Wilson, Davis mentioned that their *dahabiyeh* had "a new and very good piano and Nettie has her usual Nile voice." He summarizes their activities: "We are happy on this wonderful Nile, with its warm, certain and hospitable sun and mild sweet airs. We eat, drink, sleep, read, study, write, talk and sing! Our minds and bodies are taking a winter off from the cares, anxieties and frets which the gradual furnace of the World consumes us with."[97]

Egypt had won Davis's heart, and he and Emma began discussing building their own boat for annual visits. He commissioned the construction of a luxurious *dahabiyeh* before he left the country, and he and Emma planned its details and finishes. He wrote to newlywed Nellie Knagenhjelm from the Reef in April 1896 that "the more I contemplate spending the next few winters in Egypt the better I feel and the wiser I hold my conclusion. Emma is doing a great deal of work in the matter of furnishing the dahabiyeh and its internal fittings; I am quite sure it will be turned out in a most charming fashion. We are having carpets and rugs made for it, spring beds, silk curtains for doors and windows, etc."[98]

When they arrived at Shepheard's again on December 9, 1896, "we had a great disappointment," Emma records. "Our boat was a month behind time—painters and carpenters still at work—the boom not raised, and general helplessness." Davis went after the contractor "with such well-directed effort and so much energetic talking that the foreman is scared out of his life and the workmen are jumping about like monkeys." The *Beduin* was completed a month later. Emma watched the eighty-foot-long *dahabiyeh* approach down the Nile from the terrace at Shepheard's on January 11, 1897: "stately, tall and shapely . . . Several people gathered on the terrace to see her go by—and I heard her pronounced 'the handsomest craft on the river.'" The *Beduin* proved to be "a rattling good sailor"; Davis beat the best and largest tour boat on the river in an impromptu race south of Luxor.

Their annual visits to Egypt followed the same pleasant pattern in coming years: "the usual things—races, visits to ruins, etc.," as Emma put it. Lunches and dinners with guests on boats or in hotels, games of cards and chess, enjoying the scenery and exploring excavation sites filled their days. "I can never weary of this— night or day," Emma wrote. "Each hour has its own charm, and I do not want to leave."

As they sailed down the river, Theo and Emma visited every significant ancient site. In Tel el-Amarna in 1895 they saw the beautiful painted pavement of Akhenaten's palace, which Petrie and Carter had found four years before (the archaeologists had painstakingly conserved the masterpiece and built a roof over it; twenty years later local farmers, fed up with tourists trampling their crops on the way to the site, hacked the floor to pieces in one night). When their boat was tied up at Beni Hassan and a dispute arose with the locals over *baksheesh* (tips or bribes expected by the Egyptians), "Theodore put some cartridges in his pocket," Emma wrote, "and took his gun and sat down in a conspicuous position with it on the upper deck." Davis's gun was used more often for bird-hunting excursions with Jones and male guests.

Theo and Emma wined and dined the archaeologists up and down the Nile, finding them interesting and helpful. Dinner guests in February 1899 were the two young British archaeologists Percy Newberry and Howard Carter. Their conversation led to friendships and eventually resulted in the night in January 1901 when Newberry brought on board the small bronze bowl he had found in the forecourt of Rekhmire's tomb chapel. The vacationing millionaire became the explorer who discovered the tombs of Thutmose IV, Hatshepsut, Yuya, KV 55, the Gold Tomb, Horemheb, and a dozen others.

On December 21, 1908, Emma noted in her journal that "the days are so quiet and monotonous there is little to chronicle." Harold

Jones, Davis's new excavator, had started digging in November where they had stopped the season before, at the tomb of Horemheb, and as the trench moved past KV 35 and KV 12 only minor finds emerged: bits of broken glass, a piece of a *shabti,* and a few beads. On January 10, 1909, however, Jones made his greatest discovery. He came upon a vertical shaft dug into the rock floor of the valley and sent for Davis and Inspector Weigall; Davis spent the afternoon there, and at the end of the day Weigall and artist Joe Smith slept in front of the new discovery to guard it. They sent Harold Jones back to the dig house; his health seemed too precarious to risk sleeping outdoors.

As the crew began clearing the shaft the next day, Jones noted that they found "very interesting fragments of furniture all thrown about in the debris and of an interesting period—the end of the 18th dynasty, the objects bearing cartouches of Pharaoh Aye and of another called Tut-Ankh-Amon, the latter of whom has not yet been discovered or his tomb."[99] Davis wrote, "At the depth of 25 feet we found a room filled almost to the top with dried mud, showing that water had entered it."[100] The tedious, painstaking work of clearing out the fill began with some promise; Emma noted after two days of work they had found "bits of gold foil, stamped with the cartouches of Thut-ankh-amen, Ai and S-ankh-aten, wife of T.A.A."

The tomb took ten days to clear and proved to be a single, undecorated chamber. The primary finds were some twenty pieces of gold foil; Joe Smith recalled "that evening Jones and I straightened out the crumpled gold sheets, and in the process discovered the names of two kings, together with pictures of one of them in his war chariot shooting enemies with bow and arrow, a very spirited scene."[101] Davis, Maspero, and Nellie Knagenhjelm visited the valley site on January 20 and Jones recorded finding an "alabaster statuette in male costume (feet broken, otherwise intact)."[102] Emma was especially charmed by the statuette, writing on the twenty-first that "Harold found yesterday in the last corner of the pit tomb a most lovely alabaster statuette of a woman—about 9 in. high, the most perfect specimen of Egyptian art I have ever seen, and in perfect condition. To think of her lying under that hard mud for nearly 3000 years!" (The uninscribed statuette is a *shabti* of a man.) In Davis's publication, Egyptologist Georges Daressy guessed it depicted king Ay before his elevation to the throne, when he succeeded Tutankhamen; both their names were on the gold foil.

The tomb—designated KV 58—remains a mystery. Scholars have concluded the gold foil was from one or more chariots originally placed in Ay's tomb (already known, in the West Valley) and that KV 58 was dug in association with Horemheb's tomb. When Ay's mummy was later relocated to a cache in Horemheb's tomb, the chariot and its foil followed. Another theory makes KV 58 the tomb of Ay's son.[103]

Davis had a different idea, however. He concluded that the jars in KV 54 and the blue cup with Tutankhamen's name on it had all been removed from KV 58, and that they were all that remained of the burial. Harold Jones, Davis decided, had discovered the tomb of Tutankhamen. Davis's guess was not an unreasonable one; the list of kings who should be in the valley had been whittled down to two, Tutankhamen and Thutmose II (whose tomb has still not been positively identified to this day, though there are several candidates). Maspero and the other experts all agreed with the American—except for Howard Carter.

Ironically, at the same time Davis was claiming to have found King Tut, Carter was joining forces with the patron who would help prove the American wrong. He wrote a friend on January 16,

"I have just been offered an enormous fee by Lord Carnarvon to undertake a month's excavation . . . I have accepted and shall try to do my best."[104] For Carter it was a heaven-sent opportunity; after years of scraping by selling his paintings, guiding tourists, and accepting charity from friends, he was again going to excavate—at a salary of £400 per year. Carnarvon's agreement to hire "a learned man" to conduct his digs was greatly influenced by Davis's example—and caused Davis's public obscurity after 1922.

After clearing KV 58, Jones moved the digging crew on, extending the trench beneath the shed which sheltered donkeys rented to valley tourists. He found little but fragments deemed unimportant. By February 19 he was attacking a steep mound of sand and chippings that took up the rest of the season. The work stopped on March 7 with no finds recorded, and the Davis party moved on to Europe.

Twelve-year-old Pierre Boal spent the summer of 1909 at the Reef when Davis returned while his parents were in Spain fighting a legal battle over Mathilde's inheritance from her aunt—a chapel from the Columbus castle that was eventually disassembled, moved to Boalsburg, and erected inside a building Terry designed. Terry sent Davis a letter in July thanking his uncle for another loan—"in a few months my affairs will be in shape," he promised—and explained their legal fight against Mathilde's father was "on account of his hatred for his son-in-law."[105] Mamie Newberry and her daughter, Doris, also spent the summer in Newport, joining Davis in his box at the horse show.

Davis's book *The Tomb of Siphtah* appeared that summer. One review raved that "Exquisite is probably the only adjective which will even faintly convey the artistic charm pervading this production."[106] The Gold Tomb's influence on Egyptomania was cited in a syndicated newspaper account: "the present craze for jewelry fashioned after old Egyptian pieces is likely to receive a fillip from the discoveries of the American explorer, Theodore Davis."[107]

It was around this time that Davis's passion for horses began to be supplanted by a love of automobiles. In 1910 he bought one of the most luxurious cars of the time, a Packard Model 30 limousine with white leather upholstery, natural wood trim, and brass fixtures; the car had an open compartment for the chauffeur and a top speed of fifty miles per hour. He also parked in the rebuilt stables two Pierce-Arrows, a Brougham, and a touring car. Davis's Packard cost as much as eight of the new Model T Fords, which had just come on the market.

At age seventy-one, Davis was beginning to show signs of slowing down. He stopped writing letters in 1909, due to failing eyesight. On September 21, however, he visited his old friend and lawyer John Parsons, now retired, at his home in Lennox, Massachusetts, and delivered a lecture on his Egyptian finds. He gave the same talk at the Miantonomi Club in Newport: "[T]he finds have been of much greater interest than many that have been made by other explorers,"[108] the *Newport Mercury* noted. When he visited Berenson at his Italian villa in 1910 after several years of separation, Berenson wrote that before seeing Davis he "was afraid of the ravages of time on his aging face. But he looked scarcely a day older, and was full of his usual jokes and quips."[109] The connoisseur had written to his wife, however, that "One could only wish he would die. He refuses to be pleased with anything."[110]

The 1909–10 season in Egypt was even less exciting than the previous year, although Davis's party was joined on the way by a photographer Emma had met years before in Florence named Henry "Harry" Burton, whom Davis paid to photograph Horemheb's tomb. Harold Jones began excavating in November near the animal tombs and found nothing of interest except an unfinished, fourteen-inch-high stele dated to the Nineteenth or Twentieth dynasties, depicting Amenhotep I; Maspero gave it to Davis, and the Metropolitan judged it "accomplished but rather lifeless."[111]

On January 6, 1910, hopes rose briefly when Jones came across a shaft that led to a doorway on the left side of the path leading to the tomb of Thutmose III. The fill in the shaft appeared to be undisturbed and the doorway was sealed to the top with stones, but after two days of clearing Jones peered through the door and saw only a "small, ill-hewn chamber half filled with debris." He cleared the chamber until "every corner of the tomb was bare, and bare were the results—for never even a potsherd was found." The tomb—which might have been sealed in anticipation of a burial that never took place—was designated KV 61. It was the last tomb found in the valley until 1922 and the last Davis discovered. It was the eighteenth the American had revealed—a record that made him the most successful explorer the valley had ever seen (he had also paid for clearing a dozen more). Digging stopped on January 26, but the *Beduin* stayed moored in Luxor as Jones and Burton continued to work recording Horemheb.

Tension with Davis was taking the fun out of things for Jones— "He is old and I might say almost stupid at times through his stubborn arrogance," Jones wrote home, but the archaeologist had more serious concerns—his own health. "I really don't feel up to the work and don't know what I shall do next year," Jones wrote. "I don't feel up to taking it on again—if I live so long."[112]

When ex-president Theodore Roosevelt visited the valley on March 22, however, Jones took him through the tombs of

Hatshepsut and Horemheb before Roosevelt lunched with Davis at the dig house; in Cairo later that month, the two Theodores toured the museum together. In a joking thank-you to Inspector Weigall, Roosevelt wrote, "If you see your fellow savage, Theodorum Daviz, give him my love. I think particularly good is the fact that the unfortunate Mr. Jones is believed to be preparing a tomb for Mr. J.P. Morgan, with my approval."[113] Davis and Emma were also visited in Luxor by Alexander Agassiz. It was the last time they saw each other; Agassiz died on board his ship home.

The 1910 season marked the symbolic end of the Davis excavations in the valley. His diggers returned and worked at full strength at other locations, but Davis and Maspero recognized that they had accomplished what they had set out to do. The entire system of wadis, paths, and dry waterways that was the Valley of the Kings had been exposed to bedrock. Davis dated his (probably most quoted) comment—"I fear that the Valley of the Tombs is now exhausted"[114]—in 1912, but in early 1910 everyone agreed there was nothing left to find.

Arthur Weigall tapped out the smoldering embers from his ever-present pipe and tucked it into his pocket before crossing the familiar *Beduin* gangplank in March 1910. It had been eight years since he had begun spending evenings on Davis's boat. The day he and Davis had gaped through a hole in a wall at Yuya's treasures seemed long ago.

Weigall appeared nervous much of the time now. He was a man of energy, of action, of creativity and tremendous enthusiasm—but ambition caused him great problems. Much of his anxiety had to do with a plot he was hatching, a backdoor attempt to advance his career by ousting Maspero, but Weigall's reason to be nervous at the moment was Davis and how he would react to plans for the next season.

While Maspero and Weigall had concurred on what they felt was the only logical way to proceed, the inspector was worried that old Davis might not want to cooperate. The American could be difficult at times; he still refused to agree with Weigall about the occupant of KV 55. Seated at the oversized card table with Davis and Weigall were Emma and Harry Burton; Howard Jones was in his bed back at the dig house. After drinks were served, various tobaccos ignited, and pleasantries exchanged, Davis brought the meeting to order by abruptly asking Weigall what the antiquities service recommended for his workers to do when they returned in eight months.

Weigall explained carefully, as he unrolled a map on the table, that the area known as the Valley of the Kings had now been completely explored. He indicated on the map the places different diggers had worked. The past two uneventful seasons had been spent in the last unexcavated areas. The job in the valley was done, Weigall said. He proposed Davis next send his forces to the West Valley—a less populated outgrowth of the valley cemetery proper. Weigall said there were several likely spots he wanted to try where he thought tombs of Twenty-first Dynasty kings might be found.

It is unlikely Davis did much to conceal his irritation with Weigall's suggestion. It had been the American's pride since 1905 that he did not look in "likely spots"; his style was systematic and thorough, using relentless plodding to reach his objective. For Weigall to suggest a program that Davis had dismissed years before as "looking hither and thither" suggests Weigall either lacked awareness of Davis's opinions (unlikely for a man so bright) or he was deliberately attempting to assert his authority by dictating an approach that would irritate his funding source.

Davis asked Burton if he had any thoughts. The photographer had taken over for Jones when necessary and planned to return the next season. Not surprisingly, Burton agreed with Weigall's proposal but, with his usual good-spirited charm and tact, raised the possibility of waiting until the time came to decide exactly where they would dig. Davis leaned back in his chair, looked at the men, and concurred with Burton.

Davis and Maspero had already agreed, of course, that the main valley was finished and that the West Valley would be next. Davis knew Burton already had a plan in mind for October. The question had been settled before Weigall ever came aboard, but the niceties of the situation had been observed, everyone's position had been honored, and—as Weigall knew he would—Davis still served a magnificent dinner.

There was never any question about whether Davis would return for another season. Egypt had long been the best part of his life; isolated with Emma from Annie and her family, insulated from the business battles his fortune inevitably caused, living a glamorous life of luxury in an exotic land, Theo and Emma had created a unique private kingdom for themselves. In Egypt, social proprieties did not stop people from calling on them—especially when a pharaoh's golden treasure was on display belowdecks. Because Egypt was such an idyll for Davis, he was willing to come back and wield his checkbook year after year, and that in itself was one of his most important contributions to archaeology.

Excavating ancient ruins was a relatively costly undertaking, and the people who paid for the work were notoriously fickle. Phoebe Hearst funded three years of George Reisner's digs at

Giza—and then abruptly withdrew her support, leaving the archaeologist in the lurch. The first woman to excavate in Egypt—Margaret Benson, in 1895—spent three seasons excavating the temple of Mut at Karnak before quitting. The Frenchmen Maspero had let dig in the valley in 1906 quit after a few weeks. James Breasted's support from John D. Rockefeller for his epigraphic work had suddenly been withdrawn in 1907. Money from the Egypt Exploration Fund depended on gifts from donors, and the uncertainty of the source caused even Petrie (whom Emma suspected received unfair preference) to form his own organization. When the EEF money was cut off in 1906, Henri Edouard Naville's work at Deir al-Bahri had only been rescued by Davis's introduction to the *Sun*'s publisher. Most famously, Lord Carnarvon decided to quit paying for work in Egypt in 1921; the discovery of Tutankhamen was only achieved by Carter's impassioned plea for one more season.

Davis, in contrast, had committed to the work for the long haul. For a dozen years he continued to pay the diggers, and the result was his record number of discoveries. He again set an example for how the science of archaeology should be conducted—with a view to the long term, affording systematic study of a site. It was an example that was followed later; Reisner worked at Giza for forty more years after replacing Mrs. Hearst with Harvard and the MFA; Breasted's epigraphic work was resumed by the University of Chicago in 1924 and continues to the present day; the Brooklyn Museum has been working at the temple of Mut since 1976; and the American Research Center in Egypt has been funding exploration and conservation projects since 1962. Sponsors now recognize the need to pay for extended periods of proper digging.

The first long-term campaign of excavations was the result of Davis's vision, however. Expensive as it was, the spectacular results revealed the value of continuing work. It had taken eight years to finish the Valley of the Kings, but the American would continue to explore—and have a wonderful time.

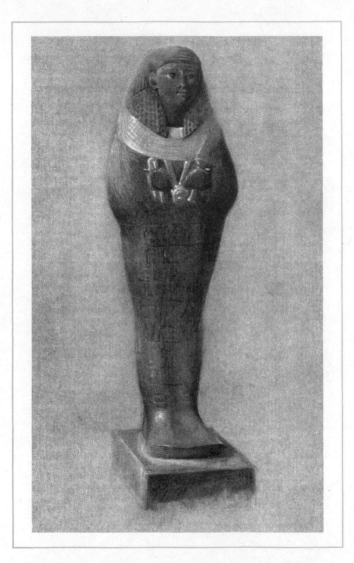

"Wooden Shawabti Figure of Iouiya," painted by Howard Carter.
From Davis, The Tomb of Iouiya and Touiyou.

Six

YUYA'S
VANISHED SHABTIS

Eighteen beautiful *shabti*s were found in the tomb of Yuya and Thuyu in 1905. The statuettes, each around ten inches tall, were inscribed with magical spells intended to bring them to life in the afterworld, where they would do the bidding of their owner. They are all exceptionally well carved—in calcite, ebony, and cedar—and exquisitely modeled. One of Yuya's, painted by Howard Carter for Davis's book on the tomb, is in wood, covered with two plates of beaten copper; the wig is painted black and the eyes feature white pupils and black irises. A pectoral necklace is of gilt stucco. In 1905 three of the *shabti*s were given to Davis as "keepsakes" (now in the Metropolitan) and the rest, including the lovely piece with the gilt pectoral, were retained for the Egyptian Museum.

On January 28, 2011, revolution raged in Tahrir Square outside the museum as massive rallies and demonstrations against the government became violent battles between the people and the police.

In the chaos that night, the museum was ransacked by looters who broke in (reportedly through the skylights), smashed display cases, and stole at least sixty priceless antiquities. Among the stolen items were ten of Yuya's and Thuyu's *shabti*s.

The *shabti*s stolen from Cairo have not reappeared. Davis the discoverer would have been disappointed; Davis the crook would have been unsurprised. The statuette painted by Carter was not among the stolen treasures, however; it was in New York that night, with two other *shabti*s from the tomb, part of a traveling exhibit on display in Times Square.

Henry "Harry" Burton was not an archaeologist, but as he crossed the gangplank onto the *Beduin* in early December 1910, he was as grateful for the job Davis had given him as any of the archaeologists had been in previous years. The thirty-one-year-old son of a cabinetmaker from Lincolnshire, Burton had effectively been adopted around the age of fifteen by a wealthy local art historian named Robert Henry Hobart Cust. In 1896 Cust and Burton had moved to Florence, where the connoisseur worked on scholarly subjects and Burton acted as his secretary and companion. Like Emma, Burton was interested in photography and the two had discussed the medium passionately when they had first met at Nettie Buttles's villa in 1903; Emma noted seeing his "beautiful photographs" in her journal. Burton quickly became a regular part of Davis's social circle. By 1905 he had established himself as one of the finest art photographers in Italy.

It had been an adventure for the photographer in 1909 when Davis had brought him from Florence to Egypt, more as a friend than an employee, to take pictures in Horemheb's tomb. Over the summer, however, Cust had married and decided to leave Italy and return to England. Now, to continue the life he had become accustomed to, Burton needed a new patron.

He joined Davis and Emma on deck, along with Harold Jones's brother Cyril. The melancholy topic of conversation was Harold's tuberculosis, which had grown worse—so bad the archaeologist could not join them on the boat. A few months before, Harold had written to Percy Newberry that "the slightest exertion puts one out of breath . . . Thus ends the career of E. Harold Jones!"[1] He was "so poorly, so weak, quite incapable of work, even painting," Emma noted. Harold was still on the payroll, ostensibly leading the excavations, but clearly incapable of taking part, and Davis had hired Cyril and Burton to supervise the work. Gaston Maspero had approved hiring Burton, charmed by the poised, clever, hardworking photographer. Burton was the least experienced digger Davis ever hired; with only one season observing Jones's uneventful trench-extending, Burton still had much to learn. He would win archaeological immortality in 1922, but for his photography: Burton's pictures of the excavation of Tutankhamen's tomb are of an importance and quality never surpassed.

It was a quiet night on the *Beduin*. All the steamers on the river tied up at night, so the evening silence, as in the old days, was interrupted only occasionally by the sounds of Luxor from across the Nile. Candles and oil lamps, like those of his childhood, lit the deck as Davis and his men discussed the season's plan.

To pacify Arthur Weigall, Davis asked Cyril to do some desultory work near the dig house in the "likely spots" the inspector had identified. Cyril agreed, realizing the assignment would allow him to stay closer to his dying brother.

The main work for the next few months was assigned to Burton. He was to lead the crew of diggers in another systematic and thorough exploration, this time in the West Valley. "Theo has established Harry Burton in his new concession in the 'Priest Kings' Valley," Emma recorded. It was a huge undertaking for the inexperienced Burton, but with confidence and a droll sense of humor—and no other job prospects—the Englishman was happy to take it on.

Burton began digging along the gullies and cliffs near the tomb of Amenhotep III (KV 22). He then proceeded southwest. It was an immense project, requiring hundreds of trenches delving down to bedrock and stretching more than a mile through the dumps of debris from previous excavations. Day after day the work proceeded, for three long, hot, and dusty months, but nothing was revealed except the remains of an ancient workmen's camp.

Davis moved Harold Jones to the Winter Palace across the river for a few days in December; on the eighteenth Emma gave a tea for the dying archaeologist and some of his friends. "The poor fellow looked very tired when it was over," she noted. The social life of Luxor continued for the Americans; they had Weigall to dinner with his visiting sister, who wrote that instead of the "glorious splendor" she had expected as they sailed across the river to the *Beduin,* "a fussy old butler dragged us on board, and his still more fussy old master bored us with lengthy discourses on the obvious."[2] On January 28, 1911, painter Mary Cassatt came to tea but wrote to a friend disapprovingly about Emma: "that woman pirate . . . There is no life in her and such cold eyes . . . and he telling he has given her $100,000 string of pearls."[3] The necklace, if that is what Davis said, was likely a joke Cassatt did not get; $100,000 would have been extravagant even for him.

Theo and Emma visited Carter in the house Carnarvon was providing him—"it looked like the abode of an artist and a scholar," Emma noted; she commissioned a painting by their old friend of a scene from the tomb of Mena. On March 1, J. P. Morgan (now the president of the Metropolitan Museum) and his sister arrived in Morgan's *dahabiyeh*. Morgan had been Davis's Newport neighbor since 1895, when he had bought a fifteen-acre "fishing box" next to the Reef, which he staffed with four permanent servants for his stops once or twice each year. They had lunch together at the dig house; a photo of the visit has survived, including the Metropolitan's Herbert Winlock (who was guiding Morgan) and Burton. Morgan's sister wears a floor-length white gown and broad-brimmed hat topped by an enormous bouquet of flowers; the men wear three-piece suits; Davis sports a broad-brimmed hat and Morgan a pith-helmet.

The West Valley finished and the unproductive season over, Davis briefly discussed the next season's work with Maspero and set off north. On March 12 the *Beduin* tied up for the night to the riverbank and received a telegram that Harold Jones, age thirty-four, had died three days before in the dig house. His brother and Lord Carnarvon arranged his burial in the Foreigners' Cemetery in Luxor; the funeral was attended by Carter and Professor Archibald Sayce. In 2009 the cemetery was moved to an area near the Luxor airport and the bodies given new coffins. The original cemetery site is now a park.

When Davis arrived back at the Reef in June 1911, two crises were reaching a head. Although his friends did not yet seem concerned, Davis recognized his mind was starting to fail (his doctors ultimately diagnosed his affliction as "dementia"). The difficulties of his ménage à trois had also finally reached a breaking point. Baby de Lagarde recalled he seemed "worried, and there was an air of mystery about the house."[4] The Reef was crowded with an assortment of guests that summer—lawyer Herbert Parsons, broker

Thomas Manson, Davis's secretary, Terry and Mathilde, Keweenaw Association board members and staff from the Metropolitan Museum, the museum people making an inventory of the objects that would come to them when Davis died.

Davis placed all his holdings in a trust, his business affairs to be managed by the Rhode Island Hospital Trust Company, and decided to revise his will one final time. As before, Manson and Parsons were to be his executors when he died, and Annie and Emma both had equal rights to occupy the Reef until their deaths. He gave a small house in Newport and $10,000 to his coachman, Andrew Dwyer, and divided up his jewelry and silverware among various friends. He left bequests of $100,000 each to Emma and Annie, $50,000 to Mamie Newberry, $10,000 each to Terry, Mathilde, Mary, and Janet Buttles, $5,000 to valet Daniel Jones, $5,000 to the Reef's gardener, and $3,000 to Emma's maid, Amelie Burgnon. He anticipated a lengthy period sorting out the estate and dictated immediate annuities of $2,000 per year to his sister Gertrude and $5,000 to Nellie Knagenhjelm.

The big dispersal of Davis's wealth would happen after Annie and Emma were dead. Everything he held was to be sold and divided into "parts," each to be worth $50,000 (equivalent to around $1 million today). Six parts went to Nellie, three to Mamie, and two each to his half-sister Kate Atwood, Terry, Mathilde, Jean Hardy, and his secretary. Single parts were set aside for Carrie Buchanan and her school in Luxor, for Maspero, valet Daniel Jones, Baby de Lagarde, and Harry Burton. Smaller amounts were left to nine others, including a half part to his butler. As before, if the "parts" did not each equal $50,000, enough of the collections left to the Metropolitan was to be sold to cover the balance.

The trust arrangement may have relieved Davis's mind over the future of his money, but it did nothing to ease the strain between

Annie's and Emma's camps at the Reef. Annie returned to the mansion in July and later testified that Emma forced her to sign a document supposedly naming Terry's son Pierre as Davis's main beneficiary by telling her she would have to leave the Reef if she did not; what Annie signed, if anything, has disappeared.

On August 17, according to Terry, Emma summoned him to the Reef. The situation for Theodore had become unbearable, she said. Terry testified that Emma told him "it would be necessary for me to take my aunt away as soon as possible . . . I was told that I

Theodore M. Davis, around age seventy. Reproduced with the permission of the Redwood Library and Athenaeum, Newport, Rhode Island.

must persuade her to go away from the Reef."[5] On the twentieth Annie left the Reef after living there (when not traveling with her sister Sarah) for thirty years, taking along her maid to stay with her and Sarah in Atlantic City. She would never return.

Davis and Emma left the Reef in November and, along with Mary and Nettie Buttles, arrived in Luxor in December 1911. The scene had changed in the eight months since they had left; Consul General Eldon Gorst had retired due to ill health and had been replaced by military hero Lord Horatio Herbert Kitchener. The change contributed to the intrigues against Maspero at the antiquities service; Kitchener made it clear he disapproved of the generous allocations of antiquities to foreign explorers and, prodded by sniping British actors including Weigall and Carnarvon, started preparing to remove Maspero. Inspector Weigall had suffered a nervous breakdown in September and was convalescing at home.

Convinced their exploration of the valley was complete, Davis and Burton were in no rush to begin work. Davis's entourage visited the tourist sites and socialized until February 1912, when they decided to clear two known but blocked valley tombs. KV 3— tomb of an unknown son of Rameses III—had been open since antiquity but was filled to within three feet of its ceiling by rubble. Burton spent two weeks there, finding only pieces of two collapsed columns in the fill.

The major work of the season was a return to the tomb of Siptah, which Davis and Ayrton had abandoned due to its dangerous condition in 1905. An inspection showed no further deterioration, so Burton undertook completing the excavation. The tomb was filled with sand and rubble "so tightly packed and tough that it was scarcely possible to distinguish it from the living rock,"[6] Burton wrote. J. P. Morgan came to lunch on the *Beduin* on February

5 and the Carnarvons called on the thirteenth. By February 23, Burton's crew had reached the final corridor leading to Siptah's burial chamber, finding only two *shabti*s, and the abbreviated season was finished.

Burton traveled with Davis south to Aswan, and stayed with the group when they went on to Italy. In London they met Nellie, who "was so very kind and devoted to her uncle, played bridge interminably with him and was so useful and kind, a great comfort," according to Emma. Their return home was delayed by the disruptions caused to Atlantic shipping after the *Titanic* sank in April; of the tragedy, Emma only noted that "all the boats take a long southern course to avoid the ice."

Arriving in the United States in June, Davis was met at the dock by Terry Boal, who wanted to discuss Annie's return to the Reef. Davis and Emma went home and took Mamie with them, who sent Terry a letter on June 12. "In the brief time that I've been here I have seen enough to feel that beyond the shadow of a doubt the thing that cousin Theodore ought most to have is peace," she wrote. "Is there not some arrangement that could be made for cousins Annie and Sarah—say at some of the fascinating places on the Massachusetts coast?" She pointed out that all of Annie's friends were now dead or gone from the Reef, and that Davis "has reached the limit of his endurance." She asked Terry to reply to Emma, "with whose knowledge and approval I am writing this."[7]

The split divided the family—Mamie was on Emma's side, of course—and also antagonized friends. The daughter of a Davis neighbor wrote that "After Mrs. Davis's eviction, Mrs. Andrews accompanied him everywhere, she assumed control of the entire place and slowly sapped his superb mind. She professed to have embraced the Christian Science religion [as had Longyear and his wife], the teachings of which she applied to all others; in her own case the slightest cold necessitated at least two nurses. In time Mr. Davis was wholly under her domination . . . She was not young, pleasant, nor attractive in any wise. It was pure hypnotism."[8] Annie never returned, spending the summer of 1912 with Sarah in Stroudsburg, Pennsylvania.

Terry took Annie's side—he was now her only heir, trying to negotiate between the warring parties and enrich himself. Rev. Arthur Powell, visiting the Reef that summer, recalled that Davis "constantly referred to Mr. Boal's applications for money . . . He didn't seem to be able to get along without constant help."[9] Terry wanted money to invest in a real estate development near Washington and enlisted Emma in a scheme to get the cash from Davis in return for keeping Annie away from the Reef. Emma tried, but Davis replied "he would neither lend nor give Terry any more money while he was living on borrowed money that he couldn't repay." Mamie testified Terry became angry with Emma for failing to keep her end of the deal.

Terry did get some money, however. Davis gave Annie $25,000 in September to establish her new home and agreed to pay her an annual allowance of $14,000. Annie gave the money to Terry, who used it to build her a house in the development he had been trying to buy into, at Bethesda, Maryland.

Davis's physical decline was becoming noticeable; his secretary recalled his eyesight was failing and he could read only newspaper headlines. Mamie noted his memory was not good and he frequently forgot numbers and people's names. Nonetheless he completed work on his final book—*The Tombs of Harmhabi and Touatankhamanou*—and a review called it "the most magnificent Egyptological book published in recent years . . . The record of his discoveries will be his glory for all after ages . . . The United States have every reason to be proud of their son."[10] Sadly, Davis made at least one mistake in the chapter he wrote for the book (the rest was written by Maspero); he credited Harold Jones's 1909 discovery of KV 58 to Ayrton in 1907.

The book has held up well; in 2001 scholar Nicholas Reeves called it "a classic of Egyptian archaeology and a work of fundamental importance."[11] Davis's brief introduction includes his statement "I fear the Valley of the Tombs is now exhausted."[12] Although later criticized as an arrogant boast, it is in fact simply a statement of all the archaeologists' opinions. The ironic final page of Davis's final publication was a color plate of a painting of the blue glazed vase with Tutankhamen's name, which Davis had found under a rock in 1905.

Theo and Emma again left for Egypt in November, this time taking along Mamie and her twenty-three-year-old daughter, Doris, as well as Jones and Amelie. Davis refused to let the ladies go ashore when the ship stopped in Algiers; Mamie recounted the conversation in a letter to her son. "They're all of them beasts in that town. There's no knowing what they might say to you," Davis argued. "Not with me there, sir," said Jones the Great, but Davis did not relent.

In Naples, as the private coach sent by the Grand Hotel carried them from the dock, Mamie noted they were "suddenly held up by two leaping, shouting bandits who turned out to be Harry Burton, the delightful young Englishman who goes with us to Egypt"[13] and one of her son's Yale classmates. After landing in Alexandria they boarded a train with "two comfortable compartments reserved in loud red letters for 'Davis Pasha.'" Mamie was especially impressed with the way Davis's servants managed the luggage: "They both speak Arabic and Jones, imperative but courteous, and Amelie, moving about like a battering-ram and hissing out vicious syllables, accomplished the impossible."

Checking into Shepheard's, Mamie noted that "Cousin Theodore has been coming to this hotel for 20 years so we are a sort of Royal Party here." Emma, whose journal entries became shorter as she aged, noted simply, "Egypt at last, and once again. How glad we were for Theodore's sake—and he was so happy to find himself once more here!"

Their first full day in Cairo was spent at the Egyptian Museum. "We had one of the sensations of our lives inspecting the wonders and the beauties of the Theodore M. Davis Room," Mamie wrote. They met Maspero, and Emma noted he had found someone capable of restoring "the magnificent cover of the so-called Tiyii's coffin . . . it will be a grand addition to Theodore's exhibit at the Museum." When they visited the pyramids, Davis refused to allow Mamie and Doris to climb them because they would have been boosted up the monuments by native guides.

Burton took the train to Luxor and resumed work in Siptah's tomb while Davis sailed there in the *Beduin,* arriving on December 21. Much of the pleasure had vanished from sailing down the river; instead of cruising by the shore with its ever-changing scenes of peasant life, now boats were towed by steamers to avoid sitting becalmed when the wind failed. As Sayce wrote, "It was now necessary to remain always in the middle of the stream and to substitute the smoke of the steamer for the sights and scents of the fields. The excitement of watching the winds and the evolutions of the sailors was gone. Even the great sail was folded up."[14]

It took Burton's crew five weeks to finish clearing Siptah's tomb; Carter noted that, while looking for Tutankhamen, it took 10 men and 140 basket boys to move the mounds of rubbish the Davis team had removed from the tomb and dumped. Mamie grew very fond of Burton—"he's one of the most amusing persons I've ever known"—and she spent four nights in the dig house, sleeping in Burton's room. "It may smell of disinfectant," he told her, "but it's all right. It doesn't mean anything except that the last chap died here, you know."

As Burton burrowed toward Siptah's burial chamber, social life on the *Beduin* continued at its usual pace. Davis was visited by Edward Tuck, a retired New York banker and founder of the Tuck School of Business at Dartmouth. Tuck showed the sculpted head of Akhenaten he had just bought from Weigall, now recovered and assigned to a job in Cairo. Weigall had bought the head in a dealer's shop. The sale to Tuck was completely unethical and Weigall knew it. He wrote his wife, "I can't help feeling I have fallen from a pedestal."[15] At the same time he was still criticizing Maspero in a letter to scholar Alan Gardiner: "It is hateful to me always to see the splendid things in dealers' shops all going into private hands or into distant American museums,"[16] he complained, criticizing Maspero as "a Philistine."

Joe Smith was in Egypt and visited regularly; he noted Davis "had visibly aged, even more mentally than physically. He led a quiet routine on the Beduin and rarely saw visitors . . . [He] did not talk much, just sat, with a contented look on his face, that too often these days had a lack of animation and lusterless eyes."[17] John Longyear and his wife were touring Egypt that season and came by; sitting on the deck of the *Beduin,* the two old landlookers' thoughts must have gone back to their days in the wilderness in the Upper Peninsula, where Davis had started his career sixty years before.

When Carter came to visit, he got off to a bad start with Mamie. "He can be perfectly charming, I'm told," she sniffed. After arguing with Emma about fleas in Egypt—Carter maintained there were none—he then burst out to Mamie, " 'Play that piece!' pouncing on me as I was playing dominoes with cousin T," she wrote. "It annoys me excessively to be watched when I'm playing dominoes, and more so to be ordered about during the process. So I played another piece and lost the game. 'Why didn't you play the piece I told you to?' he demanded. (It was the first time I had ever talked to the man in my life.) 'Because you told me to,' I replied. Whereupon he laughed and began to be pleasant."

J. P. Morgan was in Luxor but did not visit Davis; his "eccentric behavior has caused a buzz of comment and conjecture," Mamie noted. "Mr. Morgan engaged suites of rooms at the Winter Palace for his party and before they had time to move into them he whisked them all down to Cairo in a special train." Morgan was suffering from an even more serious decline than Davis; he had a breakdown with paranoid, suicidal delusions in Cairo, which caused the U.S. stock market to plummet when the news got out on February 17, 1913. He managed to make it to Rome, where he died on the thirty-first. The next day flags on Wall Street flew at half-staff.

Morgan's abrupt departure from Egypt caused another problem for former-Inspector Weigall; he and two British officers had bought a smuggled Persian bronze statuette for £800 and had hoped to sell it to Morgan for £20,000. When the story got out it caused a scandal that within a year ended Weigall's career in Egypt forever.

On January 2, 1913, Burton broke through to Siptah's burial chamber. "The aspect of this chamber was alarming," he wrote. "It looked as if the ceiling might fall at any moment and we were obliged to build a strong column of stones to support the most dangerous part."[18] On January 7 Mamie wrote that the *Beduin* received "an exciting note from Harry" announcing he had found a red granite sarcophagus. "Intact, with the exception of small portions of the sides which had been broken away when the lid was forced off by the plunderers in ancient times," Burton reported. Six feet high and ten feet long, the cartouche-shaped sarcophagus was covered with carved figures and hieroglyphs and was the last great object Davis ever found. It failed to excite the sponsor: "Cousin Theodore has lost all interest in the tomb," Mamie sadly noted. "When he came in to breakfast and I said 'Isn't it thrilling about the sarcophagus?' he merely said, 'Ha!' "

Maspero arrived soon after and pronounced the sarcophagus "a treasure" he might put in the Cairo museum—if Davis would pay the £250 to move it there. "We are divided between our hopes it will be so fine that Maspero will want it in the Cairo Museum," Mamie wrote, "and that it will fail by a hair's breadth to meet that requirement so that we can give it to the Metropolitan." Maspero decided to keep it, and the box is still in the tomb today. He did present the patron with eleven *shabti*s, a carved alabaster canopic chest, and fragments of the sarcophagus, which all went to the Metropolitan. Davis was also given another *shabti,* a jar for eye makeup, and two fragmentary stelae, which he gave to Jones the Great; they were sold for $25 by Jones's son to the Museum of Fine Arts in 1949.[19]

Having finished clearing Siptah, Burton moved on, as Maspero and Davis had agreed, from the valley to the temple at Medinet Habu. "It was finally decided that we might best devote our attention to clearing the site of the so-called 'Palace' of Rameses III, which lies on the southern side of the temple," Burton wrote. Davis spent February 27 at the site and told Mamie they had found "some extraordinary windows." The openwork, limestone window fragments were later sent to Cairo and, as Burton recorded, "it proved possible to reconstruct from them, with a certain amount of restoration, three complete windows," which featured intricate carvings within the grill frames centered on the cartouche of Rameses III flanked by solar falcons. One of the windows was allocated to Davis; having illuminated the ceremonies and deliberations of the king and his courtiers in the throne room in 1170 B.C., the forty-square-inch window is today in the Metropolitan.[20]

Burton found some other fine things at the palace, including glazed tiles, three throne bases, and three bathrooms. "To the casual and frivolous eye," Mamie commented, "it would seem that the king divided his time between sitting on his throne and a-washing of hisself." The excavation was not well done, however. "Burton was a far better photographer than excavator," a scholar noted in 2000. "His digging caused much damage."[21] Burton destroyed mud brick walls from the Ramesside period, erasing the footprint of the later structure. Nonetheless, in 1913 Mamie wrote that the current inspector had told her, "our finds this winter have been the only ones of any importance in this region. Having lofty souls ourselves we are sorry the others have been unsuccessful, but considering how Howard Carter sneered to us one day about Harry Burton's capacity as a digger, we are too enchanted that it was Harry who made the important finds, and Harry himself is so happy he looks like a different man." When the *Beduin* left for Cairo on March 12, Mamie noticed "many handkerchiefs and scarves fluttered farewell—friends of the crew, tradesmen we had patronized, and an acquaintance or two."

In his increasingly infrequent lucid moments, Davis realized he might be saying good-bye to Egypt forever when he left in 1913. The terror of realizing he was losing his mind can scarcely be imagined, but perhaps he found comfort in the belief that he had forever revealed the last secrets of the Valley of the Kings. Every foot of the valley walls had been dug and every king accounted for; as his mind drifted into oblivion his fading memories included not only the things he had found necessary to do in New York but the things he had chosen to do in Egypt. In the Valley of the Kings the tycoon had behaved with honesty, responsibility, and generosity.

Burton joined Mamie and Doris with Theodore and Emma, Jones and Amelie as they returned through Europe. In Florence on April 16, Emma wrote in her journal, "Theo has been almost every day motoring, with Harry Burton and some one or two of the girls . . . He has loved going to the Villino and hearing Nettie sing . . . Above all I have enjoyed the companionship of the two dear nieces, Nettie and Mary. We go tomorrow at 5 P.M. via the Mt. Cenie pass to London." It was the final entry in the diary she had kept since 1889. Mamie asked her son not to meet the *Kronprinz Wilhelm* when it arrived in New York on May 27. "Every extra person only adds to poor Cousin T's confusion of mind."

Terry Boal met the boat and recalled, "I was impressed with the change that had taken place in the course of the winter, mentally . . . He was less sure about names and people." Davis's secretary, however, believed that "his logic was very good but he had trouble with his words and the meaning of some words."[22] That summer at the Reef was a grim one, as Davis's mental condition deteriorated daily.

Mamie came to visit in June and rode the train from New Haven with Terry, who wanted a private meeting to talk about Davis's will and the people he thought had no claim to the estate, like the Wilsons. "He didn't like it at all because there were so many people remembered in the will; that it was going to divide the estate up so that we who had a prior claim wouldn't get as much as we ought to," Mamie later testified. He told her, "I don't think you are getting very much, anyhow." He felt Emma had double-crossed him on the Maryland real estate deal. "He said, 'If it comes to a fight we want you on our side' . . . I said, 'Cousin Emma has been very kind to me and I cannot take sides against her.'"

Davis was still capable of changing his will; he eliminated the $5,000 for the Reef's gardener when he quit or was fired; a later account referred to his "mysterious death." Even Mamie testified that Emma had become "drunk with power"; her maid Amelie Burgnon, who had traveled with her bosses to Egypt since 1895, quit and returned to France and was also eliminated from the will. Mamie wrote that Davis "looked so shocking it sent my heart into my mouth." He failed to recognize Baby de Lagarde when she arrived; Nellie Knagenhjelm arrived for her last visit to the Reef and stayed until August. It was the last time she and Davis saw each other.

On September 10 another tragedy occurred at the Reef. Mamie wrote to her son on the fourteenth, "Something so dreadful has happened—I can hardly bear to tell you. Jones, [the valet] dear Jones killed himself four nights ago at the Reef. He had been having trouble with his head and he must have gone crazy for the time. He shot himself in the hall outside of his room and the servants found him in the early morning. I think it would have killed Cousin Theodore too had he known the full truth." Davis was told his companion of twenty years had grown ill and gone to the house he shared with his wife; the next day he was told there was no hope, and the next day that Jones was dead. "In all my life I have known few men as worthy of admiration and affection," Mamie wrote. Davis revised his will a few days later, establishing a $20,000 trust for Jones's widow, Hilda, and their children.

• • •

Despite Davis's deteriorating condition, he and Emma returned to Egypt for one more season. They were accompanied by Davis's secretary, Annie Ghio (previously secretary to a U.S. Supreme Court justice) and Davis's butler Henry Kidd. Mamie was also with them, more to care for Davis than out of any desire of her own to return.

In Luxor in December 1913, Burton was photographing Siptah's tomb. Davis had sent instructions the next job should be the clearance of KV 7, the tomb of Rameses II, which had been open since antiquity. It was a considerable challenge; the tomb had never been fully explored because flood damage had caused the shale rock it was dug into to swell and disintegrate, making it especially dangerous. Major sections of the wall decorations had flaked off and the tomb was filled with rock-hard debris. Burton had to pull down much of the ceiling in the first passage.

By December 28 he had reached the burial chamber, which he wrote was "in a very bad state. All the eight columns have fallen and brought down much of the roof with them."[23] Conditions were difficult; Burton noted the temperature in the tomb was ninety degrees, and a recent flood had soaked the mud on top of the fill, creating suffocating humidity. By January 14, 1914, Burton had given up, finding only a few broken fragments of a statue, some calcite, and glass. The clearing did provide a dramatic, if highly imaginative, drawing of the excavation in progress, which appeared in the British newspaper *The Graphic* on February 21. Titled "Where the Pharaoh of the Oppression Was Buried," the caption stated the tomb had been "thoroughly cleared by Mr. Theodore Davis." It was the last published news account of a Davis excavation.

Burton went on to do a desultory clearing of the gully between KV 6 and KV 8, although the area had already been explored. His final entry in his excavation journal, on February 11, simply stated "Nothing of importance." It was the end of the Davis excavations, but Davis's final season did produce one remarkable irony. In 1923, after the discovery of Tutankhamen, Burton told *The Manchester Guardian,* "If Mr. Theodore Davis for whom I was excavating in 1914 had not stopped his last 'dig' too soon I am convinced he would have discovered the present tomb of King Tutankhamun. We came within six feet of it. Just then Mr. Davis feared that further digging would undermine the adjacent roadway and ordered me to cease work."[24] Considering Davis's condition, Burton's imperfect archaeological technique, the chaotic situation at the antiquities service, and the imminent start of World War I, it is fortunate the tomb escaped notice until 1922—but the prospect of Tut being excavated by Burton with Carter assisting, instead of vice versa, is intriguing.

When Davis returned to Cairo, he told Maspero he was done with work in Egypt, a quiet end to a spectacular career. In June, when Maspero granted the right to work in the valley to Lord Carnarvon, Carter noted that the Frenchman agreed with Davis that the valley had nothing left to reveal. Unlike Davis's deal, Carnarvon was given a share of all finds to "sufficiently recompense him for the pains and labour of the undertaking," except in the extremely unlikely event of finding an intact tomb. Maspero, exhausted by bureaucratic infighting, resigned the following month and returned to Paris. He had a heart attack in August.

Davis—or perhaps Emma—realized he would never return to Egypt. They decided to sell the *Beduin,* and with Carter as a go-between the *dahabiyeh* was bought by Percy Newberry, now a professor at the University of Liverpool, for $10,000. Newberry returned to Egypt to teach at Cairo University in 1929.[25]

At Shepheard's on March 14, Davis had grown so much worse that two nurses were added to his entourage. Emma and Mamie were also ill; when they finally left for home at the end of April it concluded what Mamie called "the long Cairo nightmare." Davis said good-bye to Burton in Naples; they would never meet again, but Davis spoke to Albert Lythgoe about finding a job for him with the Metropolitan's team, and Burton was hired by the Metropolitan to undertake a thorough photographic recording of the Theban monuments (the money was provided by Robb de Peyster Tytus's mother, in her son's memory). Burton was still with the Metropolitan in 1922 when he was loaned to Carter, and used KV 55 as a dark room.

Shortly after they arrived home at the Reef, Davis bowed to the urgings of his board members and resigned as chairman of the Keweenaw Land Association after thirty-six years in charge. As he lapsed further into oblivion, Nettie and Mary Buttles arrived from Florence to help care for him in June, joining Terry there, and Mamie returned in July. "It is very hard for me to bear," she wrote to her son. "He is so sad, so silent and remote . . . It is more desperate here than I have ever known it." Davis might not have understood when word arrived of the death of Edward Ayrton, who after leaving Davis's employ had been appointed director of the Archaeological Survey of Ceylon (now Sri Lanka). Ayrton had gone on a shooting expedition on Lake Tissa Tank, fallen overboard, and drowned at age thirty-one.

On June 24 a gala joint meeting was held of the Garden Association and the Newport Horticultural Society. The papers reported that "almost everyone at Newport in the villa colony was present and the occasion furnished the first display of the season for the latest mode in dress."[26] The military band from Fort Adams played for the well-dressed crowd as the guests dined on cake and ice cream under umbrella-shielded tables. Davis won four first prizes for entries from his gardens.

Four days later an assassin killed the Austrian crown prince in Sarajevo and the collapse of Europe into World War I began; Mamie wrote that "Cousin Theodore doesn't know at all whom you mean when you say 'the Germans,' he only understands if you say 'the devils.' 'The Allies' means nothing to him; we always have to say, 'Our Side.'"

In October 1914, the probate court appointed Terry and Dudley Dean (of the Keweenaw Association board) to act as Davis's conservators. Mamie wrote that when trying to play cards, Davis "can generally recognize hearts and diamonds, but when it comes to spades and clubs he has to be told over and over again." Emma dictated that Terry organize a move to Florida for the winter, although Terry was a bit preoccupied; his son, Pierre, and Baby de Lagarde had both gone to France, where Baby served as a nurse (as Emma's former maid Amelie was also doing) and Pierre joined a cavalry regiment.

Terry learned that the Miami mansion of Secretary of State William Jennings Bryan was available, and traveled to Florida with Bryan (a three-time progressive candidate for president who had made a fortune speaking on the Chautauqua circuit). Terry rented Villa Serena, home of the "Great Commoner," located on what the locals called "Millionaires' Row." Bryan, under fire in Washington, cited the rental to reporters as proof he was not considering resigning.

Davis's sad last season at the Reef, with middle-aged women gathered to watch him die, ended on December 6 when he left for the final time, taking a private train car to New York. His last entourage included Emma, secretary Annie Ghio, butler Henry Kidd, a nurse, and Emma's new maid. They spent a few days at the St. Regis and attended the theater; Ghio thought Davis understood what was happening. Nathaniel Wilson came to New York and joined Davis for the train trip as far as Washington; they talked the entire time.

Davis's last days in Miami were orchestrated by Terry to support a scheme he had been working on for at least two years. As soon as the group arrived at Bryan's mansion Terry set about getting the other beneficiaries to leave. He was in constant communication with lawyer Parsons, and wrote him in December that he hoped by refusing to treat Emma as "the mistress of everything" she would "lose interest and herself decide to leave."[27] He succeeded in less than a month, when Emma abruptly left the house and took the train to Washington without telling him she was leaving; Nathaniel Wilson met her at the station. Terry wrote to Annie that "both she and the Wilsons are, as you know, unfriendly, and I am writing you this word of warning in case you should meet her or them."[28] When Terry ordered secretary Annie Ghio to leave, it led to a tear-filled argument.

Terry began generating documents for the legal fight he planned to mount over Davis's estate. His idea was to create evidence that the will Davis had spent so much time on had been the result of Emma's domineering influence. He bullied the staff into signing affidavits he wrote describing Emma's "hypnotic" control of the old man, supposedly driving him to tears and whimpering by staring or waving her hands. His lawyers later realized it would have been disastrous to introduce the documents in court.

On January 12, 1915, Terry wrote to Parsons that Davis was "a person out of his mind." Parsons's father, who sat at Davis's side at the congressional investigations in 1874 and 1880 and helped fight the Ocean Bank battles against the Averys, died of pneumonia four days later. The death of his father, one of Davis's oldest friends, would have lessened Herbert's worries about conspiring with Terry to defeat Davis's intentions for his money. Terry sent a telegram on February 10 to Emma, Nathaniel Wilson, and Mamie: "conversation vague and incoherent, occasionally a momentary flash of understanding." Mamie offered to come to Miami, but Terry said with three nurses on duty it was unnecessary; he wrote of "Uncle's last request before lapsing into semi-coma to send for Annie," but said he did not because "Uncle is entirely unconscious of surroundings."

On the eighteenth Terry wrote a document that was signed by the maid he had hired in Miami two months before. It stated that after waking from a nap Davis said "Find her—find her." When the nurse asked who he wanted, Davis supposedly replied, "Mrs. Davis. I want her love. Nobody loves me! Oh Lord! Oh Lord! Deliver me!" as he began weeping and praying.

Finally, on February 23, Terry sent telegrams to Emma, Mamie, and Wilson: "Uncle died this morning. The end was peaceful after the painful illness." To Parsons he wrote that Davis "had no moments of lucidity since those in which he asked for aunt Annie." Butler Henry Kidd, who had already signed several of Terry's affidavits, testified later that as Davis died he called for Annie.

The day Davis died, according to wire service reports, there was tremendous anxiety in Egypt over the nineteen thousand Turkish troops that had crossed the Sinai Peninsula and attacked the Suez

Canal. "Cairo never before presented such a dismal and melancholy aspect," according to the dispatch. "From Shepheard's Hotel to the Mena House, every establishment which tourists associate at this time of year with riotous living is deserted."[29]

Terry claimed to have found a document expressing Davis's desire to be cremated and brought the body on the train to the Massachusetts Cremation Society, near the Forest Hills Cemetery in Boston. He telegraphed Wilson that "it has been understood between Mrs. [Mamie] Newberry, Mr. Parsons and Mrs. Davis that Mrs. Andrews will not be present at the service" at the crematorium on March 2. Annie did not attend either, but Mamie and Doris did. "I feel dreadfully about this cremation," she wrote her son. "My reason approves, but when it comes to anyone I have loved it's horrible to me." Davis's ashes were buried in a grave at Island Cemetery in Newport, where he had bought a plot for himself and Annie. Terry took responsibility for obtaining a tombstone, extremely modest by robber baron standards. Above a carving vaguely resembling a pyramid, Davis's name is inscribed with the date of his birth carved incorrectly (as 1837 rather than 1838).

Obituaries for Davis focused exclusively on his career in Egypt. *The New York Times* titled its piece "Theodore M. Davis, Egyptologist, Dead." It cited the discovery of Yuya's tomb and described KV 55 as "literally full of gold, the walls, ceiling and even the floor being covered with plates of the precious metal."[30] The *Newport Mercury* called him "an Egyptologist of world-wide fame." There was no mention of the Ocean Bank, the Lake Superior Ship Canal, the three congressional investigations, or anything else before Yuya and Thuyu's discovery. Davis would likely have been pleased.

Davis might have frozen to death when his canoe was stolen in

Michigan in 1853; if his schedule had been slightly different, he might have drowned with a number of his Newport neighbors when the *Titanic* went down in 1912. In between, he spent half his life fighting with tenacity and ruthlessness to get what he wanted and the other half indulging his every whim and fancy. The world has been fortunate ever since that one of his fancies involved Egypt.

Davis's incorrectly inscribed tombstone had not even been placed over his ashes when the battle over his money began on March 8, 1915. The contesting sides had been drawn up for a long time, and most of the parties were present at a meeting in executor Parsons's office that day. Annie's sole heir was Terry Boal; Terry's last surviving brother, Montgomery Davis Boal (who had been traveling with Davis when he bought the "Leonardo"), had died during an evening with friends in 1898 when he removed a derringer from his pocket that went off accidentally and killed him instantly. Annie and Terry were supported by her sister Sarah and Terry's sister-in-law, Baby de Lagarde. Emma's partisans included the Wilsons and Mamie. They were joined in Parsons's office by Davis's broker, Thomas Manson, the other executor of the estate.

The central character at the meeting, Herbert Parsons, was struggling with a life in decline. Parsons had attended St. Paul's School with Terry, but had gone on to Harvard Law School, become a partner in his father's firm, and begun a successful political career. He had been elected to Congress in 1904, formed an alliance with Teddy Roosevelt, and become chairman of the New York Republican Committee (the *Times* called him "the absolute boss" in 1907), but he failed to deliver the delegation for Taft at the 1908 Republican convention and been defeated in his reelection bid in 1910. His marriage had collapsed, as well; after several of Herbert's rumored affairs, his wife Elsie Clews Parsons had left him to pursue an extraordinary career as an anthropologist in New Mexico (she was the first woman elected president of the American Anthropological Association, in 1941). Parsons had been Davis's attorney since his father retired. At the meeting, he dropped Terry's bombshell.

A document that the subsequent legal proceedings and the press dubbed the "Million Dollar Agreement" was produced. The original, supposedly a letter to Annie by Davis, had mysteriously disappeared, but the paper (in Terry's handwriting) was presented as a copy signed by Davis. Dated October 9, 1911 (shortly after Annie had left the Reef), the letter stated that Davis had decided to increase the immediate bequest in his will to Annie from $100,000 to $1 million. Everyone in the room was taken aback except Terry, Annie, and Parsons; since the total estate was less than $3 million, the terms of the new document would have made the rest of Davis's gifts and bequests impossible to pay. "I shall be in luck if I get one-half what Cousin Theodore thought he was leaving me," Mamie wrote to her son.

Parsons also announced he was declining to serve as executor; he would shortly sign on as attorney for Annie and Terry. It later came out Terry had shown him the "agreement" in 1913; as Davis's attorney, Parsons understood that it would completely alter the existing will Davis had filed, but in his midlife crisis the forty-four-year-old lawyer had concealed Terry's gambit and continued to represent Davis, never mentioning the blockbuster letter. It had been completely unethical—and promised a large fee from Terry at the end of the proceedings.

The Million Dollar Agreement was more than suspicious; it was illogical and entirely out of character for Davis, who had spent much time carefully crafting his plan. Davis had never mentioned it to anyone (except Annie and Terry, according to them), although he enjoyed frequently talking about the gifts he would give his heirs. If the copied letter was upheld, however, as Annie's sole heir it would bring Terry well over $1 million instead of the $200,000 Davis had left him.

It quickly united the other players against Terry and Annie. "I am not the only one who does not trust said nephew for a moment," Mamie wrote of the man she had lived with as a sister in Davis's home for seven years; Manson called Terry a "viper." Parsons filed a suit on March 24 to institute the Million Dollar Agreement. As the case of *Annie B. Davis vs. Thomas L. Manson* began, the newspapers recognized one of the major implications; the story in *The New York Times* was headlined "Davis Museum Bequest Clouded," and *The Washington Post* announced "Gold-Lined Tomb May be Sold with Mummy of Egyptian Monarch" (an arresting, if not accurate, anticipation).

The beneficiaries all lawyered up. There were a dozen attorneys at a probate hearing in Providence on May 7; it was not mentioned the day would have been Davis's seventy-seventh birthday, but the participants did hear that the passenger ship *Lusitania* was torpedoed by a German submarine that day, killing 128 Americans among the 1,200 who died.

Nathaniel Wilson was the guiding mind for Terry's opponents; his children stood to gain a half million dollars if the will was upheld. He had other concerns at the same time; an old friend and client named Edith Bolling Galt had been proposed to by President Woodrow Wilson and she had lunch with her lawyer to get his advice on May 11, when Nathaniel took her hand and told her, "Child, I don't know why, but I feel you are destined to hold in this woman's hand a great power—perhaps the weal and woe of a country."[31] Edith married Woodrow (who had replied that he was glad "a man of such insight and vision should bear the name of Wilson") and after the president's stroke in 1919 was rumored to have become "the first woman President."

Emma moved back to the Reef that summer. Annie chose not to, although the will allowed her the option. Emma shocked Mamie at one meeting where she claimed she "could live with Annie even if Theodore could not." The court decreed the Davis estate pay for guards to patrol the grounds to protect the art still inside the mansion. Emma continued her gardening, and in 1917 won a silver cup at the Horticultural Society exhibition for her ferns, palms, and foliage plants and blue ribbons for her grapes and raspberries.

As *Davis vs. Manson* began its journey through the courts, the litigants did agree on a few points; Davis's clothes were given to butler Henry Kidd, the Reef was put up for sale, and some items were distributed by the court. Mamie wrote that "when the silver left to me is turned over to me I have to promise to return it on demand." What Davis had called his Egyptian "Apepi ring," made from a scarab of the Hyksos period (ca. 1550 B.C.), was given by the court to Emma, as his will decreed. Strangely, such a ring was given by Emma to the Metropolitan that year and is still in the collection,[32] but Nettie Buttles wrote that the ring was the most valuable item in the collection in the Buttles's Florence villa ("so valuable did he consider it that he apportioned it in his Will, as a separate item, leaving it to our aunt, who in turn gave it to us"[33]).

Nathaniel Wilson sent a lawyer to Germany in December 1915, to take his daughter Nellie's deposition. It gave rise to an article in *The Washington Post* about the erstwhile "Washington Girl." The paper stated she had "completely identified herself with European life"; her three sons were "brought up with the royal sons of Saxony," and mentions that her oldest child, Davis's godson Nils Theodore Knagenhjelm, "though only 16 is with the German army and was recently decorated with the iron cross because of conspicuous gallantry in action."[34]

While Nellie's son was winning the Iron Cross, Pierre Boal was distinguishing himself on the Allied side by joining the Lafayette Flying Corps, a group of American aviators who flew in French uniform. Terry was visiting him in France when Annie Davis died on March 7, 1916, of cancer of the lower bowel. She is buried in Newport next to Theodore's ashes. She left the house Davis had bought her and the income of $200,000 to her sister Sarah; everything else went to Terry, who became the complainant in *Davis vs. Manson.*

The trial began in earnest on June 14, 1916. There were forty-six individuals involved in the suit and more than twenty lawyers in the courtroom. On June 30 another of the beneficiaries passed away; as Gaston Maspero rose from his chair to address the French Academy he collapsed and died of a stroke. Friends believed his spirit had been broken when his son had been killed in battle the year before.

The lengthy proceedings included testimony by most of the principals. Terry was on the stand for six days; the judge later found him "not prepossessing," with "little or no personal magnetism . . . In a most marked and gentlemanly manner [he] endeavored to keep personal hostility out of his testimony." Baby de Lagarde showed "a keen mind," a "gracious manner," and "a very pleasing voice." Davis's secretary, Annie Ghio, "betrayed a stronger partisanship than some counsels'" on behalf of Terry's opponents (she stood to win $100,000 and the TMD-inscribed silver coffee set if Terry lost) and showed "a very strong antipathy to Mrs. Davis and said she had not liked Mrs. Andrews for many years."[35]

The trial continued until September 27, concluding with testimony from four handwriting experts, two of whom called the Davis signature on the Million Dollar Agreement a forgery (the other two were unsure). The court's decision came on January 19, 1917, and found the agreement to be a fake. Although not stating Terry had committed fraud, the judge concluded he had not told the whole truth and "wandered far from the path of veracity."[36] Terry's gamble had failed; newspapers assumed the case was over and ran articles calling Carrie Buchanan "the $50,000 missionary." Terry and Parsons did not give up, however; an appeal was immediately filed.

The United States entered the war in April 1917, and Terry joined the army in France where he served as aide-de-camp to two generals, saw combat, and won the Distinguished Service Cross. Pierre was made a captain in the U.S. Army and won the Purple Heart, the Legion of Honor, and the Croix de Guerre. Baby de Lagarde married a war correspondent she had met in France, in the Columbus Chapel at the Boalsburg mansion wearing her Red Cross uniform; she died in childbirth in May 1918. Her husband, Owen Johnson, wrote a novel in 1921 about the war titled *The Wasted Generation*. Davis's sister, Gertrude, died intestate in 1917 and her half-sister Kate Atwood was named her executor.

The Rhode Island Supreme Court ruled on Terry's appeal on January 9, 1918, upholding the lower court's decision. "The testimony of Mr. Boal and Miss de Lagarde, if not untrue, must be deficient in the recital of important facts,"[37] the court found. The legal fight continued, however. Executor Manson died in May and the Rhode Island Hospital Trust Company took over the case, and Terry and Parsons joined forces with Davis's half-sister Kate Atwood in a new suit that attempted to get Davis's will thrown out on technicalities; if they succeeded, Davis would be considered to have died without a will and Rhode Island law would dictate the entire estate be divided between them as the two surviving family members. Their effort failed, in March 1920, but they appealed the decision and also sued the Metropolitan Museum (where Davis's collection was displayed on loan, pending the lawsuits' resolution) because they felt the Metropolitan, "by its attitude" (entering the case to win the collection) had "forfeited all rights to receive anything."[38]

Ultimately, there were at least eight lawsuits filed in the matter and appeals won and lost, one going to the U.S. Supreme Court. The final decision on Davis's will and trust was reached in 1927, when the Federal Circuit Court of Appeals ruled they were valid. Terry's fight against the Metropolitan went on until 1930, when the Newport Probate Court granted the museum permanent possession of the collection Davis had called "the child of my mind." When the Supreme Court refused to hear Terry's appeal, it was Theodore Davis's final legal victory.

The museum did not follow Davis's request that the entire collection be displayed together under his name, and was unable to mount a special exhibit bringing together the paintings, Egyptian items, classical antiquities, rugs, furniture, textiles, porcelains, and amber he had donated "because of the serious disruption this would cause in so many departments of the Museum." The Metropolitan published a thirty-four-page edition of its *Bulletin* highlighting the most important of the thousand-plus objects it finally owned, as a "tribute, however inadequate, to the memory of Theodore M. Davis, distinguished lawyer and financier, eminent Egyptologist and collector, generous benefactor."[39]

Terry's litigation lasted longer than many of the people he tried to take Davis's money from. Emma divided her time between Newport and Washington, where she rented a home on Sixteenth Street (a mile and a half from the U.S. Capitol) for the extravagant rent of $7,500 per year. She died in Washington on January 19, 1922, at age eighty-four. Her will, written in 1918, recognized that the Davis collections were hostage to Theodore's requirement that each "part" in his will total $50,000 and she designated up to $50,000 of her estate (estimated at $600,000) be used to make up any difference needed; the Metropolitan did receive $25,000 from her. Another of Nathaniel Wilson's sons, Clarence, was her executor; she left her estate, an impressive collection of jewelry, and her 1916 Locomobile to her nieces Helen Powell, Nettie, and Mary Buttles.

She is buried in Green Lawn Cemetery in Columbus in the Buttles family plot, with her parents and siblings. Her life had been luxurious and eventful, but perhaps her happiest moments had been like one she described in her Egyptian journal: "At sunset Theodore and I walked to the extremest verge of this sand island, enjoying the stillness and the lonely desert scene. Ah me, what delicious moments of quiet these are."

Nathaniel Wilson died the following October, a month before the Tutankhamen discovery took over the headlines. Annie's sister Sarah—who never got along with Davis—died in Boalsburg a year later, probably pleased to have lived long enough to see Davis's claim of having "exhausted" the valley disproved. Herbert Parsons died in 1925 after falling off a motorized bicycle he had just given his son, striking his kidneys with the handlebar. His partners never received payment from Terry for their years of work.

Terry Boal continued to live at the Boalsburg mansion, although he eventually had to sell much of the land surrounding it. He had placed his wife, Mathilde, in a mental hospital near Boalsburg in 1915, but she managed to extricate herself and returned to France, where she died in 1951. Terry used three boxcars of souvenirs he had brought home from France to form the "28ᵗʰ Pennsylvania Division Shrine" in Boalsburg, which he left to the state (in 1968 it was converted to the Pennsylvania Military Museum). On his deathbed in 1938 he was reportedly asked by a neighbor if he would do anything differently in his life and replied, "I had the honor of inheriting three fortunes and the pleasure of spending them"⁴⁰ (presumably his father's, his wife's, and Annie's). He is buried in a vault beneath the Columbus Chapel with Annie's sisters Malvina, Sarah, and Julia and "Baby" Cecile de Lagarde.

Pierre Boal, whose teeth Davis had paid to straighten, went on to a distinguished career in international diplomacy, serving as the U.S. ambassador to Nicaragua and Bolivia. He returned to Boalsburg in 1952 and turned the home into the Columbus Chapel and Boal Mansion Museum; it operates today as a marvelous testimony to the family and the region's history, under the guidance of Pierre's grandson Christopher Lee. One room of the museum features some Theodore Davis memorabilia, including a bust (possibly by Mary Buttles) dated 1897; unlike most of his photos, in the bust Davis is smiling.

Nellie Wilson Knagenhjelm died at age sixty in Dresden in 1927. Her son Nils Theodore moved to America, lived in New York and Connecticut, and during World War II became a prominent "anti-Nazi German," serving as editor of a newspaper published by the Psychological Warfare Branch of Allied Headquarters for German troops in Norway, urging them to surrender.

Mamie Newberry moved to Milwaukee to be with her son, Roger, following daughter Doris's marriage. When she finally received her bequest from Davis she bought a home on the Milwaukee River that she named Windfall. She employed a cook and a chauffeur and was known affectionately as "Nonie" to her six grandchildren (who were allowed to believe Cousin Theodore and Cousin Emma were man and wife). She died in November 1945, at age eighty.

Janet and Mary Buttles lived in Florence the rest of their lives. In 1925 they established a day care nursery for children of poor working mothers, which in 1930 won gold medals from the city and commendations from the Italian government. They stayed in touch with the old circle; in 1933 Harry Burton visited their villa and gave them a copy of a stone plaque depicting Queen Ahmes, which they put on display. Janet died in 1947; Mary in 1956.

After their deaths, their heirs disposed of their 250-piece collection of antiquities, which included what was left of the mask and heart scarab from Userhet's tomb (Carter's 1902 discovery), foundation deposits from Hatshepsut's tomb, 4 blue-glazed ankhs from the tomb of Thutmose IV, a bit of Thuyu's mummy cloth, gold pieces from a KV 55 necklace, and 1 of Siptah's *shabti*s. The collection was offered to the Oriental Institute, which declined to purchase it, and the pieces were sold at auction by Sotheby's in 1976 and 1986.[41] Another of their items—the forged "Leonardo da Vinci" painting—was last seen in a New York apartment in 1963.[42]

The Reef finally found a buyer after Emma's death in 1922, a Packard motorcar executive named Milton Budlong. He bought most of the furniture, although Terry moved the dining room table and Davis's Packard limousine to Boalsburg (the car is now in a private collection near Chicago). Budlong had a roving eye, and his wife (whom *The New Yorker* described as a woman who loved "perhaps not too well, but wisely"[43]) sued him for divorce twenty-one times, the marriage finally ending in 1928. Fifty-nine-year-old Milton stayed at the Reef with his new wife, a woman thirty years younger named Lolita. He died in 1941, and the army took over the vacant mansion, installing antiaircraft guns and spotlights on the grounds to defend nearby navy facilities. Gunnery soldiers lived in the house during World War II and were its final occupants.

In 1951 the site was proposed for a World War II memorial park but Newport voters overwhelmingly rejected the $100,000 bond issue. By 1957 the vacant house had become a target of vandals. Most of the windows had been broken; furniture, pipes, and fixtures had been stolen; and the floors were covered with debris. Even the wall Davis had jumped over and Emma's gardens were gone. "[T]he stone wall, damaged by several hurricanes, has never been repaired. The grounds bear evidence of disuse for years."[44]

After decades of neglect and clandestine teenagers' parties, the Reef burned to the ground on July 16, 1960. The fire distracted a golfer on the neighboring course; as President Dwight D. Eisenhower putted the fifth green of the Newport Country Club, the papers reported, "smoke from the inferno billowed overhead."[45] The last visitors to the Reef, and the possible cause of the fire, were law enforcement officials who regularly stood guard on the third floor of the mansion's tower when the president played; it offered a perfect view of the golf course and "any fanatic with ill purpose could take position from it."

The ruins were demolished three years later and the state took possession of the property, creating the Brenton Point State Park in 1974. The fireproof stables Terry built survived and were spared demolition, reportedly because the cost of mitigating the hazards of the asbestos shingles was too high (they had been touted as "the roof that outlives the building" by the manufacturer in a 1911 advertisement that pictured the stables). Today they are in ruins, surrounded by chain-link fence. The servants' quarters have been turned into office space for park staff, and the stone-faced brick clock tower Davis built stands as well.

Davis's dig house in the valley had a kinder fate. Although reduced to a ruin by 1970, the house was excavated and rebuilt in 1978 by archaeologist John Romer, who recovered a number of plate-glass photo negatives from the Davis era from the piles of mud plaster—as well as a 1906 map by Ayrton showing the areas he had excavated. The house has served as a home for archaeologists and inspectors, and today is a storage facility.

The Keweenaw Land Association closed its last iron mine in 1995, after the company had drawn more than a hundred million tons of ore from sixteen different mines. The association still owns 150,000 acres of timberland, markets nine different types of wood, and is a recognized industry leader in sustainable forestry. In 2012 the government issued a permit to an association leaseholder to begin mining copper on the land. The association's CEO is Frederick Ayer's great-grandson.

The discovery of Tutankhamen's tomb in 1922, in one golden moment, effectively erased the memory of Davis's career (and of all other Egyptian archaeologists) from the public mind. Carter was described in one 1922 wire service story as an American to whom in 1902 "Davis offered the command of the expedition of scientists, engineers and diggers who invaded the Valley,"[46] but Davis's name soon vanished. The Salle Theodore M. Davis in the Egyptian Museum had disappeared by 1919, when the galleries were reorganized; today the space displays Tutankhamen's treasures. To the extent he is remembered at all, it is with surprising dislike by archaeologists and Egyptologists, although their professional forebears found him helpful and charming.

The catalog of the blockbuster exhibition "Tutankhamun and the Golden Age of the Pharaohs," which toured the world for a decade in the early twenty-first century—with nearly a quarter of the objects, like Yuya's *shabti* and Thuyu's coffin, from Davis discoveries—mentions him only as "not an easy man to work for."[47] Egyptologist John Romer wrote that his "brusque and pushing manner won him few friends . . . Often rude and overbearing."[48] Before he was deposed as head of the Supreme Council of Antiquities after the 2011 revolution, Zahi Hawass called Davis "a very difficult man to work with and work for."[49] He has been called an amateur and a dilettante, been blamed for botching excavations, and been ridiculed for thinking everything in the valley had been found. Even his name was mangled; in most Egyptological accounts his middle name is given as "Monroe," possibly a scholar's confusion with another New York lawyer who had been a member of the Union League Club at the same time as Davis.

He has fared even worse in popular fiction, called a "pompous, arrogant ignoramus"[50] in one bestseller; in another Carter hisses, "I despise you, Davis!" to the "pretentious and tyrannical man."[51] His legacy remains, however, and it is doubtful the carping of people he never met would have bothered Davis any more than the complaints of ruined business rivals did. During the 1874 congressional hearings, Avery had pursued a line of questioning emphasizing his bad reputation. Davis had replied by simply asking, "That was rather my misfortune than my fault, was it not?"[52]

American history has been seen as the process of a nation's transformation through the self-transformations of its citizens. Davis transformed himself from an uneducated landlooker into a fabulously wealthy New York robber baron, then into an art collector, and finally into a patron of archaeology and a "generous benefactor." Over his twenty-seven years in Egypt he transformed himself from another rich tourist seeking a mild winter climate into an important part of the history of the Valley of the Kings. He set standards for future diggers that fostered genuine professionalism, thorough and long-term excavation planning, full and useful publication of results, and the generous dispersal of objects found. Museumgoers around the world are fascinated and moved by his discoveries every day.

Davis had been the right man in the right place. The valley was ripe for exploration when he began, and the way he undertook it benefited the science, added immensely to scholarly knowledge, and greatly increased interest among the general public in one of the most fascinating eras of human history. Davis was a rogue, a criminal who found that great wealth did not bring personal fulfillment, and like other robber barons of the Gilded Age he tried to fill his soul with fine art and romance. It was only in exploring the world of the pharaohs, however, that he finally found hope of achieving the great deeds that would win him the immortality the ancient kings had dreamed of.

He was a crook like many others of his time, but he transformed himself into a man who—despite his past—contributed unselfishly and honorably to the world's heritage. His personal redemption, although accomplished with little sacrifice, was genuine and lasting. He was self-indulgent, relentless, and sometimes ruthless. Whatever latter-day criticisms may be made about the man or his career, however, the world and posterity were well served by the Egypt-loving robber baron archaeologist.

Notes

One: Thuyu's Golden Coffin

1. Egyptian Museum CG 51006.
2. "Theodore M. Davis" in New York City Bar Association, *The Memorial Book and Mortuary Roll,* 1915. Although his middle name is given as "Monroe" in many later sources, Davis's middle name as stated on his passport application, etc., is the same as his father's, "Montgomery."
3. Theodore M. Davis, Gaston Maspero, Percy E. Newberry, and Howard Carter, *The Tomb of Iouiya and Touiyou* (London: Archibald Constable, 1907), xxv.
4. Arthur Weigall, *Tutankhamen and Other Essays* (New York: George H. Doran, 1924), 20.
5. Now designated KV 46.
6. Arthur Weigall, *The Glory of the Pharaohs* (New York: G. P. Putnam's Sons, 1923), 143.
7. (and following) Emma B. Andrews, "A Journal on the Bedawin, 1889–1913" (unpublished manuscript, quoted by permission of the Metropolitan Museum of Art).
8. Davis, 1907, xxvi.
9. Ibid.

10. Joseph Lindon Smith, *Tombs, Temples and Ancient Art* (Norman: University of Oklahoma Press, 1956), 22.

11. Davis, 1907, xxvii.

12. Ibid.

13. Gaston Maspero, *New Light on Ancient Egypt,* translated by Elizabeth Lee (New York: Appleton, 1909), 241.

14. Ibid.

15. Weigall, 1923, 144.

16. Weigall to Hortense Weigall, February 16, 1905. Quoted in Julie Hankey, "Arthur Weigall and the Tomb of Yuya & Thuyu" in *Kmt: A Modern Journal of Ancient Egypt,* 9:2 (Summer 1998), 43.

17. Maspero, 1909, 244.

18. Davis, 1907, xxviii.

19. Smith, 1956, 33.

20. Archibald Henry Sayce, *Reminiscences* (London: Macmillan, 1923), 323.

21. Davis, 1907, xxix.

22. Alumni file, Archives of the Burke Library (Columbia University), at Union Theological Seminary, New York.

23. Jacob Knapp, *Autobiography of Elder Jacob Knapp* (New York: Sheldon, 1868), 77–78.

24. Davis to Nellie Knagenhjelm, August 3, 1902, exhibit C-29, *Davis v. Manson.*

25. Smith, 1956, 37.

26. *New York Times,* March 26, 1905.

27. *Illustrated London News,* supplement to March 17, 1906.

28. *Sandusky Star Journal,* June 19, 1905.

29. Henry Copley Greene, "A Great Discovery in Egypt," *Century Magazine,* November 1905, 68.

30. William Randolph Hearst to Phoebe Apperson Hearst, 1899. Phoebe Apperson Hearst Papers. Bancroft Library, University of California, Berkeley. Quoted in Judith Robinson, *The Hearsts: An American Dynasty* (San Francisco: Telegraph Hill Press, 1991), 325.

31. Theodore M. Davis, Gaston Maspero, Edward Ayrton, George Daressy, and E. Harold Jones, *The Tomb of Siphtah: The Monkey Tomb and the Gold Tomb* (London: Archibald Constable 1908), 1.

32. Joseph Lindon Smith, "Egypt, My Winter Home" (unpublished manuscript, 1950), 270.

33. Zahi Hawass, *Tutankhamun and the Golden Age of the Pharaohs* (Washington, D.C.: National Geographic, 2005), 158–59.

Two: Rekhmire's Bronze Bowl

1. MMA 30.8.67; William C. Hayes, *The Scepter of Egypt,* vol. 2 (New York: Metropolitan Museum of Art, 1959), 205–206.
2. Davis to Nellie Wilson, January 3, 1895; exhibit D-1, *Davis v. Manson.*
3. (and following) Andrews.
4. Percy Newberry to Davis, August 1900. Newberry Papers, Griffith Institute. Quoted in H. E. Winlock, "An Egyptian Flower Bowl," in *Metropolitan Museum Studies,* vol. 5, no. 2 (September 1936), 147.
5. James J. Hagerman, unpublished memoir. Quoted in John Jay Lipsey, *The Lives of James Hagerman, Builder of the Colorado Midland Railway* (Denver: Golden Bell Press, 1968), 11.
6. Davis to Nellie Knagenhjelm; exhibit in *Davis v. Manson.*
7. John Munro Longyear, *Landlooker in the Upper Peninsula of Michigan* (Marquette: Marquette County Historical Society, 1960), 71.
8. Memoir of E. B. Ward, in Charles Moore, *History of Michigan* (Chicago: Lewis Publishing, 1915), 520.
9. Henry Rowe Schoolcraft, *Narrative Journal of Travels Through the Northwestern Regions of the United States* (Albany: E. and E. Hosford, 1821), 178.
10. W. P. Clarke, material written by Clarke tipped in to a biography of Lincoln held with Clarke's papers by the Historical Society of Iowa, Iowa City.
11. U.S. House of Representatives, Committee on Banking and Currency, "Hearings in the Matter of the Receivership of the Ocean National Bank," first session of the Forty-third Congress, June 1874.
12. *Davis v. Bronson,* in "Reports of Cases in Law and Equity Determined in the Supreme Court of the State of Iowa," vol. 6 (1859).
13. Semitic Museum #91.9.1.
14. Howard Carter to Percy Newberry, n.d. (1899), Newberry MS, Griffith Institute, Oxford; quoted in Nicholas Reeves and John H. Taylor, *Howard Carter Before Tutankhamun* (New York: Harry N. Abrams, 1993), 55.
15. Howard Carter, unpublished biographical sketch, Carter MSS, notebook 16, sketch VI; Griffith Institute, Oxford; quoted in Reeves and Taylor, 71.
16. Ambrose Lansing, quoted in *The Discovery of Tutankhamun's Tomb,* edited by Polly Cone (New York: The Metropolitan Museum of Art, 1976), v.
17. Davis to Nellie Knagenhjelm, March 2, 1902; exhibit 0–12, *Davis v. Manson.*
18. MMA #30.95.258.

19. Maspero, 1909, 241.

20. Weigall to F. Llewelyn Griffith, October 1, 1908; Griffith correspondence, Griffith Institute, Oxford; quoted in Julie Hankey, *A Passion for Egypt: Arthur Weigall, Tutankhamun and the 'Curse of the Pharaohs'* (London: I. B. Tauris, 2001), 127.

21. Davis to D. G. Lyon, February. 24, 1902; on file at Redwood Library, Newport, R.I.

22. Davis to Lyon, March 1, 1902.

23. Janet Buttles, in unpublished notebook (n.d.) at the Oriental Institute, University of Chicago; quoted by John Larson in *Kmt: A Modern Journal of Ancient Egypt,* vol. 1, no. 1 (spring 1990), 50.

24. Donald P. Ryan, *Beneath the Sands of Egypt: Adventures of an Unconventional Archaeologist* (New York: William Morrow, 2010), 188.

25. Semitic Museum, #2840–44.

26. Davis to Nellie Knagenhjelm, March 2, 1902; exhibit 0–12, *Davis v. Manson.*

27. Davis to Lyon, March 1, 1902.

28. Davis to Lyon, June 23, 1902.

29. Davis to Nellie Knagenhjelm, January 18, 1903; exhibit T-17, *Davis v. Manson.*

30. Mary B. Newberry to Roger Newberry (unpublished), December 1912.

31. MFA #03.1035, 03.1036 a–b.

32. Davis to Nellie Knagenhjelm, January 18, 1903; exhibit T-17, *Davis v. Manson.*

33. Howard Carter, *Annales du Service des Antiquites de l'Egypte* (Cairo), no. 4 (1903), 176.

34. For a complete analysis, see Dennis C. Forbes, "The Re-Search for Hatshepsut's Mummy" in *Kmt: A Modern Journal of Ancient Egypt,* vol. 23, no. 1 (Spring 2012), 65.

35. Pierre Loti, *Egypt* (New York: Duffield, 1909), 297.

36. (and following) Howard Carter, MSS at Griffith Institute, Oxford, notebook 16, sketch VI; quoted in Reeves and Taylor, 73–75.

37. Gaston Maspero, *Egypt: Ancient Sites and Modern Scenes* translated by Elizabeth Lee (London: T. F. Unwin, 1910), 188.

38. Egyptian Museum CG 46069.

39. CG 46097.

40. CG 46526.

41. Davis to Nellie Knagenhjelm, February 16, 1903; exhibit U-18, *Davis v. Manson.*

42. Carter, notebook 16, sketch V; quoted in H. V. F. Winstone, *Howard*

Carter and the Discovery of the Tomb of Tutankhamun (London: Constable, 1991), 319.

43. MFA # 03.1137a–b.
44. MFA # 03.1129a–b.
45. *New York Times,* March 30, 1903.

Three: Hatshepsut's Quartzite Sarcophagus

1. Carter, notebook 16, sketch VI; quoted in Reeves and Taylor, 78.
2. Theodore M. Davis, Edouard Naville, and Howard Carter, *The Tomb of Hatshopsitu* (London: Archibald Constable, 1906), xiii.
3. Ibid., xii.
4. (and following) Andrews.
5. Reprinted in *The New York Times,* April 2, 1904.
6. Ellen Mary Newberry to Roger Newberry, January 24, 1913. Unpublished.
7. Charles Wilbour to Charlotte Beebe Wilbour, 1888; Wilbour, *Travels in Egypt: Letters of Charles Edwin Wilbour,* edited by Jean Capart (Brooklyn: Brooklyn Museum, 1936), 460.
8. Ellen Mary Newberry to Roger Newberry, op. cit., 1912.
9. Jeremiah Lynch, *Egyptian Sketches* (New York: Scribner and Welford, 1890), 18.
10. Ellen Mary Newberry to Roger Newberry, op. cit.
11. *Davis v. Manson,* Andrews deposition.
12. Ellen Mary Newberry to Roger Newberry, op. cit.
13. History of Johnson County (Iowa City, Iowa), 277.
14. Samuel J. Kirkwood, quoted in Daniel Gordon, *The Robber Baron Archaeologist: An Essay About the Life of Theodore M. Davis* (Baltimore: Department of Near Eastern Studies, Johns Hopkins University, 2007), 19.
15. Smith, 1950, 65, 223.
16. Frederic Jesup Stimson, *My United States* (New York: Charles Scribner's Sons, 1931) 69.
17. James D. McCabe, *Lights and Shadows of New York Life: Or, the Sights and Sensations of the Great City* (Philadelphia: National Publishing, 1872) 135, 520.
18. George Templeton Strong, *The Diary of George Templeton Strong, 1820–1875,* edited by Allan Nevis and Milton Helsey (New York: Macmillan, 1952) 178.

19. *Davis v. Manson,* testimony.
20. U.S. House of Representatives, Committee on Banking and Currency, "Failure of National Banks" (second session of the Forty-second Congress, February 12–March 23, 1872), 23.
21. Ibid., 14.
22. Gordon, 33.
23. U.S. House of Representatives, 1874, 316.
24. Ellen Mary Newberry to Roger Newberry, op. cit.
25. Ellen Mary Newberry to Roger Newberry (unpublished), December 1912.
26. See Hankey, 49.
27. Davis, 1907, 4.
28. Howard Carter, Carter Papers, Griffith Institute, V., 139; quoted in T. G. H. James, *Howard Carter: The Path to Tutankhamun,* revised edition (London: Tauris Parke, 2001), 125.
29. Davis, 1907, xxvi.
30. MMA #30.8.93.
31. Davis to Carter, February 10, 1905 (Griffith Institute, Oxford; Carter Papers V, 124), quoted in James, 127–28.
32. A. A. Quibell, *Some Notes on Egyptian History and Art* (Cairo: C. M. S Bookshop, 1919), 98.
33. *New York Times,* March 26, 1905.
34. *Century Magazine,* November 1905, 76.
35. Smith, 1956, 42.
36. *The American Antiquarian and Oriental Journal,* vol. 32, no. 4 (October 1910), 205–208.
37. C. N. Reeves, "Introduction" in *The Tomb of Queen Tiyi,* second edition (San Francisco: KMT Communications, 1990), iv.
38. Davis, 1907, xxx.
39. MMA #30.6.5658; 30.8.5960; 10.84.1a, b; 11.155.7; 11.155.9.
40. MMA #7.316.2–3.
41. Arthur Weigall Archive held by Julie Hankey; printed in Hankey, 347–48.
42. Davis to Weigall, June 20, 1905, Weigall Archive, quoted in Hankey, 64.
43. Weigall, 1924, 20.
44. Davis, 1908, 3.
45. A. B. De Guerville, *New Egypt* (London: W. Heinemann, 1906), 211.
46. MMA #30.95.268.

47. Henry Hall, "Edward Ayrton," in *Journal of Egyptian Archaeology,* vol. 2 (January 1915), 22.

48. Theodore M. Davis, Gaston Maspero, Georges Daressy, and Lancelot Crane, *The Tombs of Harmhabi and Touatankhamanou* (London: Archibald Constable, 1912), 2.

49. Davis, 1908, 8.

50. Ibid., 2.

51. Charles Breasted, *Pioneer to the Past: The Story of James Henry Breasted, Archaeologist* (New York: Charles Scribner's Sons, 1943), 160–61.

52. For a modern discussion of this, see Aidan Dodson, *Poisoned Legacy: The Fall of the Nineteenth Egyptian Dynasty* (New York: American University in Cairo Press, 2010).

53. Davis, 1908, 12.

54. Smith, 1956, 46.

55. Loti, 180.

56. Davis, 1908, 4–5.

57. Smith, 1956, 49.

58. Loti, 279.

59. Davis, 1908, 23.

60. Walter Tyndale, *Below the Cataracts* (Philadelphia: J. B. Lippincott, 1907), 160.

61. *Pall Mall Gazette* (London), April 1906; reprinted in the *Daily Oklahoman* (Oklahoma City), April 29, 1906.

62. Maud Gage Baum, 1907; quoted in L. Frank Baum, *Sam Steele's Adventures: The Treasure of Karnak* (San Diego: Hungry Tiger Press, 2009), 235.

63. Theodore M. Davis, Gaston Maspero, G. Elliot Smith, Edward Ayrton, and Georges Daressy, *The Tomb of Queen Tiyi* (London: Archibald Constable, 1910), 7.

64. Ibid., 1.

65. E. R. Ayrton, "The Tomb of Thyi" in *Proceedings of the Society of Biblical Archaeology,* vol. 29 (November 13, 1907).

66. Davis, 1910, 1.

Four: Kiya's Alabaster Jar

1. MMA #30.8.54.

2. Ellen Mary Newberry to Roger Newberry, 1912, op.cit.

3. Davis, 1910, 8.
4. Arthur Weigall, *The Treasury of Ancient Egypt* (Chicago: Rand McNally, 1912), 208.
5. Davis, 1910, 8.
6. Ibid., 2.
7. Smith, 1956, 56, 61.
8. Weigall, *Century Magazine,* September 1907.
9. *New York Times,* March 26, 1905.
10. Janet R. Buttles, *The Queens of Egypt* (New York: Appleton, 1908), 110–13.
11. Dominic Montserrat, *Akhenaten: History, Fantasy and Ancient Egypt* (London: Routledge, 2000), 85.
12. Davis, 1910, 2.
13. Weigall, *Century Magazine,* op. cit.
14. Maspero, 1909, 292.
15. Tyndale, 185.
16. *New York Herald,* June 29, 1869.
17. U.S. House of Representatives, 1872, 340.
18. (and following), Ibid., 15–17, 25.
19. Davis, 1910, 9.
20. Charles Trick Currelly, *I Brought the Ages Home* (Toronto: Royal Ontario Museum, 1956), 142.
21. Davis to Weigall, January 13, 1907, Weigall Archive, quoted in Nicholas Reeves, *Valley of the Kings: The Decline of a Royal Necropolis* (London: Kegan Paul, 1990), 333.
22. Tyndale, 192–94.
23. Smith, 1956, 59.
24. Ibid., 53.
25. Arthur Weigall, "The Mummy of Akhenaten" in *Journal of Egyptian Archaeology,* vol. 8 (1922), 196.
26. Davis, 1910, 2.
27. Ibid.
28. Maspero, 1909, 294.
29. Davis, 1910, 2.
30. Davis to G. Eliot Smith, July 1907. Quoted in Aldred and Sandison, "The Pharaoh Akhenaten: A Problem in Egyptology and Pathology," in *Bulletin of the History of Medicine,* vol. 36, no. 4 (July 1962), 301.
31. Martha Bell, "An Armchair Excavation of KV 55" in *Journal of the American Research Center in Egypt,* vol. 27 (1990), 133.
32. Smith, 1956, 66.

33. *New York Herald,* December 15, 1871.
34. U.S. House of Representatives, 1874, 366.
35. *Davis v. Manson,* 25.
36. *New York Herald,* January 20, 1872.
37. (and following) U.S. House of Representatives, 1872.
38. Oswald Garrison Villard, *Fighting Years: Memoirs of a Liberal Editor* (New York: Harcourt, Brace, 1939), 181.
39. U.S. House of Representatives, Committee on Banking and Currency, second session of the Forty-sixth Congress, "Investigation of the Failure of the Ocean National Bank and the Alleged Improper Management of Theodore M. Davis, Receiver" (May 1880), 211.
40. Ibid., 190
41. Ibid., 297.
42. *Davis v. Manson,* depositions, 21.
43. U.S. House of Representatives, 1880, 224.
44. Davis to Malvina Boal (undated), Boal Papers.
45. Kate Bosse-Griffiths, *Amarna Studies and Other Selected Papers* (Fribourg, Switzerland: Univ. Press; Gottigen, Vandenhoeck und Ruprecht, 2001), 97.
46. Sixth Earl of Carnarvon; from an undated talk, Highclere Castle; quoted in Reeves and Taylor, 86.
47. Arthur Weigall, "Excavating in Egypt" in *Putnam's Magazine,* vol. 6, no. 4 (July 1909), 397.
48. Sixth Earl of Carnarvon, undated draft of an article, Highclere Castle Egyptian Archive; quoted in Nicholas Reeves, *The Complete Tutankhamun: The King, the Tomb, the Royal Treasure* (London: Thames and Hudson, 1990), 47 (hereafter cited as Reeves, 1990a).
49. Carnarvon to Weigall, April 14, 1907, Weigall Archive; quoted in Reeves, 1990a, 48.
50. Howard Carter, Griffith Institute, I. C. 145; quoted in Elizabeth Thomas, *The Royal Necropolis of Thebes* (Trenton, N.J.: privately printed, 1966), 154.
51. Mary Berenson to Isabella Gardner, November 10, 1902, Harvard University and Villa i Tatti, quoted in Rolin Van N. Hadley, *The Letters of Bernard Berenson and Isabella Stewart Gardner, 1887–1924* (Boston: Northeastern University Press, 1987), 306.
52. (and following) U.S. House of Representatives, 1874.
53. *New York Times,* March 17 and 24, 1874.
54. (and following) U.S. House of Representatives, 1874.

55. Quoted in Christopher Lee, "The Boals of Boalsburg" in *Pennsylvania Heritage* (Fall 1989).

56. (and following) Boal correspondence.

57. U.S. House of Representatives. *In the Matter of the Investigation into the Affairs of the Ocean National Bank, Majority and Minority Reports,* March 3, 1875.

58. U.S. House of Representatives, 1880, 83.

59. Ibid., 87.

60. Ibid., 215.

61. Ibid., 217.

62. Frederick L. Heinrich, *A History of Keweenaw Land Association, Limited* (Boston: privately printed, 1981), 5.

63. *Proceedings of the Society of Biblical Archaeology,* February 13, 1907.

64. *New York Times,* February 24, 1915.

65. William Dana Orcutt, *Celebrities Off Parade* (Chicago: Willett, Clark, 1935), 114.

66. *New York Times,* June 13, 1907.

67. Weigall, 1923, 156.

68. Weigall, "A New Discovery in Egypt: The Recent Uncovering of the Tomb of Queen Tiy" in *Century Magazine* (September 1907).

69. Weigall to Hortense Weigall, undated, Weigall Archive; quoted in Hankey, 91–92.

70. Sayce to Weigall, October 20, 1907, Weigall Archive; quoted in Nicholas Reeves and Richard H. Wilkinson, *The Complete Valley of the Kings: Tombs and Treasures of Egypt's Greatest Pharaohs* (London: Thames and Hudson, 1996), 78.

71. Weigall, *Journal of Egyptian Archaeology,* vol. 8 (1922), 194.

72. Davis, 1910, 3.

73. Cyril Aldred, *Akhenaten, King of Egypt* (New York: Thames and Hudson, 1988), 95.

74. Weigall, 1924, 33.

75. Weigall, 1923, xvi.

Five: Tawosret's Golden Earrings

1. Egyptian Museum CG 52397–98.

2. *Washington Post,* May 27, 1907.

3. Davis, 1910, 4.

4. Davis, 1912, 3.
5. Davis, 1908, 31.
6. Arthur Weigall, *Egypt from 1798 to 1914* (London: Blackwood, 1915), 234.
7. Winlock, 1941, 5.
8. Maspero to Weigall, January 17, 1908; Weigall Archive, quoted in Hankey, 106.
9. Davis, 1908, 3.
10. Davis to Nellie Knagenhjelm, January 20, 1908; exhibit BB-26, *Davis v. Manson.*
11. Nicholas Reeves, "The Amarna Dead in the Valley of the Kings," a lecture delivered in Imola, Italy, on April 12, 2003. Posted on www.nicholas reeves.com, June 2011.
12. Winlock, 1941, 5.
13. Ibid., 17.
14. John Romer, *Valley of the Kings* (New York: Henry Holt, 1981), 223.
15. Dennis Forbes, *Tombs, Treasures, Mummies: Seven Great Discoveries of Egyptian Archaeology* (Sebastopol, Calif.: KMT Communications, 1998), 321.
16. Jones to his family, January 31, 1908, National Library of Wales; quoted in Reeves and Wilkinson, 79.
17. Jones to his family, February 27, 1908, National Library of Wales; quoted by Lyla Pinch-Brock, "The Short, Happy Life of Harold Jones" in Diane Fortenberry, ed., *Who Travels Sees More: Artists, Architects and Archaeologists Discover Egypt and the Near East* (Oxford: Oxbow Books, 2007), 37.
18. Ayrton to Davis, December 31, 1908; Weigall Archive, quoted in Reeves, 1990, 337.
19. *New York Times,* February 23, 1908.
20. Ellen Mary Newberry to Adeline, February 23, 1913 (unpublished).
21. Ayrton to Weigall, February 22, 1908, Weigall Archive; quoted in Reeves, 1990, 336.
22. Weigall, 1912, 228.
23. Davis, 1912, 1.
24. Ibid.
25. Weigall, lecture text (1923); Weigall Archive, quoted in Hankey, 281.
26. Davis, 1912, 2.
27. Weigall, 1912, 229–30.
28. Personal communication to the author, 2011.
29. Davis, 1912, 2.

30. George B. Johnson, "Painting with Light" in *Kmt: A Modern Journal of Ancient Egypt,* vol. 8, no. 2 (Summer 1997), 59.

31. Weigall, "A New Egyptian Discovery: The Tomb of Horemheb," in *Century Magazine,* June 1909, 297.

32. Jacke Phillips and Aidan Dodson, "Egyptian Antiquities of Chiddingstone Castle" in *Kmt: A Modern Journal of Ancient Egypt,* vol. 6, no. 1 (Spring 1995), 55.

33. Weigall to F. L. Griffith, October 1 [1908], #362, Griffith Institute, Oxford; quoted in James, 154.

34. Smith to his mother, March 19, 1908; Smith correspondence, Smithsonian Institution; quoted in Hankey, 109.

35. MMA #30.8.66.

36. Smith, 1950, 223.

37. Arthur Stanley Riggs, *The Romance of Human Progress* (New York: Bobbs-Merrill, 1938), 28.

38. *Evening News* (Ada, Okla.), April 10, 1908.

39. Davis to Weigall, November 23, 1908, Weigall Archive; quoted in Reeves and Wilkinson, 79.

40. *Hartford Daily Courant,* August 13, 1886.

41. *New York Times,* November 29, 1877.

42. John Munro Longyear, 1960, 62–67.

43. (and following) U.S. House of Representatives, 1880.

44. *New York Times,* November 8, 1879.

45. U.S. Supreme Court, *Meddaugh v. Wilson,* 151 U.S. 333 (1894).

46. (and following) U.S. House of Representatives, 1880.

47. *New York Times,* April 12, 1878.

48. Nancy Newberry Kamlukin, introduction to Mary B. Newberry, *A Winter on the Nile* (privately printed, 1996).

49. *Davis v. Manson,* op. cit.

50. Ibid., 21.

51. *William and Henry James, Selected Letters* (Charlottesville: University of Virginia Press, 1997).

52. Henry James to Hendrik Andersen, November 5, 1905, and July 6, 1914, quoted in Susan E. Gunter and Steven H. Jobe, *Dearly Beloved Friends: Henry James's Letters to Younger Men* (Ann Arbor: University of Michigan Press, 2001), 56, 79.

53. (and following) James Breasted to Harriet Breasted, September 17, 1903. Transcribed by archivist John Larson of the Oriental Institute, University of Chicago, and located in the Newport Historical Society.

54. Davis to Nellie Knagenhjelm, *Davis v. Manson*; quoted in Gordon, 49.

55. Davis to Nellie Knagenhjelm, July 9, 1901.

56. U.S. House of Representatives, 1884, 314.

57. Longyear, *Keweenaw Canal Company*, 7–8.

58. Bernard Berenson to Mary Berenson, November 9, 1894; quoted in Ernest Samuels, *Bernard Berenson: The Making of a Connoisseur* (Cambridge, Mass.: Belknap Press, 1979), 205.

59. Hagerman to William Lidderdale, September 24, 1890; quoted in Lipsey, 99.

60. Stimson, 68.

61. Terry Boal to Malvina Boal, December 23, 1896; Boal correspondence.

62. Alexander Agassiz to James MacNaughton, November 19, 1906; quoted in Larry Lankton, *Cradle to Grave: Life, Work, and Death at the Lake Superior Copper Mines* (New York: Oxford University Press, 1991), 210.

63. Terry Boal to Malvina Boal, April 8, 1905; Boal correspondence.

64. Davis to Malvina Boal, September 1, 1906; Boal correspondence.

65. Davis to T. D. Boal, September 13, 1906.

66. Davis to Nellie Knagenhjelm, October 15, 1906; exhibit Z-23, *Davis v. Manson*.

67. T. D. Boal to Davis, undated; Boal correspondence.

68. Ellen Mary Newberry to Terry Boal, January 4, 1888; Boal correspondence.

69. *Davis v. Manson*, testimony.

70. Ibid.

71. Alexander Agassiz; journal, September 15, 1899; quoted in G. R. Agassiz, ed., *Letters and Recollections of Alexander Agassiz with a Sketch of His Life and Work* (Boston: Houghton Mifflin, 1913), 354.

72. Mary Cassatt to Louisine Havemeyer, January 28, 1911; quoted in Millicent Dillon, *After Egypt: Isadora Duncan & Mary Cassatt, a Dual Biography* (New York: Dutton, 1990), 12.

73. Ruth Ellen Patton Totten, *The Button Box: A Daughter's Loving Memoir of Mrs. George S. Patton* (Columbia: University of Missouri Press, 2005), 32.

74. MMA #30.95.256.

75. *New York Times*, December 8, 1890.

76. *Washington Post*, December 30, 1915.

77. Davis to Nellie Knagenhjelm, August 3, 1902; exhibit C-29, *Davis v. Manson*.

78. *Davis v. Manson*.

79. Ibid., testimony, 1446.
80. Maspero, 1910, 117.
81. Laura Elizabeth Howe Richards and Maud Howe Elliot, *Julia Ward Howe, 1819–1910,* vol. 2 (Cambridge, 1916), 251.
82. Lewis Mumford, *The Golden Day* (New York: Boni & Liveright, 1926).
83. Agassiz, 382.
84. Bernard Berenson to Senda Berenson, April 23, 1893; quoted in Samuels, 1979, 166.
85. Ibid.
86. Davis to Berenson, April 18, 1894; quoted in Samuels, 1979, 182.
87. Mary Berenson, journal of American trip, 1903–1904; quoted in Meryle Secrest, *Being Bernard Berenson: A Biography* (New York: Holt, Rinehart and Winston, 1979), 225.
88. Barbara Strachey and Jayne Samuels, *Mary Berenson: A Self Portrait from Her Letters and Diaries* (New York: Norton, 1983), 110.
89. Berenson to Isabella Gardner, May 29, 1898; quoted in Hadley, 139.
90. Berenson to Gardner, July 6, 1898; quoted in Hadley, 143.
91. Berenson to Gardner, December 4, 1899; quoted in Hadley, 196–97.
92. Tyndale, 3.
93. MMA #30.8.6869; identified in 2012 by Nicholas Reeves as from the tomb of Amenhotep, overseer of the builders of Amen during the reign of Amenhotep II (ARCE Conference presentation, Providence, R.I.).
94. Agassiz, 435.
95. Martin Brimmer, *Egypt: Three Essays on the History, Religion and Art of Ancient Egypt* (Cambridge, Mass., 1892), 1–3, 9, 17, 86.
96. Sayce, preface, to Heinrich Schliemann, *Troja: Results of the Latest Researches and Discoveries on the Site of Homer's Troy* (New York: Harper, 1884), iv.
97. Davis to Nellie Wilson, January 3, 1895; exhibit D-1, *Davis v. Manson.*
98. Davis to Nellie Knagenhjelm, April 2, 1896; exhibit F-3, *Davis v. Manson.*
99. Jones to his family, January 14, 1909, National Library of Wales; quoted in Reeves and Wilkinson, 186.
100. Davis, 1912, 2.
101. Smith, 1956, 104.
102. Quoted in C. N. Reeves, "The Discovery and Clearance of KV 58" in *Gottinger Miszellen* 53 (1982), 35–36.

103. D. Bickerstaff, "The Enigma of Kings Valley Tomb 58" in *Kmt: A Modern Journal of Ancient Egypt,* vol. 28, no. 3 (Fall 2010), 35–44.

104. Carter to Mrs. Kingsmill Marrs, January 16, 1909; Massachusetts Historical Society; quoted in James, 486.

105. T. D. Boal to Davis, July 14, 1909; Boal correspondence.

106. *The African World* (Summer 1909).

107. *Daily Courier* (Waterloo, Iowa), August 4, 1909.

108. *Newport Mercury,* October 30, 1909.

109. Berenson to Isabella Gardner, April 17, 1910; quoted in Hadley, 470.

110. Berenson to Mary Berenson, August 25, 1909; Archives of American Art, quoted in Samuels, 1987, 90.

111. MMA #14.6.182; see Hayes, 384.

112. Jones to his family, January 30, 1910, National Library of Wales; quoted in Reeves and Wilkinson, 79–80.

113. Roosevelt to Weigall, May 30, 1910; Weigall Archive, quoted in Hankey, 151.

114. Davis, 1912, 3.

Six: Yuya's Vanished Shabtis

1. Jones to Percy Newberry, June 15, 1910; National Library of Wales, quoted by Pinch-Brock in Fortenberry, 38.

2. Geraldine Weigall, unpublished journal, early 1911, Weigall Archive; quoted in Hankey, 152.

3. Cassatt to Louisine Havemeyer, January 28, 1911; quoted in Dillon, 12–13.

4. *Davis v. Manson,* 35.

5. Ibid.

6. Henry Burton, "The Late Theodore M. Davis's Excavations at Thebes in 1912–1913" (Part I) in *Bulletin of the Metropolitan Museum of Art,* vol. 11, no. 1 (January 1916).

7. *Davis v. Manson.*

8. Pages from Davis memorabilia at the Newport Historical Society; quoted in Gordon, 61–62.

9. (and following) *Davis v. Manson.*

10. *The American Antiquarian,* vol. 13 (1912), 92.

11. *The Tombs of Harmhabi and Touatankhamanou* (reprint), London, 2001; foreword by Nicholas Reeves.

12. Davis, 1912, 3.

13. (and following); Ellen Mary Newberry to Roger Newberry (unpublished), December 1912.

14. Sayce, 338.

15. Weigall to Hortense Weigall, early 1913, Weigall Archive; quoted in Hankey, 176.

16. Weigall to Gardiner, Griffith Institute; quoted in James, 180.

17. Smith, 1950, 268.

18. Burton, op. cit.

19. MFA #49.1071–1074.

20. MMA #14.6.232.

21. Reeves, 2000, 119.

22. *Davis v. Manson,* 117–18.

23. Burton's excavation journal, December 28, 1913; quoted in Reeves and Wilkinson, 140.

24. *Manchester Guardian,* January 27, 1923.

25. Thanks to John Larson and Sarah Ketchley for this information.

26. *Washington Post,* June 26, 1914.

27. Terry Boal to Herbert Parsons, December 19, 1914; Boal correspondence.

28. Terry Boal to Annie Davis, January 7, 1915 (and following quotations); Boal correspondence.

29. *Evening Gazette* (Cedar Rapids, Iowa), February 25, 1915.

30. *New York Times,* February 24, 1915.

31. Edith Bolling Galt to Woodrow Wilson, May 11, 1915; quoted in Edwin Tribble, ed., *A President in Love* (Boston: Houghton Mifflin, 1981), 24–25.

32. MMA #15.171.

33. Janet Buttles notebook held by the Oriental Institute Archives, University of Chicago.

34. *Washington Post,* December 30, 1915.

35. *Boal v. Manson,* Rhode Island Superior Court Decision (January 19, 1917), 9–10.

36. *Newport Journal,* January 26, 1917.

37. Supreme Court of Rhode Island, *Davis v. Manson, et al,* no. 384, January 9, 1918.

38. *New York Times,* March 19, 1924.

39. Metropolitan Museum of Art, *The Theodore M. Davis Bequest,* New York, 1931.

40. Lee in *Pennsylvania Heritage,* 30.

41. John A. Larson, "Theodore M. Davis, Pioneer to the Past" in *Kmt: A Modern Journal of Ancient Egypt,* vol. 1, no. 1.

42. Secrest, 206.
43. *New Yorker,* March 7, 1925.
44. *Newport Daily News,* July 24, 1957.
45. Ibid. July 16, 1960.
46. *Bridgeport Telegraph,* January 9, 1923.
47. Hawass, 159.
48. Romer, 183, 125.
49. Hawass, 97.
50. Peters, 1997, 88.
51. Christian Jacq, *The Tutankhamun Affair* (London: Pocket Books, 2003), 160, 167.
52. For a discussion of Davis's posthumous reputation, see John M. Adams, "Generous Benefactor or Arrogant Ignoramus? Theodore M. Davis and His Excavators," in *Kmt: A Modern Journal of Ancient Egypt,* vol. 22, no. 2 (Summer 2011), 54 ff.

Bibliography

Agassiz, G. R., ed. *Letters and Recollections of Alexander Agassiz with a Sketch of His Life and Work.* Boston: Houghton Mifflin, 1913.

Aldred, Cyril. *Akhenaten, King of Egypt.* New York: Thames and Hudson, 1988.

Andrews, Emma B. "A Journal on the Bedawin, 1889–1912." Unpublished manuscript. Used with permission of the Metropolitan Museum of Art.

Annie B. Davis (Theodore D. Boal, Executor) v. Thomas L. Manson, Executor, et al. Superior Court, Newport County, R.I. Equity. Case No. 1602.

Baker, Darrell D. *The Encyclopedia of the Egyptian Pharaohs.* Oakville, Conn.: Bannerstone Press, 2008.

Baum, Maud Gage. *In Other Lands Than Ours.* Chicago: Privately printed, 1907.

Boal Family Papers, 1850–1940. Historical Collections and Labor Archives, The Pennsylvania State University, State College, Pa.

Breasted, Charles. *Pioneer to the Past: The Story of James Henry Breasted, Archaeologist.* New York: Charles Scribner's Sons, 1943.

Brimmer, Martin. *Egypt: Three Essays on the History, Religion and Art of Ancient Egypt.* Cambridge, Mass.: 1892.

Burrows, Edwin G. and Mike Wallace. *Gotham: A History of New York City to 1898.* New York: Oxford University Press, 1999.

Buttles, Janet R. *The Queens of Egypt.* New York: Appleton, 1908.

Currelly, Charles Trick. *I Brought the Ages Home*. Toronto: Royal Ontario Museum, 1956.

Davis, Theodore M., Howard Carter, Percy E. Newberry, Gaston Maspero, and G. Elliot Smith. *The Tomb of Thoutmosis IV*. London: Archibald Constable, 1904.

Davis, Theodore M., Gaston Maspero, Edward Ayrton, Georges Daressy, and E. Harold Jones. *The Tomb of Siphtah: The Monkey Tomb and the Gold Tomb*. London: Archibald Constable, 1908.

Davis, Theodore M., Gaston Maspero, Georges Daressy, and Lancelot Crane. *The Tombs of Harmhabi and Touatankhamanou*. London: Archibald Constable, 1912.

Davis, Theodore M., Gaston Maspero, Percy E. Newberry, and Howard Carter. *The Tomb of Iouiya and Touiyou*. London: Archibald Constable, 1907.

Davis, Theodore M., Gaston Maspero, G. Elliot Smith, Edward Ayrton, and Georges Daressy. *The Tomb of Queen Tiyi*. London: Archibald Constable, 1910.

Davis, Theodore M., Edouard Naville, and Howard Carter. *The Tomb of Hatshopsitu*. London: Archibald Constable, 1906.

Dillon, Millicent. *After Egypt: Isadora Duncan & Mary Cassatt, a Dual Biography*. New York: Dutton, 1990.

Dodson, Aidan. *Poisoned Legacy: The Fall of the Nineteenth Egyptian Dynasty*. New York: American University in Cairo Press, 2010.

Forbes, Dennis. *Tombs, Treasures, Mummies: Seven Great Discoveries of Egyptian Archaeology*. Sebastopol, Calif: KMT Communications, 1998.

Fortenberry, Diane, ed. *Who Travels Sees More: Artists, Architects and Archaeologists Discover Egypt and the Near East*. Oxford: Oxbow Books, 2007.

Gordon, Daniel. *The Robber Baron Archaeologist: An Essay About the Life of Theodore M. Davis*. Baltimore: Department of Near Eastern Studies, Johns Hopkins University, 2007.

Hadley, Rolin Van N. *The Letters of Bernard Berenson and Isabella Stewart Gardner, 1887–1924*. Boston: Northeastern University Press, 1987.

Hankey, Julie. *A Passion for Egypt: Arthur Weigall, Tutankhamun and the 'Curse of the Pharaohs.'* London: I. B. Tauris, 2001.

Hawass, Zahi. *Tutankhamun and the Golden Age of the Pharaohs*. Washington, D.C.: National Geographic, 2005.

Hayes, William C. *The Scepter of Egypt*. Vol. 2. New York: Metropolitan Museum of Art, 1959.

Heinrich, Frederick L. *A History of Keweenaw Land Association, Limited*. Boston: privately printed, 1981.

History of Johnson County, Iowa, Containing a History of the County and Its Townships. Iowa City, Iowa: 1883.

James, T. G. H. *Howard Carter: The Path to Tutankhamun* (revised edition). London: Tauris Parke, 2001.

Knapp, Jacob. *Autobiography of Elder Jacob Knapp.* New York: Sheldon, 1868.

Lankton, Larry. *Cradle to Grave: Life, Work, and Death at the Lake Superior Copper Mines.* New York: Oxford University Press, 1991.

Lipsey, John Jay. *The Lives of James John Hagerman, Builder of the Colorado Midland Railway.* Denver: Golden Bell Press, 1968.

Longyear, John Munro. *Keweenaw Canal Company.* Unpublished article, provided courtesy of Keweenaw Land Association, n.d.

———. *Landlooker in the Upper Peninsula of Michigan.* Compiled by Helen Longyear Paul. Marquette, Mich.: John M. Longyear Research Library, Marquette County Historical Society, 1960.

Loti, Pierre. *Egypt.* New York: Duffield, 1909.

Lynch, Jeremiah. *Egyptian Sketches.* New York: Scribner and Welford, 1890.

Maspero, Gaston. *Egypt: Ancient Sites and Modern Scenes.* Translated by Elizabeth Lee. London: T. F. Unwin, 1910.

———. *New Light on Ancient Egypt.* Translated by Elizabeth Lee. New York: Appleton, 1909.

McCabe, James D. *Lights and Shadows of New York Life: Or, the Sights and Sensations of the Great City.* Philadelphia: National Publishing, 1872.

Montserrat, Dominic. *Akhenaten: History, Fantasy and Ancient Egypt.* London: Routledge, 2000.

Moore, Charles. *History of Michigan.* Chicago: Lewis Publishing, 1915.

Newberry, Mary B. *A Winter on the Nile.* Unpublished letters, 1912–1914, compiled by Nancy Newberry Kamlukin. Made available through the kind courtesy of Lady Eileen Baker Strathnaver, Alice Newberry Hall, and Mary Newberry Matthews.

Orcutt, William Dana. *Celebrities Off Parade.* Chicago: Willett, Clark, 1935.

Peters, Elizabeth. *Seeing a Large Cat: An Amelia Peabody Mystery.* New York: Warner Books, 1997.

Reeves, Nicholas. *Ancient Egypt: The Great Discoveries.* New York: Thames and Hudson, 2000.

———. *The Complete Tutankhamun: The King, the Tomb, the Royal Treasure.* London: Thames and Hudson, 1990. (In notes, "1990a.")

———. *Valley of the Kings: The Decline of a Royal Necropolis.* London: Kegan Paul, 1990.

Reeves, Nicholas, and John H. Taylor. *Howard Carter: Before Tutankhamun.* New York: Harry N. Abrams, 1993.

Reeves, Nicholas, and Richard H. Wilkinson. *The Complete Valley of the Kings: Tombs and Treasures of Egypt's Greatest Pharaohs.* London: Thames and Hudson, 1996.

Riggs, Arthur Stanley. *The Romance of Human Progress.* New York: Bobbs-Merrill, 1938.

Romer, John. *Valley of the Kings.* New York: Henry Holt, 1981.

Ryan, Donald P. *Beneath the Sands of Egypt: Adventures of an Unconventional Archaeologist.* New York: William Morrow, 2010.

Samuels, Ernest. *Bernard Berenson: The Making of a Connoisseur.* Cambridge, Mass.: Belknap Press, 1979.

———. *Bernard Berenson: The Making of a Legend.* Cambridge, Mass.: Belknap Press, 1987.

Sayce, Archibald Henry. *Reminiscences.* London: Macmillan, 1923.

Schoolcraft, Henry Rowe. *Narrative Journal of Travels Through the Northwestern Regions of the United States.* Albany: E. and E. Hosford, 1821.

Secrest, Meryle. *Being Bernard Berenson: A Biography.* New York: Holt, Rinehart and Winston, 1979.

Smith, Joseph Lindon. "Egypt, My Winter Home." Unpublished manuscript. 1950.

———. *Tombs, Temples and Ancient Art.* Norman: University of Oklahoma Press, 1956.

Stimson, Frederic Jesup. *My United States.* New York: Charles Scribner's Sons, 1931.

Strong, George Templeton. *The Diary of George Templeton Strong, 1820–1875.* Edited by Allan Nevis and Milton Helsey. New York: Macmillan, 1952.

Thomas, Elizabeth. *The Royal Necropolis of Thebes.* Trenton, N.J.: privately printed, 1966.

Totten, Ruth Ellen Patton. *The Button Box: A Daughter's Loving Memoir of Mrs. George S. Patton.* Columbia: University of Missouri Press, 2005.

Tyndale, Walter. *Below the Cataracts.* Philadelphia: J. B. Lippincott, 1907.

U.S. House of Representatives. Committee on Banking and Currency. "Failure of National Banks." Second session of the Forty-second Congress, February 12–March 23, 1872.

———. Committee on Banking and Currency. "Hearings in the Matter of the Receivership of the Ocean National Bank." First session of the Forty-third Congress, June 1874.

――――. Committee on Banking and Currency. Second session of the Forty-sixth Congress. "Investigation of the Failure of the Ocean National Bank and the Alleged Improper Management of Theodore M. Davis, Receiver." May 1880.

――――. Committee on Public Lands. First session of the Forty-eighth Congress. "Investigation of the Portage Lake and Lake Superior Ship-Canal Company." April 1884.

Weigall, Arthur. *The Glory of the Pharaohs.* New York: G. P. Putnam's Sons, 1923.

――――. *The Treasury of Ancient Egypt.* Chicago: Rand McNally, 1912.

――――. *Tutankhamen and Other Essays.* New York: George H. Doran, 1924.

――――. *Egypt from 1798 to 1914.* Edinburgh: William Blackwood and Sons, 1915.

Wilbour, Charles Edwin. *Travels in Egypt: Letters of Charles Edwin Wilbour.* Edited by Jean Capart. Brooklyn: Brooklyn Museum, 1936.

Winlock, H. E. *Materials Used at the Embalming of King Tut-Ankh-Amun.* New York: Metropolitan Museum of Art, 1941.

Winstone, H. V. F. *Howard Carter and the Discovery of the Tomb of Tutankhamun.* London: Constable, 1991.

Index

abolitionists, 41–43, 84
adultery, 251–52
Agassiz, Alexander, 229–30, 247, 252, 265, 276
Akhenaten, 14, 48, 125, 143, 148, 270
  Tiyi as, 188–89
Amarna-era mysteries, 190, 193
amduat, 74
Amenhotep I, 275
Amenhotep II, 48–49, 118
Amenhotep III, 2, 14, 143
American Institute of Architects, 235
American Missionary School for Girls, 78
Andrews, Abner (husband of Andrews, E. B.), 47, 81–82, 251
Andrews, Emma B., 9, 60–61, 65, 96, 120–21, 162, 233–34, 239, 311
  Beduin furnished by, 270
  on *Beduin* visitors, 168

Boal, T. D., description of, 305
  Brenton Point mansion and, 232
  Davis, T. M., gift of crown to, 150
  Davis, T. M., relationship with, 47, 251, 252–53
  Davis, T. M., will and, 257–58
  death of, 315
  drunk with power accusation, 300
  Egyptian peasants viewed by Davis, T. M., and, 76–77
  floor plan made by, 146
  husband's illness, 81–82
  journal of, 265, 299
  move into Davis, T. M., home, 251
  neighbor's criticism of, 291–92
  tensions between wife and, 253–54, 288–90
animal mummies, 117–18
Annie B. Davis vs. Thomas L. Manson, 310, 311, 312–14
Apepi ring, 311

archeology. *See also* Egyptology;
  excavation; *specific tombs*
  Davis, T. M., contribution to, 54,
    278, 279, 321
  early twentieth-century, 53
art collection, 259–65
artifacts, EEF donor agreement
  concerning, 173. *See also specific
  objects*; *specific tombs*
Atwood, Warren, 252
automobiles, 274
Avery, Perez, 91–92, 134, 139, 174
  bribery conviction of, 182
Avery, William, 91, 92, 134, 139,
    183–86, 223–24
  Ayer and, 154–56
  bribery conviction, 136–37
  surrender of, 182
Avery-Davis interactions
  Avery, W., deal failure, 185–86
  Avery bankruptcy plan, 160–61
  Avery bonds, 139–40, 153,
    154–56, 159, 163, 183–84, 227
  campaign against Davis, 165–66
  hearings, 174–78, 223
  hearings against Averys, 174–78
Aye (pharaoh), 271–72
Ayer, Frederick, 185, 215, 253, 319
Ayer, James ("Sarsaparilla King"),
    154, 158–59, 161, 183
  in Avery hearings, 175, 176, 177
  in syndicate, 155–56, 158–60,
    163–65, 176, 178, 181
Ayrton, Edward Russell, 105, 108–9,
    112, 113, 115–16, *145,* 192,
    196
  Davis, T. M., verbal abuse of,
    203
  death of, 303

Gold Tomb and, 199–201, 210
Hatshepsut mummy left behind
  by, 119
improvements brought by, 114
strained relations with, 197, 201
Tiyi tomb and, 122–23, 128–31,
    132, 146–48, 187
Weigall, A., and, 113, 210–11

Bank of the Metropolis, 88–90,
    137–38, 157
Baum, L. Frank, 121
beautiful suicide, 152–53
Beduin (yacht), 6, 7–8, *9,* 77. *See also
  dahabiyeh*
  Aswan journey, 61
  Carter visits to, 48–49
  furnishing of, 270
  Morgan's visit to, 287, 290–91
  sale of, 302–3
  socializing on, 73, 101, 198–99,
    295–96
  visitors, 168, 290–91
Bell, Martha, 149
Bellini, Giovanni, 254
Belmont, August, 231
Belzoni, Giovanni, 53, 104, 119
Bennett, James Gordon, 231
Benson, Margaret, 53, 279
Berenson, Bernhard (art critic),
    261–65
Berenson, Mary, 262–63
Bickel, Susanne, 25
Boal, George, 44, 81, 93, 162, 179,
    242–43
Boal, John, 82
Boal, Malvina, 44, 93, 180
Boal, Pierre (son of Boal, T. D.,),
    248, 273, 313, 316

Boal, Theodore Davis ("Terry"),
    179–81, 235, 254, 304, 315–16
    Davis, T. M., disappointment over,
        245–49
    Davis, T. M., will and, 288, 292,
        299–300, 305–6, 308–14
    in Reef dispute, 291
Bol, Ferdinand, 261–62
Book of the Dead scrolls, 11, 48, 104,
    266
Boutwell, George S., 175–76
bowl, bronze, *28, 29,* 32–33
Breasted, Charles, 115
Breasted, James Henry, 111–12,
    237–38, 279
Brenton Point, 232, 318
Brenton's Reef, 229, *233*
bribery, 136–37, 157, 176, 177, 182
bricks, magical, 118, 143
Brimmer, Martin, 266–67, 268
bronze bowl, *28, 29,* 32–33
Brown, John, 41–43
Bryan, William Jennings, 304
Buchanan, Carrie, 78–79, 288, 313
Budge, E. A. Wallis, 23, 60–61, 205,
    268
Budlong, Milton, 317
Burton, Henry ("Harry"), 76,
    274–75, 277, *278,* 293, 299
    adoption by Cust, 284–85
    excavation inexperience of, 285
    farewell and subsequent work,
        303
    1911 excavation headed by, 286,
        287
    photography of, 285
    in Rameses II tomb, 301
    Siptah tomb cleared by, 290–91,
        294–98

    on Tutankhamen discovery and
        irony, 302
Busk, Jo, 244
Butler, Benjamin, 166
Buttles, Ellen Mary ("Mamie").
    See Newberry, Ellen Mary
    ("Mamie") Buttles
Buttles, Janet ("Nettie"), 56, 122,
    290, 317
Buttles, Joel Benoni ("Judge"), 44,
    46, 47, 93, 235

Cairo, 59–60, 68
Callender, Charles, 92, 140, 151, 157,
    161, 176, 177
canal. *See* Keweenaw canal; Soo canal
candles incident, 15
canoe hooking incident, 36, 153
canopic jarheads, 56, 57, 125, 131,
    143, 203–4. *See also* jars,
    alabaster
Carnarvon, Earl of, as donor, 54,
    168–69, 279
Carnarvon Tablet, 54
Carnegie, Andrew, 80, 216–17
Carter, Howard, 10, 24, 50–52, 60,
    94, 169, 270, 295–96
    Beduin sale and, 302–3
    Beduin visits by, 48–49
    career of, 48, 51
    criticism of, 57
    Davis, T. M., letter to, 101–2
    laborers not acknowledged by, 75
    Maspero and, 52, 95, 103, 203
    mummies overlooked by, 57, 119
    party incident, 68
    Saqqara incident, 100, 101–2, 112
    Thutmose I tomb excavation and,
        71–75

Carter, Howard *(continued)*
  Thutmose IV project, 49–50, 51,
    62–67
  tomb missed by, 55
  transfer of, 95, 96–97
  Tutankhamen discovery by, 54,
    204, 272–73, 294, 319
  unemployment of, 112
  Yuya *shabti* painted by, *282,* 283
casino, Newport, 231–32, 235, 239
Cassatt, Mary, 286
Catena, Vincenzo, 52
chair incident, 105–6
chariot yoke, 7, 8
Chase, Salmon P., 82
Chicago Method, 112
cigarette card, 130
Civil War, 80, 81, 82
Clark, George W., 39, 40–41, 44,
    80–82, 164
Clarke, William Penn, 38, 39, 40, 42,
    80
  Davis, T. M., partnership with, 43
  dispute and lawsuit, 82–84
Clay, Henry, 34
Cleopatra, 130
Cleveland, Grover, 242
coffins, 12–14. *See also* sarcophagus
  of Thuyu, 1–2, 14–15
  Tiyi gold-lined, 147–48
Colorado Midland railroad, 242–45
Committee on Banking and
    Currency, 167, 175, 222
congressional hearings, Averys-
    Davis, T. M., 174–78
Conkling, Roscoe, 185
Connaught, Duke of, 22, 206, 208–9
Cooke, Jay, 165
Cooper, James Fenimore, 17

copper mining, 20–21, 229–30, 247
Cordozo, Albert, 142
corruption, in New York City,
    89–90, 136–39, 158, 182
Crane, Lancelot, 210
Cromer, Lord, 8, 54, 100, 168
crown, from tomb of Tiyi, 149, 150,
    168
Cushing, Caleb, 176
Cust, Robert Henry Hobart, 284–85

dahabiyeh (houseboat), 5–6, 7, 10,
    265. *See also Beduin*
  construction of personal, 269
Daressy, Georges, 272
DaVinci, Leonardo, 263–65, 317
Davis, Angellica, 17
Davis, Annie Buttles (wife of
    Davis, T. M.), 45–47, 79, 84, 93,
    267–68
  departure from Reef, 288–90,
    291–92
  estrangement from husband, 94,
    251
  husband's semi-retirement and,
    234–35
  husband's will and, 257–58,
    292
Davis, Gertrude Matilda (sister of
    Davis, T. M.), 18, 313
Davis, Jefferson, 140
Davis, Richard Montgomery (father
    of Davis, T. M.), 16–17, 18
Davis, Theodore Montgomery, *45,
    145, 289. See also* Avery-Davis
  interactions; *Beduin*; Keweenaw
  canal; Ocean National Bank;
  the Reef; *specific excavations*;
  specific topics

adopted son "Terry" and, 179–81,
    245–49, 305–6
ambition of, 69, 82
Andrews, E. B., relationship, 47,
    251, 252–53
archeology contribution of, 54,
    278, 279, 321
art collecting by, 259–65
automobiles of, 274
Ayrton hired by, 112–13
Ayrton verbally abused by, 203
Bar admittance of, 40–41
birth and childhood, 18–19
books published by, 106–7, 272,
    292–93
Brenton Point purchased by, 232
Britain trip with Avery, W., 185
bronze bowl received by, 32–33
Buttles, E. M., helped by, 250
card playing, 37, 179
career development, 33–44
Carter and, 48–52, 94, 112
during Civil War, 80, 81
Clark, G. W., and, 39, 40–41, 83,
    164
Colorado trip with Moffat, 244–45
connections through Andrews,
    E. B., 82
cremation and obituaries, 307
crown given to Andrews, E. B.,
    by, 150
death and funeral of father, 16
death of, 306–7
decision to excavate, 13
as donor, 278, 279
Egypt companions, 6
Egyptian collection of, 120, 172–73
Egyptian government agreement
    with, 3, 108–10

Egyptian relations, 76–79
Egypt-New York comparison of
    actions by, 299
estrangement from wife, 94, 251
excavation role of, 99–100, 105, 108
fake DaVinci painting purchased
    by, 263–65, 317
first discovery, 65
first Egypt trips of, 265–70
forgotten accomplishment of,
    25–26, 54
girls' school funded by, 78
Gorst note to, 199
half-sister of, 92–93
interviews of, 188, 196
Knagenhjelm marriage paid for
    by, 255–56
lack of offspring, 93–94
as landlooker, 34–38
last days of, 305–6
last excavation by, 209, 275, 276,
    302
last words of, 306
lawsuit over money and will of,
    306, 308–14
letter to Knagenhjelm, "Nellie,"
    268–69
library of, 232
limerick taught to Berenson, B.,
    by, 262
Maspero's defense of, 200
mental deterioration of, 287, 298,
    299, 303
mistress of, 6–7, 213
mummy case bought by, 48
museum room named after, 108
Newport mansion of, 232–34, 233
paternalism towards Beduin crew,
    77

Davis (continued)
  personality of, 85–86, 87, 236
  physical decline of, 292
  posthumous gifts of, 173
  publicity of discoveries, 22–23, 74,
     110–11, 186–87, 212, 301
  Rembrandt painting purchase by,
     111
  reputation of, 320
  Saqqara incident and, 101–2
  search policy of, 13, 24, 25, 99, 121
  secretary of, 301, 305, 312
  self-education of, 236–37
  self-transformation of, 320–21
  semi-retirement lifestyle, 234–35,
     237–39
  servants of, 293–94
  silver gloves washed by, 201
  social disapproval of Andrews,
     E. B., and, 253
  suicide by half-sister of, 152–53
  on Thuyu mummy, 15–16
  Titus influence on, 33–34, 37, 38
  Tiyi and, 129, 130, 142–50,
     188–89, 191, 193, 196
  tomb treasures given to, 108, 187,
     283, 297
  tombs discovered by, listed, 270
  tombstone of, 308
  trust arrangements, 288–89
  Tutankhamen tomb and, 272–73,
     319–20
  valet of, 63, 126–27
  wealth of, 4, 90, 94, 110, 186, 259,
     288–89
  wedding of, 44–46
  Weigall, A., and, 3–4, 100–101,
     199–200, 205, 211
  wilderness ordeal of, 34–36

  will revisions and estate of,
     257–59, 288, 292, 300
  Wilson, E. S., and, 255–57
  wreaths torn by, 203
Davis & Edsall office, 137
Denis de Lagarde, Mathilde,
     246–47, 248, 254
Denver & Rio Grande, 243
Devonshire, Duke and Duchess of,
     204
Dickens, Charles, 236–37
Dickinson, Donald, 220
dig house, 113–14, 202, 319
divorce, 252
donkeys, 2
donors, 173. See also funding,
     excavation
  fickleness of, 278–79
Douglass, Frederick, 18
Drost, Willem, 111
Dwyer, Andrew, 288

earrings, of Tawosret, 194, 195,
     201
Edsall, Thomas Henry, 87, 140, 153,
     242
Edwards, Amelia, 31
EEF. See Egypt Exploration Fund
Egypt
  first trips to, 259, 265–70
  first woman to excavate, 53, 279
  idyllic lifestyle in, 278
  last stay in, 303
  New York and, 299
  pattern of visits to, 269–70
  supreme god of, 66
Egypt: Three Essays on the History,
     Religion and Art of Ancient
     Egypt (Brimmer), 266–67

Egypt Exploration Fund (EEF), 31,
    48, 113, 120. *See also* funding,
    excavation
donor agreement with, 173
Egyptians, 76–79
Egyptian collection, Davis, T. M.,
    120, 172–73. *See also* Salle
    Theodore M. Davis
Egyptian government, Davis
    agreement with, 3, 108–10
Egyptian Museum, on Ismailia, 58
2011 robbery of, 283–84
Egyptology
    controversial episode in, 123,
        127–28
    KV 55 controversy and, 190–91
    publications and reports issue in,
        106
    Yuya tomb influence on, 104
Egyptomania, 23–24, 273–74
embalming cache, 204
Erskine, David, 127
Eugenie (empress), 105–6
excavation. *See also* KV 55
    controversy; Valley of the
    Kings; *specific tombs*
    amateur, 54
    authority issues in 1907, 192–93
    Ayrton in charge of, 108–9, 192,
        196
    Burton's 1911, 286, 287
    controversial 1907, 123, 127–32
    December 1907, 197–98
    first long-term campaign of, 280
    first woman to excavate Egypt, 53
    funding, 24, 31, 50–52, 120
    improvements, 114
    ironic end of Davis, T. M., 302
    laborers, 75–76

last, 209, 275, 276
1910 West Valley, 276–78, 285–87
of 1905, 2–5, 101–6
of 1907, 122–23
of 1908, 199–210, 270–71
of 1909, 271–73
of 1913, 301
policy and approach, 13, 24, 25,
    99, 121
role in, 99–100, 105, 108
technical limitations and, 192
exhibitions, 1, 25, 26, 204

filigree work, 201
Filipinos, taunting incident at
    World's Fair, 95–96
financial dealings, of Davis, T. M.,
    See also Avery-Davis interactions;
    Ocean National Bank
auction of bonds by, 163
charges against Davis, 167
Clark, G. W., 39, 40–41, 83
Clarke dispute, 82–84
Clarke partnership, 43
Colorado trip with Moffat,
    244–45
Edsall partnership, 87, 140, 153
first financial score, 88–90
fortune estimate of 1908, 259
Frost lawsuit, 217–21
investigations into, 181–82,
    221–27, 239–42
last major undertaking, 242–45
law practice, 21, 39, 40–43, 79–81
Michigan land sale, 183–84, 185
mid-1880 battle against, 239–42
mining millions made by, 217
in New York City, 84–94, 136–39,
    178–79

financial dealings (continued)
  Rutter's visit, 137–38, 156–57
  silver mine stock of, 245
  syndicate, 155–56, 158–60,
    163–65, 178, 181, 228
  Tweed and, 90–91
  Washington, D.C., visit, 87–88
financial panic
  of 1873, 165
  of 1893, 246
Fisk, Jim, 222
Frick, Henry, 159–60
Frost, George S. ("railroad
    wrecker"), 34, 93, 155, 176,
    217–21, 223–25
funding, excavation, 24, 31, 50–52,
    120
  donor fickleness, 278–79

galabiyas, 170–71
Galloway, Gertrude Davis (sister of
    Davis, T. M.), 18, 44–45, 153
Galt, Edith Bolling, 310–11
Gardiner, Alan, 295
Garstang, John, 196, 197
Germans, 304
Ghio, Annie (secretary), 301, 305, 312
Gilded Age period, 230, 231
Gilman, ("Mr."), 86, 151–52, 179
gloves, silver, 201
Gogebic Range, 219, 230
gold foil, 271–72
gold leaf inscriptions, from KV 55,
    142, 146–47, 190
Gold Tomb (1908), 199–205, 210
  Egyptomania influenced by,
    273–74
gold watch, 246
Gorst, Eldon, 199, 202, 213, 290

Gould, Jay, 80
Grant, James, 41
grave robbers, 4, 8, 12, 64, 209
Great Strike, 214–15
guides (dragomen), 59, 79

Hagerman, James J., 33, 217, 242, 243
Haggard, H. Ryder, 95
Hardy, Jean, 6, 74, 98
Harvey, Charles, 133
Hassan ("donkey boy"), 22
Hathor cow, 120
Hatshepsut, 71. See also tomb,
    of Hatshepsut
  left behind mummy of, 119
Havemeyer, T. A., 239
Hawass, Zahi, 320
Hearst, Phoebe, 278–79
Hearst, William Randolph, 23
heretic pharaoh, 125
Horemheb, Harmhabi, 66, 206–7,
    275. See also tomb,
    of Horemheb
Houghton, Douglass, 19
houseboat, Davis's. See Beduin;
    dahabiyeh (houseboat)
Howe, Julia Ward, 231, 259
Hubbell. Almerin, 225
Hulburd, Hiland, 82, 89, 92, 182, 215
  death of, 228
  receivership deal, 141–42
  resignation of, 158
  Rutter carriage gift to, 137–38,
    156–57

Iddings, Lewis M., 212–13
inscriptions
  copying, 112
  gold leaf, 142, 146–47, 190

Iowa City, 38, 39–40, 43, 83
Iowa Territory, 79
iron mines, 217, 220, 239, 319

James, Henry, 231, 237
James, William ("father of American
    psychology"), 231, 237
jars, alabaster, 67–68. *See also*
    canopic jarheads
jewelry, 60
    from Gold Tomb, 201–2
Jones, Cyril, 285
Jones, Daniel (valet) ("Jones the
    Great"), 63, 126–27, 168, 239,
    300
Jones, Ernest Harold, 118, 147, 168,
    271
    Burton replacing, 278
    death of, 287
    Horemheb tomb and, 207, 210
    1909 discovery by, 271, 273
    as painter, 196–97
    Roosevelt escorted by, 275–76
    tomb souvenirs of, 167
    tuberculosis of, 196, 275, 285, 286

Keweenaw canal, 36–37, 92, 137,
    159–65. *See also* Lake Superior
    Ship Canal, Railway and Iron
    Company
    advantages of, 162
    Avery bonds, 139–40, 153,
        154–56, 158, 183–84
    bankruptcy, 160–61
    completion, 166
    Davis-Avery meeting over, 154
    iron mining, 217, 220, 239, 319
    land survey by Longyear, 216
    legality investigation, 240–42

selling of, 243
stock, 218
timber harvest, 215
Keweenaw Land Association, 242,
    255, 304, 319
Khedive Abbas Himli II, 68, 212–13
Kidd, Henry (butler), 301, 311
Kipling, Rudyard, 51–52
Kirkwood, Samuel, 40, 83–84
Kitchener, Horatio Herbert, 213,
    290
Kiya. *See* Tiyi
Kleber, Jean Baptiste, 58–59
Knagenhjelm, Eleanor ("Nellie")
    Salome, 61, 164, 186, 213,
    254–56, 300
    Davis, T. M., letter to, 268–69
    death of, 316
    in lawsuit over will, 311–12
    letters from Davis, T. M., to, 257
    valley site visited by, 271–72
Knagenhjelm, Nils ("Knogs"),
    254–56, 257
Knagenhjelm, Nils Theodore,
    311–12
Know Nothings, 38
Knox, Henry, 86
Knox, Isaac H., 155, 158–59, 161,
    164, 181
    in Avery hearings, 175, 177, 178
    canal certificates of Ayer and, 183
KV 55 controversy, 131, 142–50,
    167–68, 170–73, 186–93
    authority issues for, 192–93
    as botched excavation, 190–91
    mummy identity controversy, 131,
        144–45, 147, 149, 150, 188–89,
        191
    strained relations over, 197, 199

laborers, excavation, 75–76
Laffan, William F., 119–20
Lagarde, Cecile de ("Baby"), 287, 288, 300, 312, 313
Lake Superior Ship Canal, Iron and Railway Company, 91, 139
  forming of new, 184–85
Lake Superior Ship Canal, Railway and Iron Company, 184–85, 214, 217, 239–42
lawsuits, 82–84, 306, 308–14
Lee, Robert E., 43
Lewis, Samuel, 252
Lincoln, Abraham, 84, 94
Lipton, Thomas, 59
loincloths, 60
Longyear, John Munro, 216, 219, 241, 295
Loti, Pierre, 62, 117
Ludwig, Bruce, 55
Lyon, David G., 58
Lythgoe, Albert, 60, 69, 120, 187, 303

magical bricks, 118, 143
Maiherpri, 60
mansions, 5–6, 230. *See also* the Reef
  Boal, T. D., 247
  robber barons', 231
Manson, Thomas, 179
marriage
  scarabs, 14
  in upper classes, 252
Martin, Geoffrey, 202, 208
Martin, Randolph, 134
Maspero, Gaston, 7, 10, 12, 54, 63, 98, 259
  authority and role in 1907 excavation, 192
  Carter and, 52, 95, 103, 203

Carter transferred by, 95, 96–97
Davis, T. M., agreement with, 108–10
Davis, T. M., defended by, 200
Davis, T. M., museum room and, 108
death of, 312
intrigues against, 290
resignation of, 302
in Tiyi project, 147, 167
on tomb atmosphere, 64–65
tomb treasures given to Davis, T. M., by, 187, 211, 297
Weigall criticism of, 295
Yuya tomb and, 14, 110–11
Medinet Habu, 49, 297
Mena House, 96–97
Mentuhotep II, 113, 120
Metropolitan Museum of Art, 119, 120, 125, 314
Michigan land, 153, 182, 186, 221, 240. *See also* Keweenaw canal
  iron mining on, 217, 220, 239
  sale of, 183–84, 185
  survey, 34–38
Million Dollar Agreement, 309–10, 312–13
Millionaires' Row, 304
Minghetti, Donna Laura, 263
mistress, 6–7, 213. *See also* Andrews, Emma B.
Mohassib, Mohammed, 170, 171–72, 266
Mollie Gibson silver mine, 245
Monet, Claude, 260
monkey mummy, 117–18
Montuhirkopeshef, 61, 119
Morgan, J. P., 80, 120, 171, 173, 179
  Beduin visit by, 287, 290–91

death of, 296
Roosevelt's joke about, 276
Morse, Samuel, 18
mummies, 188–89
    animal, 117–18
    Aye's, 272
    ear piercings in, 195
    missing bands, 148
    overlooked by Carter, 57, 119
    of Siptah, 115
    slashed, 67
    of Thuyu, 15–16
    Tiyi tomb's, 131, 144–45, 147, 149,
        188–89, 191
    unwrappings, 47–48, 49, 68
museums. *See* Egyptian Museum;
    Metropolitan Museum of Art
Museum of Fine Arts, Boston, 69,
    71, 74

Napoleon, 58–59
Napoleon III, 106
National Banking Act, 88
Naville, Henri Edouard, 120, 279
Necho II, 102
Nefertari, 95
Nefertiti, 202
New York City, 84–94
    corruption, 89–90, 136–39, 158,
        182
    Davis, T. M., in Egypt compared
        to, 299
    personal life in, 178–79
New York Printing Company, 91,
    140, 141, 151–52, 171, 265
Newberry, Ellen Mary ("Mamie")
    Buttles, 234–35, 265, 273, 290
    Carter and, 295–96
    Davis, T. M., death and, 307

Davis, T. M., will and, 300
    on Davis, T. M., servants, 293–94
    death of, 317
    family split and, 291
    home built by, 316
    wedding of, 249–50
    as widow, 250, 251
Newberry, Percy, 30–33, 63, 67, 73,
    100, 270, 285
    Beduin bought by, 303
    books written by, 121
    fund-raising by, 31
    Jones, E. H., helped by, 196
    mummy case unwrappings by,
        47–48
Newberry, Wolcott, 249–50
Newport, Rhode Island, 229.
    See also the Reef (Davis, T. M.,
        mansion)
    casino in, 231–32, 235, 239
    history of, 231
    move to, 237
Newport Industrial School for Girls,
    251
Nubian sailors, 6

Ocean National Bank, 90, 92, 163, 170
    auction of shares, 218–19
    Avery bonds and, 156, 159, 183,
        227
    casualties, 227–28
    closing of, 140–42, 150–52
    depositors, 217
    Panic of 1873 and, 165
    receivership, 141–42, 150–52, 153,
        167, 174–78, 215, 227
    robbery, 133–36
    settlement, 215, 217
    shareholder assessments, 215

O'Conor, Charles, 140
Olmsted, Frederick Law, 174, 233–34
Orcutt, William Dana, 188
Osgood, John C., 247
Osiris, 208

Page, Thomas Nelson, 188
palace. See also Winter Palace Hotel
    of Akhenaten, 270
    of Khedive Abbas Hilmi Pasha,
        212–13
    of Rameses III, 297
The Panic, 165, 246
Parsons, Elsie Clews, 309
Parsons, Herbert, 287–88, 306,
    308–10, 315
Parsons, John, 221, 223, 224, 258,
    306
passenger cars, elevated, 133
patent-medicine peddlers, 87
Patton, George S., 254
Paulin-Grothe, Elina, 25
Petrie, William M. F., 48, 60–61,
    97–98
pharaohs. See also specific pharaohs
    heretic, 125
Pie Girl Dinner, 179
Pirie, Annie (wife of Quibell), 97–98
Powell, Arthur, 236
Presbyterian missionary, 78
preservation, tomb, 49–50
Priam's Treasure, 173
private suspension, 89, 157
Proctor, John, Jr., 254
professional archaeologists, 53
publicity, on tomb discoveries,
    22–23, 74, 110–11, 212, 301
Pumpelly, Raphael, 230–31
pyramids, 294

Quibell, Annie, 104
Quibell, James E., 95, 96, 97–99, 103

Rameses II, 55, 301
Rameses III, 297
Rameses IV, 145, *145,* 200
Rameses IX, 121–23
receivership, 141–42, 150–52, 153,
    167, 174–78, 215, 227
Redfield, Henrietta, 215
Redstone Castle, 247
the Reef (Davis, T. M., mansion),
    233, 251
    army use of, 317–18
    burning of, 318
    crises of 1911, 287
    death of gardener, 300
    design and building of, 232–34
    family split and dispute over,
        288–92
    gardens, 233–34, 303–4
    last visitors to, 318
    selling of, 317
    tensions in household, 256
    upkeep costs, 235
Reeves, Nicholas, 202, 204, 293
Reisner, George, 278–79
Rekhmire, 31–32
Rembrandt, 111
Republican Party, 82, 90
revolution, in Tahrir Square, 283–84
Rhinelander, Fred, 244
Richter, J. P., 260
ring, Apepi, 311
robber barons, 159, 231, 321
    art collecting compulsion of, 260
robberies, 209, 212
    ancient grave, 4, 8, 12, 64, 209
    animal mummy joke and, 117–18

contemporary vandalism, 60
jewelry and loincloth, 60
Ocean National Bank, 133–36
tomb of Tiyi, 170–73
2011 Egyptian Museum, 283–84
by workers, 107, 210
Rockefeller, John D., 80, 112, 216
funding withdrawn by, 279
Romer, John, 319, 320
Roosevelt, Theodore, 76, 159,
275–76, 308
Rothschild, Alfred de, 168–69
Rutter, George, 89, 158
carriage gift to Hullburd, 137–38,
156–57
Ryan, Donald, 57, 118–19

sailors, Nubian, 6
St. Mary's Falls Ship Canal
Company, 33–34
Salle Theodore M. Davis, 108, 188,
211, 311, 319. See also Egyptian
collection, Davis, T. M.,
Saqqara incident, 100, 101, 112
sarcophagus. See also coffins
Hatshepsut's, 70, 71, 74
Horemheb's, 208
in Siptah's tomb, 296–97
Thutmose I, 70, 73, 74
Sayce, Archibald, 7, 146, 189
Scarabs: An Introduction to the Study
of Egyptian Seals and Signet
Rings (Newberry), 121
scarabs, marriage, 14
Schaden, Otto, 25
Schiaparelli, Ernesto, 95
Schliemann, Heinrich, 53, 173, 268
Second National Bank, 221
Semitic Museum at Harvard, 57

Sennedjem (craftsman at Deir
al-Medina), 49
Service des Antiquities, 95
Seti I, 53, 197
Seti II, 195, 201
Seward, William, 43
shabtis (statuettes), 49, 57
definition of, 283
stolen, 284
uninscribed male, 271–72
of Yuya, 282, 283, 284
Shepheard's Hotel, 58–59, 294, 303
demonstration at, 77
shrine, in tomb of Tiyi, 129, 142, 143,
168, 191
silver gloves, 201
silver mines, 243, 245
silver statuette, 171
Siptah. See tomb, of Siptah
Sitamon chair incident, 105–6
Smenkhare, 189
Smith, Corinna, 8, 9, 101
Smith, Grafton Elliot, 68, 188, 189
Smith, Joseph Lindon, 8–9, 22, 101,
142, 295
controversial excavation account
of, 127–28
on gold sheets with kings' names,
271
Siptah paintings commission, 116
Sitamon chair incident, 105–6
wet gold sheets found by, 149
Soo canal, 35, 36, 38
S.S. Koenig Albert, 96
Statue of Liberty, 235
statues. See also shabtis
silver statuette, 171
Stevenson, Columbus, 134, 136, 141,
151, 228

Stimson, Frederick J., 243–44
Stone, Benjamin, 145
Strong, George Templeton, 87
sugar trust, 239
suicide, Davis, I., 152–53
Swineford, Alfred P., 239–42
The Sybil, 111

Tahrir Square, 283–84
Tappan, Arthur, 16
Tawosret
  earrings of, *194,* 195, 201
  as pharaoh, 195
  tomb of, 202
tennis, 231, 232, *233,* 238
Terry (adopted son). *See* Boal,
  Theodore Davis ("Terry")
Thutmose I, 71–75
  sarcophagus of, *70,* 73, 74
Thutmose III, 29, 32, 120, 259, 275
Thutmose IV, 74
  Davis, T. M., book on, 106
  famous dream of, 65–66
  reign of, 65
  unwrapping of, 68
Thuyu. *See also* tomb, of Yuya and
  Thuyu
  coffin of, 1–2, 14–15
  exhibition of, 1, 25, 26
  marriage scarabs with name of, 14
  mummy of, 15–16
Titanic, 291, 308
Titus, Catherine (mother of Davis,
  T. M.,), 16–17, 18–21
  loss of daughter, 153
Titus, Isabella (half-sister of Davis,
  T. M.,), suicide by, 152–53
Titus, Jonas, 19–20, 33–34, 37, 38, 45,
  184

Titus, Jonas, Jr., 81
Titus, Lucy, 19
Tiye. *See* Tiyi
Tiyi (Kiya), 14, *124,* 202. *See also*
  tomb, of Tiyi
  crown of, 149, 150, 168
  jarheads associated with, 125
  lecture on, 196
tombs. *See also* Gold Tomb; tomb,
  of Tiyi; Valley of the Kings;
  specific pharaohs; *specific tombs*
  of Amenhotep II, 48–49
  Carter's missed opportunity, 55
  discovered by Davis, T. M., 270
  of Maiherpri, 60
  mystery tomb of 1909 excavation,
    271–72
  1907 controversial discovery,
    122–23, 128–31, 132
  preservation of, 49–50
  of Rameses II, 55, 301
  of Rameses IV, 145, *145*
  of Rameses IX, 121–23
  of Rekhmire, 31–32
  of Seti I, 197
  of Tawosret, 202
  of Thutmose I, *70,* 71–75
  of Tutankhamen, 10, 11–12
  Twentieth Dynasty, 119
  of Userhet, 56–57, 317
tomb, of Hatshepsut, 61, 63, 72–75,
  96
  objects in, 67–68
  Roosevelt visit to, 276
  sarcophagi, *70,* 71, 74
tomb, of Horemheb, 206–7
  carved wall artwork, 210
  condition of, 209
  photographic record, 209

publicity, 212
re excavation of 2010, 208
sarcophagus in, 208
unfinished state of, 210
tomb, of Siptah, 196–97
Ayrton excavation of, 115–16
mummy, 115
return to, 290–91, 294–98
sarcophagus found in, 296–97
window found in, 297–98
tomb, of Thutmose IV
atmosphere, 64–65
Carter's discovery of, 62–67
Carter's project, 49–50, 51, 62–67
clearing of, 67
explorer attitudes inside, 64–65
objects found in, 66, 69
party celebrating discovery, 68
search for, 55, 60–62
tomb, of Tiyi (Kiya). *See also* KV 55
controversy
Amarna-era mysteries and, 190, 193
Ayrton and, 122–23, 128–31, 132,
146–48, 187
contents fragility, 130, 142
Davis, T. M., and, 129, 130,
142–50, 188–89, 191, 193, 196
Egyptologist conclusion about KV
55, 190–91
excavation of, 126, 127–29
gold leaf inscriptions, 142, 146–47,
190
as gold-filled, 131
gold-lined coffin, 147–48
mummy identity controversy, 131,
144–45, 147, 149, 150, 188–89,
191
objects cataloged and restored,
187–88

photography of, 144, 191–92
physician on mummy gender,
188–89
publicity, 186–87
puzzle of, 150
robbery and purchase of objects
from, 170–73
shrine pieces, 129, 130, 142, 143,
168, 191
tourists stealing from, 167
tomb, of Tutankhamen
Burton's famous photography of,
285
Davis, T. M., mystery tomb as,
272–73
tomb, of Yuya and Thuyu, 2–5,
10–12, 101–12
artifacts of, 7–8, 11, 13–16, 22–23,
107, 112
candle incident, 15
as Egyptology landmark, 104
Maspero lecture on, 110–11
objects given to Davis, T. M.,
from, 108, 284
public memory and, 25
publicity, 22–23, 110–11
shabti from, *282,* 283, 284
*The Tombs of Harmhabi and
Touatankhamanou* (Davis,
T. M.,), 292–93
Tuck, Edward, 295
Tutankhamen
Burton on discovery of, 302
Carter's discovery of, 54, 272–73,
294, 319
cartouches discovered in 1909,
271
cloth with name of, 197
Davis, T. M., book and, 293

Tutankhamen *(continued)*
Davis, T. M., ironic missing of tomb, 302
embalming and burial jars, 204
exhausted valley theory disproved by, 315
exhibition of, 25
first finds of, 114
funding for excavation, 279
funeral exhibition, 204
housing for treasures of, 108
mother of, 125
preservation issue over KV 55 and, 191
rubbish left in tomb of, 294
seal of, 128
tomb of, 10, 11–12, 319–20
"Tutankhamun and the Golden Age of the Pharaohs," 25, 319–20
Tweed, William M. ("Boss"), 90–91, 94, 133, 139–40
arrest of, 140
death of, 228
Tweed Ring, 139
Tyndale, Walter, 132, 144–45
Tytus, Robb de Peyster, 63

Underground Railroad, 41
Union League Club, 136, 139–40
unwrappings, mummy, 47–48, 68, 117
Userhet, 56–57, 317
utilitarian vandalism, 62

Valley of the Kings, 271. *See also* excavation
Davis, T. M., last discovery in, 209, 275, 276
Davis, T. M., tourist life in, 259
first visit to, 266

oldest tomb in, 74
previous exploration of, 52–53, 104
Tutankhamen and, 315
vandalism, 4, 8, 12, 60, 62, 64.
See also robberies
Vanderbilt, Cornelius, 251–52
Vanderbilt, William, 220
Varley, John, Jr., 56
Venice, 111
vulture crown, 149, 150, 168

walking stick, 211–12
Wall Street, *93,* 137, 165
Wanamaker's, 222
Weeks, Kent, 55
Weigall, Arthur, 11, *145*
Ayrton and, 113, 210–11
complaint about Davis, T. M., 211
Davis, T. M., and, 3–4, 100–101, 199–200, 205, 211
on Davis, T. M., and Tiyi/Akhenaten, 189
on Horemheb tomb, 207, 208
inspector appointment, 100–101
job of, 3
nervous breakdown of, 290
1907 tomb and, 128, 129–30, 167–68
role in 1907 excavation, 192
scandal and career end, 296
sister of, 286
Sitamon chair incident and, 106
strained relations with, 197, 201
timelessness experience of, 14
Tutankhamen seal noted by only, 128
unethical Tuck sale, 295

Index   363

West Valley proposal by, 276–78, 285
Yuya tomb and, 13–14, 102–3
Weigall, Hortense, 145
wells, 64
Wells, Henry, 92
West Valley, 276–78, 285–87
Wharton, Edith, 231
whist, 259
White, George Miles, 136
Wilbour, Charles, 91, 141, 171, 173, 268
Wilson, Alice, 6, 98
Wilson, Nathaniel, 82, 87, 94, 228, 255
    as Davis, T. M., witness, 224–25
    in Davis, T. M., plan, 164
    death of, 315
    Keweenaw stock of, 218
    land sold by, 185
    law firm of, 163
    in lawsuit over Davis, T. M., will, 306, 310
    in Michigan land scheme, 182, 184, 186

new canal company formed by Davis, T. M., and, 184–85
Wilson, Nellie. *See* Knagenhjelm, Eleanor ("Nellie") Salome
Wilson, Woodrow, 310–11
window, in Ramses III Palace, 297–98
Winlock, Herbert, 202–3, 287
    embalming cache identified by, 204
Winter Palace Hotel, 117, 147, 169, 286
winter vacations, 30
Wombley, Frederick, 168–69
World Trade Center, 133
World War I, 302, 304, 306–7, 312
World War II, 316, 318
World's Fair, 95–96
Wyoming, 139

yacht. *See Beduin; dahabiyeh*
yellow dog, 117–18
yellow mask, 198, 204
Yuya. *See* tomb, of Yuya and Thuyu